The Sacred Editors

The Women Who Shaped and Were Erased from Sacred Texts

By

Kevin L. Meyer

The Sacred Editors: The Women Who Shaped and Were Erased from Sacred Texts

Copyright © 2025 by Kevin L. Meyer

All rights reserved. No part of this publication may be reproduced, distributed, or transmitted in any form or by any means, including photocopying, recording, or other electronic or mechanical methods, without the prior written permission of the publisher, except in the case of brief quotations embodied in critical reviews and certain other noncommercial uses permitted by copyright law.

Bhavana Press
Morro Bay, California

ISBN: 979-8-9996276-6-7

First Edition

Printed in the United States of America

Contents

A Note on Language and Sources 1

Dedication 5

Introduction 7

Prologue: She Who Holds the Ink 13

Part I - The Women Within

Chapter 1: The Apostle They Erased -- Mary Magdalene 19

Chapter 2: The Nuns Who Sang -- The Therīgāthā Poets 25

Chapter 3: The Scholar Constrained -- Aisha bint Abi Bakr 31

Chapter 4: Hindu Women's Sacred Agency 37

Chapter 5: The Prophetesses Silenced - Miriam & Her Sisters . 45

Chapter 6: Sacred Voices Beyond the Center 53

Chapter 7: What If They Had Been Canon? 61

Interlude A: The Mystics' Rebellion 67

Part II - The Women Around

Chapter 8: Christian Women as Scribes and Mystics 75

Chapter 9: Islamic Women as Preservers 81

Chapter 10: Hindu Women's Sacred Labor 87

Chapter 11: ewish Women as Liturgical Guardians 93

Chapter 12: Buddhist Women in Transmission 99

Chapter 13: The Unwritten Archive 105

Interlude B: Anonymous Hands 111

Part III - Patterns of Marginalization and Resistance

Chapter 14: The Architecture of Erasure...................117

Chapter 15: The Counter-Tradition..............................127

Chapter 16: When Visions Became Texts.....................137

Part IV - Recovery and Reclamation

Chapter 17: Archaeological Angels................................151

Chapter 18: Reading Against the Grain........................163

Chapter 19: The Contemporary Conversation............177

Conclusion: To Be Remembered....................................195

Research & Methodology..209

Notes from Chapters...219

Bibliography and Index..273

Appendix A: Biographies - 116 Women Across Traditions....275

Appendix B: Key Manuscripts & Archaeological Discoveries 305

Appendix C: Glossary of Roles......................................315

Appendix D: Further Reading.......................................323

Appendix E: Guide for Book Clubs and Classrooms...............335

About the Author 347

Other Books by Kevin Meyer..349

A Note on Language and Sources

This book engages multiple religious traditions, linguistic systems, and textual lineages spanning Christianity, Judaism, Islam, Buddhism, Hinduism, and additional traditions including Zoroastrianism, Sikhism, and Indigenous oral cultures. Every effort has been made to treat each with accuracy, care, and respect.

Names and Transliterations

Where possible, names are rendered in a form recognizable to general English-speaking readers. Diacritical marks are omitted in most cases for accessibility. For example, you will see "Aisha" rather than "ʿĀʾishah," "Sita" rather than "Sītā," and "Qur'an" rather than "al-Qurʾān." In cases where alternate spellings exist (e.g., "Therīgāthā" vs. "Therigatha"), a consistent but accessible form is used throughout. When sacred texts exist in multiple versions (e.g., Hebrew, Greek, Sanskrit, Pāli, Arabic, or Chinese), the English-language title or most widely accepted rendering is used unless otherwise noted.

Scripture and Canon

The word *scripture* is used broadly in this book to refer to texts considered sacred, formative, or authoritative within a religious tradition—whether or not they are part of a fixed canon. This includes formally canonized texts (such as the Bible, Qur'an, Vedas, or Tripitaka) as well as texts revered within devotional movements, mystical lineages, or oral transmission networks. Similarly, the term *canon* is used descriptively rather than prescriptively, acknowledging that canon formation was itself a historical process influenced by theological, political, and editorial decisions. It's worth noting that what constitutes "scripture" can reflect ongoing intra-community dynamics—for instance, the Book of Enoch remains canonical in Ethiopian Orthodox Christianity while being excluded from most other Christian traditions.

Translation and Interpretation

Key religious terms such as *dharma, torah, shari'a,* and *logos* carry rich meanings that resist simple English equivalents. Where such terms appear, their contextual significance is explained. Readers should be aware that translating sacred concepts across languages inevitably shapes interpretation—a challenge that the women in this book often navigated as they transmitted wisdom across cultural boundaries.

Gender and Titles

In describing women across traditions, this book uses the terms that are most historically accurate and respectful to the context. Titles such as *prophetess, bhikkhuni, soferet, hafiza,* or *nun* are used where appropriate. In cases where women operated in roles for which there was no formal title—such as patrons, oral transmitters, or anonymous scribes—descriptive language is used instead. The phrase "women who were erased" refers to both those who were actively excluded and those whose names or works were lost due to structural neglect, anonymity, or attribution to men.

Sources and Attribution

Each chapter draws on the work of respected scholars in religious studies, textual criticism, history, and gender studies, with particular attention to including voices from women scholars, practitioners within each tradition, and non-Western perspectives. All claims are documented using Chicago Manual of Style footnotes, and each chapter concludes with a curated list of further reading for those wishing to explore the topic more deeply. The book makes no attempt to present original scholarship but rather synthesizes the insights of leading experts, always with attribution and transparency.

Methodological Considerations

Recovering women's voices from ancient and medieval sources often requires working with fragmentary, circumstantial, or indirect evidence. Where records are sparse, this book employs careful historical inference, always distinguishing between documented facts and informed scholarly speculation. Marginalia, linguistic patterns, patronage records, and oral traditions all serve as windows into women's contributions, even when their names have been lost.

Tone and Terminology

This book avoids polemic and honors the sacred nature of the traditions it discusses. It does not attempt to reinterpret doctrine or argue for theological positions. Its goal is historical and textual: to explore how women contributed to the formation and transmission of sacred texts—and how their voices were shaped, sidelined, or silenced by editorial processes, canon debates, and institutional dynamics.

The voices you will encounter in these pages come from different centuries, cultures, and spiritual perspectives. They do not always agree. But each of them mattered—and this book seeks to remember them with the dignity and attention they deserve.

Dedication

For the women whose names were lost,
whose ink dried without attribution,
whose words were carried in whispers,
and whose wisdom shaped what we now call sacred.

And for the readers and scholars
who help their voices find light again.

This book remembers you.

Introduction

For nearly thirty years, I've practiced an annual *bhāvanā*—a reflective, intentional deep dive into one subject that challenges my assumptions and expands my view of the world. Some years, that exploration was physical: marathon running, scuba diving, wilderness travel. Other years, it was intellectual: comparative mythology, moral philosophy, cultural memory. In every case, the goal was not mastery but transformation. A journey of learning, not arrival.

In 2014, I turned my attention to sacred texts.

What began as a general curiosity about how the Bible came to be soon deepened into something more demanding—and more rewarding. I began reading biblical scholars, textual critics, archaeologists, and theologians. I studied how human decision-making shaped sacred canons, how politics and theology intertwined with manuscript traditions, and how scribes, monks, and reformers altered what we now call the word of God.

The result of that journey became the first volume of *Sacred Editors*—a book about how Christian scripture was edited, translated, shaped, and contested over centuries. That project eventually grew into a five-volume series exploring similar editorial processes across Judaism, Islam, Buddhism, and Hinduism.

But somewhere along the way, another thread began pulling at me.

Again and again, across all these traditions—from ancient Jerusalem to medieval Baghdad, from Buddhist monasteries in Sri Lanka to Hindu temples in Tamil Nadu—I noticed a striking pattern: the absence of women. Or rather, their obscured presence. Their voices were not absent so much as silenced—written out of the canon, attributed to male figures, excluded from commentary, footnoted in their own stories. And yet the more I read, the more I found them: behind the manuscripts, beneath the oral traditions, between the margins.

They were there, copying texts in convents and monasteries. They were there, transmitting sacred memory in kitchens and village squares. They were there, composing poetry and mystical commentary, memorizing scripture, founding schools, funding temples. They were there in the founding stories, too—prophets, apostles, seers, teachers, healers, rebels.

And over time, I found myself haunted not by the question of *why* they were erased—that part, sadly, is easy to answer—but by the more urgent question: *What might we recover if we remembered them?*

This book is my answer.

The Sacred and the Hidden

Sacred Editors: The Women Who Shaped and Were Erased from Sacred Texts is a companion to the original *Sacred Editors* series, but it also stands alone as a work of historical recovery. It explores the role of women in shaping, transmitting, interpreting, and preserving sacred texts across Christianity, Judaism, Islam, Buddhism, Hinduism, and additional traditions including Zoroastrianism, Sikhism, and Indigenous oral cultures—both those whose names survive and those who remain anonymous.

It is not a catalog of grievances. Nor is it an effort to rewrite canon with modern values. Instead, this book listens for echoes: the stories of women who were part of the sacred literary tradition all along but were written out by the same editorial forces that shaped scripture itself. It invites readers into the silences and asks what those silences cost us—and what we might gain by revisiting them with care, humility, and courage.

Recovering women's stories often requires working with fragmentary, circumstantial, or indirect evidence. Archaeological discoveries, oral traditions, liturgical practices, patronage records, and paleographic analysis all serve as windows into contributions that formal histories overlooked. This methodological challenge is part of the story itself—a reminder of how thoroughly certain voices were marginalized.

How This Book Is Organized

The book is divided into four parts, with two thematic interludes that explore cross-cultural patterns:

Part I, The Women Within, introduces women who appear inside sacred texts—figures like Mary Magdalene, Miriam, Sita,

Draupadi, and Aisha bint Abi Bakr—whose authority was later diminished through canonization, redaction, or theological reframing. Readers will encounter detailed biographical profiles, analysis of how their portrayals evolved over time, and exploration of their enduring influence.

Part II, The Women Around, focuses on the women behind the texts: the scribes, mystics, transmitters, patrons, teachers, and oral performers who carried sacred wisdom across generations, even when they were denied authorship or recognition. These chapters combine case studies of known figures with detective work on anonymous contributions.

Part III, Patterns of Marginalization and Resistance, identifies shared themes across traditions—how women's authority was constrained and how they found ways to resist: through mysticism, oral networks, coded authorship, and lived ritual. This analytical section reveals the systematic nature of women's exclusion while celebrating their ingenious survival strategies.

Part IV, Recovery and Reclamation, brings us into the present: how women's voices are being rediscovered through archaeology, textual analysis, and feminist scholarship—and how this process is reshaping modern engagement with sacred texts.

Two **interludes**—"The Mystics' Rebellion" and "Anonymous Hands"—serve as thematic bridges that step back from tradition-specific analysis to explore patterns that transcend cultural boundaries.

Each major section ends with a **capstone chapter** that summarizes its key findings and introduces a **Scholar Debate** on contested questions. These capstones also include a "**What Would Have Changed?**" exploration, imagining how doctrine, liturgy, or religious practice might have developed differently had certain women's voices been retained as central rather than erased.

Individual chapters follow a consistent structure: a vivid narrative opening based on historical evidence, followed by scholarly analysis, a profile of "Also Remembered" figures from the same tradition, and concluding with Chicago-style footnotes and curated further reading lists.

Research and Transparency

As with the earlier *Sacred Editors* books, I am not presenting original academic research. I am not a professional scholar of religion, nor a historian of gender. What I am is a curious reader, drawing on the work of those who are—particularly prioritizing voices from women scholars, practitioners within each tradition, and non-Western perspectives. This book synthesizes and honors their contributions.

To do so, I have relied on a careful methodology that blends traditional scholarly reading with the assistance of artificial intelligence tools. In a separate **Research Methodology** section at the end of the book, I describe in detail how I used AI (including ChatGPT, Perplexity, and Claude) to help organize sources, cross-reference claims, and draft early narrative structures. Every claim was verified against published academic work, and each chapter was reviewed for accuracy and respectful tone. I remain responsible for every sentence, interpretation, and citation.

In keeping with my own annual *bhāvanā* practice, I approached this book not just as a project, but as a form of ethical attention. The process required slowing down, listening carefully, and being willing to sit with the discomfort of what was lost—and the hope of what might still be remembered.

An Invitation to the Reader

This book does not attempt to "fix" the past. It does not promise a new canon, or a revolutionary theology. Instead, it invites you to listen—to imagine the lives of those who held the ink but not the authority, who whispered sacred words into memory even when their names were forgotten, who shaped the divine story even when others claimed they had no right to.

Their voices are not entirely gone. You can still hear them if you listen closely—in the margins, in the fragments, in the footnotes of history. This book is a way of listening, and of remembering.

I invite you to listen with me.

Prologue: She Who Holds the Ink

Nalanda, 8th century. By lamplight, the parchment crackled. Outside, the night birds had gone silent, and even the temple bells were still. Inside a small chamber in Nalanda's monastic complex, Sister Padmavati dipped her reed brush once more and steadied her hand. The text was nearly complete—this copy of the *Saddharmapuṇḍarīka Sūtra*, the *Lotus of the True Dharma*. She had transcribed its 27 chapters by memory and by heart, matching every stroke to a lineage of thought and devotion stretching back hundreds of years. Her brush trembled—not from fatigue, but reverence. "May all beings find liberation," she whispered aloud, then, in tiny script at the bottom corner of the final page, she added what she always did: *"Copied by one who seeks the Way."*[1]

She did not write her name.

Canterbury, 1147. At dawn, Abbess Heloise watched the sun slide across the scriptorium floor. Two dozen women bent over vellum, their quills scratching gospel passages in golden ink. The abbey was quiet but not still; pages turned, shoulders shifted, ink was blotted and reapplied. Heloise's own manuscript lay unfinished on her desk—an annotated commentary on the letters of Paul—but she would not sign it. Not in full. She might use the old monastic formula, *anima devota*, "a devoted soul," as a signature. Perhaps not even that.

Once, in her youth, she had written love letters in her own name. Letters to Abelard. Letters that now lived beyond her reach, copied by others, taken as scandal or scripture. But here, surrounded by women illuminating sacred text by hand, she knew this was the holier work: preserving what she could, correcting what she dared, teaching those who might never be remembered.[2]

Oxford, 1945. Professor Margaret Gibson turned the brittle folio gently beneath the lamplight. It had just arrived in a shipment from the dissolved monastery of Sankt Florian in Austria—dozens of unsorted manuscripts in faded Latin and Hebrew, mostly medieval, mostly minor.[3] But this one was different. At the edge of the parchment, barely visible beneath a later gloss, was a small line in pale brown ink: *"Written by a woman who loved God more than her own name."*

No signature. No date. Just that—an anonymous testament in the margin.

It was not the first such fragment Gibson had seen. She had cataloged dozens of devotional manuscripts in her career, many bearing signs of female labor: marginal corrections in a woman's hand, softened corners from habitual use in domestic ritual, notations referencing sisters, mothers, or convent life. But something about this line stayed with her. It was not just a witness—it was a choice. To love God more than one's own name. To disappear, so the sacred might survive.

These women never met. They spoke different languages, lived in different centuries, practiced different faiths. One wrote in Sanskrit, one in Latin, one in silence. But across the boundaries of time and tradition, they shared something powerful: **they were present**.

They were present as copyists and commentators. As preservers, teachers, and transmitters of what we now call sacred. They sang scripture aloud, whispered it into children's ears, inscribed it onto parchment and memory and stone. Their fingerprints are in the margins, their choices embedded in what was kept, what was edited, what was passed down.

And yet their names are mostly gone.

Sometimes they were erased deliberately—by editors who deemed them unfit, by institutions that denied their authority. Other times they were lost through anonymity, humility, or custom. In some cases, women's words were absorbed into male attributions or survived only through oral retellings that left no signature behind. The result, across nearly every tradition, is a sacred record haunted by absence: women were there, but they are not always seen.

This book is an attempt to see them.

It does not recover every name. It does not claim to fix what history forgot. But it offers an echo, made audible. A glimpse into the lives of those who held the ink, not for fame, but for faith. Women who shaped scripture not through sermons and councils, but through devotion, labor, and love.

They were there. And now, we remember.

Part I

The Women Within

Sacred texts are filled with women—prophets, teachers, poets, and leaders whose voices shaped the earliest communities of faith. Yet over centuries of transmission and interpretation, many of these figures were recast, diminished, or pushed to the margins of their own stories. This section recovers the women who appear within scripture itself: Mary Magdalene transformed from apostle to penitent, Aisha bint Abi Bakr whose scholarly authority was later constrained, the Buddhist nuns whose enlightened poetry survived in canon but faded from memory. These are the women whose presence in sacred texts reminds us that divine revelation has always included female voices—even when later editors preferred to forget.

Chapter 1: The Apostle They Erased -- Mary Magdalene

The cave was cool and still. A single oil lamp flickered at the entrance, its light softening the rock walls and casting shadows over a painted niche. From within, a woman knelt over a wooden tablet, stylus in hand. It was sometime in the second century, perhaps near Ephesus, or maybe in a Judean monastic community long since buried. She whispered aloud as she copied the words before her:

"The Savior said, 'Blessed are you that you did not waver at the sight of me. For where the mind is, there is the treasure.'"

She paused and looked toward the image on the wall—a faint fresco of a veiled woman, right hand raised in teaching. Mary. The Magdalene. The one who first saw the risen Christ and called him "Rabboni." The one who taught the others when the men had fled. The one whose name was known but whose authority had been steadily erased.

The woman adjusted the tablet in her lap and continued. This was no ordinary Gospel—that is, no text that would later be included in the canonical collection Christians recognize today. It was a text attributed to Mary herself, one of a growing number of writings passed quietly among those who believed the story was bigger than the official collection being formed. She would never know whether the copy she made would survive. But she made it anyway.[1]

Mary Magdalene stands as perhaps the most paradoxical figure in early Christianity: simultaneously present at its most foundational moments and yet persistently recast, diminished, and dismissed across centuries. She is named in all four canonical Gospels as the first witness to the resurrection—a fact so central that it meets the highest standards of historical reliability in New Testament scholarship.[2] Yet she is also the subject of profound misrepresentation: conflated with a prostitute, stripped of apostolic status, and relegated to a symbol of repentance rather than leadership.

In the earliest strata of Christian tradition, Mary is a figure of remarkable authority. The Gospel of John portrays her as the first to encounter the risen Jesus (John 20:1–18). In that passage, she is not only the first witness but the first preacher of the resurrection—sent by Christ himself to "go to my brothers and say to them..." (John 20:17). Scholars such as Jane Schaberg and Elizabeth Schrader argue that this encounter designates her as *apostola apostolorum*—the apostle to the apostles.[3]

Her prominence, however, became increasingly uncomfortable to early church leaders. In the third century, Origen's commentary already reflects anxiety about Mary's role. By the time of Pope Gregory the Great in the sixth century, a formal conflation was made: Mary Magdalene was declared to be the same person as the anonymous sinful woman of Luke 7:36–50 and Mary of Bethany, sister of Martha and Lazarus.[4] This merging allowed the church to sideline her apostolic authority and emphasize instead a model of feminine penitence. Notably, Eastern Christianity largely avoided this conflation, maintaining a clearer distinction between these biblical figures and preserving Mary Magdalene's status as a holy woman without the overlay of repentant prostitute.

But Mary's voice persisted in texts that would later be labeled heretical. The *Gospel of Mary*, discovered in the late 19th century and published in full only in the 20th, presents Mary as a teacher and visionary.[5] In this text, she comforts the male disciples after Jesus's departure, offers insight into Christ's hidden teachings, and withstands Peter's skepticism. "Do you think I have thought these things up by myself?" she asks. "Or that I am lying about the Savior?"[6] The tension between Mary and Peter in this gospel reflects a broader tension in early Christianity: the struggle over who had the right to interpret and transmit the teachings of Jesus.

In several other non-canonical texts—such as the *Pistis Sophia* and the *Dialogue of the Savior*—Mary again appears as a favored disciple, often understanding Christ more clearly than the male apostles.[7] While some of these texts were associated with communities later deemed Gnostic, their inclusion of Mary as a primary voice is notable for both its consistency and its theological richness. Her portrayal across these diverse texts suggests a persistent memory of her authority that institutional Christianity worked steadily to contain.

Recent scholarship has uncovered even more dramatic evidence of Mary's marginalization. Elizabeth Schrader's detailed textual analysis of the Gospel of John suggests that scribes may have deliberately altered references to Mary Magdalene, replacing her name with "Martha" in key scenes to diminish her prominence.[8]

If Schrader's reconstruction is correct, Mary Magdalene originally appears in John 11:2 as the woman who anointed Jesus's feet, and her sister Martha was a later scribal addition to redirect attention away from Mary's intimate relationship with Jesus.

Why was she erased? The answer lies partly in the consolidation of orthodoxy. As the church moved toward institutional unity in the second through fourth centuries, the authority of women—especially visionary or teaching women—was increasingly marginalized. Apostolic succession was framed through male leadership. Canonical texts were selected, in part, based on their alignment with emerging ecclesial structures. And women's roles were recast to emphasize repentance rather than proclamation.

Mary Magdalene survived this process, but in altered form. She became the "reformed sinner," a model of forgiven repentance rather than authorized speech. Her feast day remained, but her voice was softened. Her gospel was lost—buried in the sands of Egypt and dismissed by bishops. Only in recent decades has her legacy begun to be revisited seriously by scholars like Karen L. King, Ann Graham Brock, and the researchers mentioned above, who have analyzed the theological, textual, and political dimensions of her marginalization.

Mary Magdalene was not forgotten. But the version of her that survived was not the one who held the ink.

The trajectory is clear: early Christianity included women in positions of authority, teaching, and spiritual leadership. But as institutional structures solidified, these roles were systematically constrained, reinterpreted, or erased. Mary Magdalene's story became the template: preserve the name, transform the role, emphasize penitence over proclamation.

Peter said to Mary, "Sister, we know that the Savior loved you more than the rest of women. Tell us the words of the Savior which you remember..." But when she shared her vision, he protested: "Did he really speak with a woman without our knowledge?" The struggle documented in the *Gospel of Mary* was not merely theological but deeply political: who had the right to speak for Jesus?[9]

The woman we call Mary Magdalene was not erased by accident. She was reshaped by theology, edited by tradition, and silenced by institutional anxiety. Her story survived, but not her voice—not fully. And yet even through centuries of distortion, the outline remains: a woman who stood first at the tomb, who spoke when others fled, who bore witness to the divine not as a footnote to male leadership, but as its necessary beginning. Her ink faded. But her echo remains.

Also Remembered

Junia (1st century CE): Described in Romans 16:7 as "outstanding among the apostles," Junia was later masculinized in manuscripts to "Junias"—a name otherwise unattested in antiquity. Like Mary Magdalene, her apostolic authority was gradually written out of the record through scribal choices.

Phoebe (1st century CE): Named in Romans 16:1–2 as a deacon (*diakonos*) and "benefactor" (*prostatis*) of Paul, Phoebe likely served as a messenger and interpreter of Paul's letter to the Romans. Her ministerial role was later downplayed in translation and commentary.

Thecla (2nd century CE): The protagonist of the *Acts of Paul and Thecla*, she was a teacher and baptizer whose story circulated widely in early Christianity. Unlike Mary Magdalene, Thecla's authority was contained not through conflation but through the eventual classification of her story as fictional rather than historical.

The Syro-Phoenician Woman (1st century CE): Appearing in Mark 7 and Matthew 15, this unnamed woman engages in theological dialogue with Jesus, challenging and expanding his mission through her wit and faith. Her theological acumen is preserved in the canonical text but rarely emphasized in interpretation.

Perpetua (3rd century CE): A Christian martyr whose prison diary (*Passio Perpetuae*) is among the earliest known writings by a Christian woman. Her visionary experiences and theological insights were preserved because they were framed within the acceptable category of martyrdom rather than ongoing church leadership.

Chapter 2: The Nuns Who Sang -- The Therīgāthā Poets

The river was quiet in the early light. Across the water, a line of forest shimmered in gold. A small group of women sat cross-legged beneath a neem tree, their ochre robes tucked neatly around their knees. One, older than the rest, began to speak—not in prose, but in verse.

> *"So freed! So thoroughly freed am I—*
> *from three crooked things set free:*
> *the mortar, the pestle, and my twisted lord..."*

The others smiled and repeated the lines aloud. They were not just listening. They were preserving. This was no ordinary gathering. It was part of a new movement within an ancient tradition: women who had left behind domestic duty to follow the Buddha's path, ordained as bhikkhunīs, or fully-ordained nuns. And what they shared that morning was not just poetry. It was scripture—carried in memory, recited in rhythm, passed from voice to voice in the oral tradition that would preserve Buddhist teachings for centuries before they were ever written down. The verses would later form part of the *Therīgāthā*, or "Verses of the Elder Nuns," among the oldest texts in any religious tradition authored by women.[1]

These women did not write for fame. They spoke to survive.

The *Therīgāthā*, part of the Pāli Canon of Theravāda Buddhism, is a remarkable compilation of seventy-three poems attributed to early Buddhist nuns. Composed between the 6th and 3rd centuries BCE, the verses offer first-person accounts of awakening, renunciation, grief, liberation, and resilience.[2] They are intensely personal yet philosophically profound—testimonies of enlightenment filtered through the lives of women who defied both caste and custom to walk the path of the Dhamma.

The preservation of these verses reflects Buddhism's unique reliance on oral transmission. Unlike textual traditions that depended on written manuscripts from their inception, Buddhist teachings were memorized, recited, and transmitted through careful oral networks for several centuries before being committed to writing. The Pāli Canon, which includes the *Therīgāthā*, was not written down until the 1st century BCE in Sri Lanka, meaning these women's voices survived through hundreds of years of communal memory.[3]

Scholars have long recognized the *Therīgāthā* as exceptional. In a tradition that privileged male voices—monks, kings, philosophers—these poems preserve the raw, unfiltered experiences of women: former wives, mothers, courtesans, aristocrats, and servants. Some, like Bhaddā Kāpilānī, had been educated and wealthy before joining the order. Others, like the poetess Puṇṇā, spoke of being "born in a family of no account." Yet each found in renunciation a source of power the world had denied them.[4]

Despite their antiquity and beauty, these verses were nearly lost to Buddhist education. While included in the *Khuddaka Nikāya* (the "Minor Collection"), the *Therīgāthā* remained marginal within the monastic curriculum. In many countries—including Sri Lanka and Thailand—the poems were rarely memorized or commented upon. Most bhikkhus (monks) focused instead on the Vinaya (disciplinary code) and Abhidhamma (philosophical teachings), with female-authored texts considered peripheral.[5]

The marginalization extended beyond Theravāda Buddhism. While some Mahāyāna texts include verses that may have been composed by women—such as certain songs attributed to female disciples in the *Lotus Sutra* and biographical accounts in Chinese Buddhist literature—these too received less attention than male-authored teachings.[6] The pattern was consistent across Buddhist cultures: women's spiritual insights were preserved but not prioritized.

Even when preserved, the *Therīgāthā* was often interpreted through male lenses. Some early commentaries softened or allegorized the women's words, stripping them of their social context. Others treated the verses as quaint testimonials rather than authoritative doctrine. The oral transmission of Buddhist scripture meant that what was repeated most often became central—and what was neglected faded.

The institutional preference for male teaching lineages played a key role in this silencing. In many Theravāda regions, the bhikkhunī order itself died out by the 11th century, due to wars, invasions, and patriarchal neglect.[7] Without women in full ordination, their texts too began to lose relevance. It was not until the 20th century that feminist scholars and reformist monks began to recover the *Therīgāthā* as a vital voice in Buddhist thought.

Translations into English, such as those by K. R. Norman and Charles Hallisey, helped bring the poems to wider audiences.[8] More recently, Buddhist scholars such as Karma Lekshe Tsomo and contemporary bhikkhunī revival movements—including the work of Dhammananda Bhikkhuni in Thailand and Ayya Tathaaloka in the United States—have reasserted the *Therīgāthā* not just as history, but as living inspiration, calling it a scripture of liberation that speaks directly to women's inner lives.[9]

In one verse, a nun named Kisāgotamī recounts her transformation after the death of her child:

> *"I ran to every home in search of mustard seed,*
> *but death had touched them all.*
> *Then I saw: my grief was not mine alone.*
> *And I let go."*

These are not abstract teachings. They are direct transmissions of insight, rendered in the breath and cadence of lived experience. They reflect what some scholars now call *embodied liberation*—a form of awakening grounded in the realities of women's lives, not just metaphysical ideals.[10]

And yet, for centuries, the voices of these nuns were not taught. Their names were remembered, if at all, as minor figures in male-authored commentaries. Their verses—some of the earliest examples of female-authored spiritual poetry in world history—were whispered rather than proclaimed.

They sang anyway.

> *"With shaven head, wrapped in the outer robe,*
> *I sat at the foot of a tree.*
> *For seven days I meditated:*
> *the arrow of craving was removed."*
> —*Therīgāthā* 5.2, translated by K. R. Norman

The elder nuns of early Buddhism sang their way into the sacred. They turned grief into clarity, poverty into peace, marginalization into awakening. Their verses survived not because they were central, but because they were memorized, repeated, and cherished by communities who understood their value. Today, their words offer more than historical insight. They offer proof that women, too, knew the Way—and left it in verse for us to follow.

Also Remembered

Mahāpajāpatī Gotamī (6th century BCE): The Buddha's foster mother and the first woman to request and receive ordination. She led the early bhikkhunī community but was later minimized in canonical narratives, with later commentaries emphasizing her initial reluctance to ordain women rather than her pioneering role.

Vijayā (date unknown): A nun whose *Therīgāthā* verses describe overcoming attachment through insight. One of the few to use militaristic metaphors to describe spiritual battle, her poetry demonstrates the diversity of voices within the collection.

Queen Sāmāvatī (5th century BCE): A royal patron of the Buddha, known for sheltering and supporting hundreds of female followers. Though her role as a lay leader was often downplayed in later texts, she represents the crucial support network that enabled women's monastic communities to flourish.

Tibetan translator-wives (8th–10th centuries CE): Women who worked alongside their husbands in translating Sanskrit sutras into Tibetan, their names largely unrecorded despite their linguistic expertise. Their anonymous contributions helped preserve Buddhist texts that might otherwise have been lost when Buddhism declined in India.

Contemporary Revival Leaders: Figures like Dhammananda Bhikkhuni in Thailand, who reestablished full female ordination there, and Ayya Tathaaloka in the United States, who founded Dharmagiri Hermitage, often invoke the *Therīgāthā* as scriptural precedent for women's spiritual authority.

Chapter 3: The Scholar They Constrained -- Aisha bint Abi Bakr

The scrolls rustled lightly as they were unrolled. A circle of men leaned forward, their expressions intent, respectful. At the center sat a woman—veiled, composed, unwavering in voice. Her name was ʿĀʾisha bint Abī Bakr, and she was not simply reciting what the Prophet had said. She was *interpreting* it, correcting others when memory failed, providing legal nuance, and occasionally questioning the narrators themselves.

"You say he ruled thus," she interrupted once. "But I was there, and it was otherwise."

The men listened. Some nodded. Others bristled. She was the Prophet's widow, the daughter of his closest companion, and one of the most authoritative transmitters of hadith in all of Islamic tradition. She was also a woman—assertive, politically engaged, theologically sharp—and her influence would spark both reverence and resentment for generations to come.[1]

Aisha's status in early Islam is without parallel. Married to the Prophet Muhammad at a young age, she lived through the formation of the Muslim ummah and became a key figure during and after his life. She narrated over 2,200 hadith (sayings or actions of the Prophet), many of which are central to Islamic jurisprudence (fiqh) and Quranic interpretation (tafsir).[2] Her intelligence, wit, and memory earned her the title *al-ṣiddīqa bint al-ṣiddīq*—"the truthful woman, daughter of the truthful man."

Yet her legacy is tangled in layers of admiration and controversy. She was revered as a teacher, but also criticized for her political activism. She was celebrated for her legal insights, but her authority as a woman was repeatedly challenged. The tension between her prominence and the constraints placed upon her speaks to a broader dynamic in Islamic textual history: the simultaneous inclusion and marginalization of female voices in the sacred record.

As a narrator of hadith, Aisha was indispensable. Major Sunni collections, including those of Bukhārī and Muslim, cite her frequently—especially on issues related to family life, purification, ethics, and women's roles.[3] Her narrations shaped not only personal piety but legal theory, and her intimate knowledge of the Prophet's household offered a window into aspects of his life that no male companion could provide. In matters of fiqh, her rulings on menstruation, prayer, and domestic relations became foundational to Islamic law. In tafsir, her explanations of Quranic verses—often based on direct observation of the circumstances of revelation—carried enormous weight among early scholars.[4]

Aisha was not alone in this scholarly role. Recent research has revealed a rich tradition of female hadith transmitters (*muhaddithat*) that persisted for centuries. Women like Karima al-Marwaziyya (d. 1070), who taught hadith to thousands of students including men, and Fatima bint Saad al-Khayr (d. 1250), whose chain of transmission was considered among the most reliable of her era, demonstrate that Aisha's scholarly authority, while exceptional in scope, was not wholly isolated in the early Islamic tradition.[5]

Yet her position was never uncontested. The most dramatic episode came during the First Fitna—the civil war that followed the assassination of the third caliph, ʿUthmān. Aisha sided with Muʿāwiya against ʿAlī ibn Abī Ṭālib, leading an army into the Battle of the Camel in 656 CE. Though she later withdrew and expressed regret, her leadership in battle shocked many, and it provided ammunition for generations of scholars who questioned the propriety of women's public authority.[6]

In Shiʿi tradition, where ʿAlī is regarded as the rightful successor to the Prophet, Aisha's political stance further complicated her reputation. Though respected as a *Mother of the Believers*, her role is often treated with caution. In Sunni tradition, however, she was long held as a model of piety and learning—until that, too, began to narrow.

By the 10th and 11th centuries, as Islamic jurisprudence (fiqh) became more formalized, the role of women as public scholars began to diminish. Male jurists increasingly dominated the production and transmission of sacred knowledge. The institutions that preserved and taught the hadith—the *madrasas* and legal schools—were almost exclusively male. While Aisha remained cited, her interpretive role faded. Later scholars often referenced her narrations without acknowledging the intellectual rigor behind them.

Her legal opinions—on issues such as menstruation, divorce, inheritance—were sometimes at odds with male consensus. In one famous exchange, she rebuked a male jurist for misunderstanding a verse of the Quran related to ritual purity. "You compare us to donkeys," she said, "but the Prophet never treated us so."[7] Her voice was sharp, her arguments grounded in firsthand experience. And yet, over time, these moments were softened in commentary, framed as anecdotes rather than arguments.

What changed was not her memory, but the framework around it.

Today, Aisha's legacy is once again being examined with fresh eyes. Scholars such as Leila Ahmed, Fatima Mernissi, and Asma Sayeed have emphasized her role not only as transmitter but as theologian.[8] Contemporary Muslim feminist scholars like Amina Wadud and Asma Barlas have drawn on Aisha's interpretive methods to argue for women's continuing authority in Islamic scholarship.[9] They note that her narrations are often self-aware, consciously framing events with moral reflection. In this, she was not simply preserving the Prophet's words. She was shaping their interpretation.

To recover her voice is to remember that sacred transmission was not a neutral process. It was personal, political, embodied—and, in Aisha's case, gendered. She bore the responsibility of being both insider and outsider: privileged by proximity, constrained by expectation.

But she spoke. And the words remain.

"The people were like donkeys regarding this matter. I and the Prophet would bathe from the same vessel, and he would not hesitate to touch me even while I was menstruating."[10] The words are Aisha's, preserved in *Sahih Muslim*, and they cut through centuries of scholarly circumvention with characteristic directness. She was not merely offering a ruling—she was asserting her authority to speak from intimate knowledge, challenging those who would constrain women's religious lives based on ignorance rather than prophetic example.

Aisha's voice echoes across Islamic tradition: sharp, reasoned, intimate, insistent. She was not merely a vessel for the Prophet's sayings, but a mind shaped by him and shaping others in turn. That her authority was later constrained does not erase her intellectual legacy. It only shows how easily even the most central women in sacred history can be recast into narrower roles. But the record still speaks. And Aisha is still teaching.

Also Remembered

Hafsa bint ʿUmar (7th century CE): The Prophet's wife who preserved one of the earliest Quranic codices, which became the basis for the Uthmanic recension. Her role as textual guardian was later downplayed in favor of male compilers like Zayd ibn Thabit.

Umm Salama (7th century CE): Another wife of the Prophet known for her political insight and hadith narration. She is remembered for arguing that women should be addressed directly in Quranic verses alongside men, leading to the revelation of verses that explicitly include women.

Fatima al-Fihri (9th century CE): Founder of al-Qarawiyyin in Fez, Morocco, often cited as the world's oldest continually operating university. Her educational vision shaped Islamic scholarship for centuries, though her founding role is sometimes attributed to male relatives.

Zaynab bint al-Kamāl (13th century CE): A renowned hadith scholar in Damascus who taught leading male jurists and whose *isnads* (chains of transmission) are still cited. She represents the continuity of women's scholarly authority well into the medieval period.

ʿĀʾisha al-Bāʿūniyya (15th–16th century CE): A Sufi mystic and prolific author of Arabic theological texts, praised for both scholarship and poetic style. Her works demonstrate women's continuing contributions to Islamic intellectual life even as formal opportunities diminished.

Chapter 4: From Devotion to Dissent -- Hindu Women's Sacred Agency

She slipped out before dawn, her anklets muffled by the folds of her sari. The temple courtyard was still empty, save for a few goats stirring in the shadows. Mirabai moved toward the shrine of Krishna, flute in hand, song in throat. Her voice broke the silence:

> *"I have found love, O my mother.*
> *I will not stay in this house."*

By day, she was a Rajput princess—a royal widow bound by the rules of caste, clan, and decorum. By night, she sang songs that made ministers bristle and priests whisper. She composed in the vernacular, not Sanskrit. She danced in public, not private. She claimed mystical union with Krishna, not submission to patriarchs. And when rebuked, she replied: *"I will not worship your stone gods. My heart belongs elsewhere."*[1]

Mirabai's life, somewhere in 16th-century Rajasthan, became legend. But she was not alone. She was part of a centuries-long current of Hindu women who resisted marginalization by turning devotion into defiance. Their tools were poetry, song, and story. Their texts—sometimes preserved in oral tradition, sometimes transcribed decades later—challenge the notion that sacred transmission in Hinduism belonged solely to Brahmins or men.

In Hindu tradition, women have long occupied an ambiguous space in relation to sacred texts. On the one hand, many foundational scriptures were authored and preserved within patriarchal frameworks. The Vedas, the earliest and most authoritative corpus of Hindu literature, were transmitted orally through male priestly lineages. Women were explicitly barred from Vedic education for much of Indian history, though some exceptions survive in memory.[2]

Yet women appear even in the earliest strata of sacred literature. The *Ṛg Veda* includes hymns attributed to women such as Ghoṣā, Lopāmudrā, and Apālā—female seers (*ṛṣikās*) who spoke of love, illness, desire, and cosmic insight.[3] Their verses, though few, offer glimpses into a time when women's voices were not entirely excluded from the sacred domain.

Over time, however, Brahmanical orthodoxy narrowed the space for female agency. The *Manusmṛti* and other Dharmashastra texts reinforced patriarchal norms, emphasizing women's dependence on fathers, husbands, and sons. Women's literacy declined. Scriptural access became increasingly limited to upper-caste males. And yet, in parallel, alternative traditions flourished—especially through the bhakti movement.

Bhakti (devotion) emerged in the first millennium CE as a spiritual path emphasizing love, personal relationship with the divine, and interior transformation over ritual purity. It often took form in vernacular poetry, and its loosened theological boundaries gave women a new kind of access to the sacred. Women like Āṇṭāḷ in Tamil Nadu (9th century), Akka Mahādēvī in Karnataka (12th century), and Mirabai in Rajasthan (16th century) became powerful voices in regional devotional traditions.

Āṇṭāḷ, the only female poet among the twelve Āḻvārs (Tamil poet-saints) of Tamil Vaishnavism, composed ecstatic hymns in praise of Vishnu, imagining herself as his bride. Her *Tiruppāvai*, still sung today during the month of Mārgaḻi, is revered as scripture in many South Indian temples.[4]

Akka Mahādēvī renounced marriage, wandered naked save for her long hair, and composed striking vachanas (short poetic aphorisms in Kannada)—about Shiva. "What can I do with a man's world?" she wrote. "My Lord, white as jasmine, is my only possession."[5]

These women's texts were not just spiritual outpourings. They were theological statements, challenging caste and gender hierarchies with bold metaphors and social critique. Yet their transmission was uneven. Much of their poetry circulated orally, and when later compiled—usually by male editors—it was sometimes sanitized or selectively preserved. Commentaries often emphasized their chastity and humility rather than their intellectual or spiritual authority.

The regional diversity of women's voices reflects the broader complexity of Hindu tradition. In North India, figures like Mirabai and Sahajo Bai (17th century) composed devotional poetry in Hindi and Rajasthani dialects. In South India, Āṇṭāḷ wrote in Tamil, while Akka Mahādēvī used Kannada. In Bengal, women like Rami (16th century) participated in the Vaishnava revival through vernacular songs. This geographical spread demonstrates that women's sacred expression was not isolated to particular regions but flourished across the subcontinent wherever bhakti movements took root.[6]

The epic heroines of Hindu scripture reflect similar tensions. Sītā, the central female figure of the *Rāmāyaṇa*, is often read as an icon of wifely virtue. But in some versions—especially regional or folk retellings—she challenges Rāma's decisions, refuses to undergo trials, or chooses exile on her own terms. In Valmiki's original Sanskrit version, she demonstrates considerable agency, while in some folk traditions, she is portrayed as an incarnation of the goddess Lakshmi with independent divine power.[7]

Draupadī, in the *Mahābhārata*, openly questions her husbands, denounces injustice, and calls upon Krishna for justice after her public humiliation. In some versions, she even vows to burn the world if vengeance is denied.[8] These moments of resistance were often interpreted as literary flourishes rather than theological contributions. But for later women readers and performers, they offered models of sacred speech.

The colonial period added another layer of complexity. British orientalists and Indian reformers alike tended to highlight "suffering woman" tropes—recasting Sītā and Sāvitrī as passive ideals while downplaying voices like Mirabai or Akka Mahādēvī. This selective emphasis shaped how these figures were taught and remembered, often diminishing their more radical expressions. In turn, postcolonial feminist scholars such as Uma

Chakravarti and Vasudha Narayanan have worked to recover the radical dimensions of these women's voices.[9]

The forms of women's religious expression evolved over time as social circumstances changed. Early Vedic women like Gārgī participated in formal philosophical debates. Medieval bhakti poets like Mirabai used devotional songs to claim spiritual authority. In the modern period, figures like Pandita Ramabai (19th century) employed memoir and social commentary to advocate for women's education and religious reform. Each generation found new ways to articulate sacred experience within the constraints of their era.[10]

Today, their songs are taught in classrooms and chanted in temples. Contemporary scholars like Madhu Kishwar and Kumkum Roy continue to uncover women's contributions to Hindu textual traditions, while practitioners across India and the diaspora draw inspiration from these historical voices. But the stories behind them—the risk, the defiance, the deliberate stepping beyond social bounds—are still being rediscovered.

These women spoke. And they were remembered. But not always as they truly were.

> *"I shall not marry a mortal man,*
> *Even if he is wise or great.*
> *I will offer myself to the Lord,*
> *The one who holds the conch and discus."*
> —Āṇṭāḷ, *Tiruppāvai* 6

The women of Hindu tradition did more than pray. They argued, sang, refused, wandered, and insisted. Their sacred agency was often cloaked in devotion, but beneath it lay critique—of caste, gender, and power. Their verses still echo in temples and on tongues, but their stories remain half-told. To remember them is not just to hear their songs; it is to recognize their courage, and to restore their place in the sacred symphony.

Also Remembered

Gārgī Vāchaknavī (c. 8th century BCE): Vedic philosopher who debated sages in the *Bṛhadāraṇyaka Upaniṣad,* one of the earliest records of women in formal philosophical discourse. Her questions about the nature of reality pushed the boundaries of theological inquiry.

Ghoṣā (Ṛg Vedic period): Female seer who composed hymns to the Ashvins, expressing both philosophical insight and personal longing. Her verses demonstrate that women's voices were part of the earliest Vedic tradition.

Āṇṭāḷ (9th century CE, Tamil Nadu): Only female Āḻvār poet-saint in the Sri Vaishnava tradition. Composed the *Tiruppāvai,* still sung in South Indian temples and considered canonical scripture by many communities.

Akka Mahādēvī (12th century CE, Karnataka): Mystic poet and Lingayat saint. Composed vachanas expressing radical detachment and divine love, challenging social conventions through her wandering lifestyle.

Sahajo Bai (17th century CE, Rajasthan): Poet-saint of the Dadu Panth who composed verses on meditation and inner realization, representing the continuation of women's devotional poetry into the early modern period.

Sītā (epic era, various retellings): Heroine of the *Rāmāyaṇa* whose agency varies significantly across versions. In some, she asserts her own divinity and rejects patriarchal judgments, while folk traditions often emphasize her independence and power.

Chapter 5: The Prophetesses They Silenced -- Miriam and Her Sisters

The dust had barely settled when she took up the tambourine.

On the far side of the sea, with the Egyptian army drowned behind them and freedom still a horizon away, Miriam raised her voice in song. The women followed, their hands clapping, feet dancing, the rhythm of deliverance echoing across the sand.

> "Sing to the LORD, for He has triumphed gloriously:
> Horse and rider He has hurled into the sea."

This was not a secondary echo. It was the first recorded act of female prophetic leadership in the Hebrew Bible. Miriam was not only the sister of Moses and Aaron. She was called *neviah*—prophetess. She was named, she was heard, she was honored.

And then she faded.[1]

In the centuries that followed, Miriam's voice became more shadow than sound. Later redactors gave her only fragments. Rabbinic midrash praised her as a righteous woman—but often as a support character, not a theologian or leader in her own right. Her name remained in sacred memory. But her voice—like those of other biblical prophetesses—was slowly tuned out.

Miriam's story reflects a broader pattern within the formation and transmission of Jewish sacred texts: early female authority acknowledged, then minimized. Named prophetesses appear in the Tanakh—Miriam, Deborah, Huldah, and others—but are rarely given extended speeches or central roles in theological discourse. Where they speak, it is often briefly. Where they lead, it is often left uncommented. And when the canon solidified under priestly and scribal control in the post-exilic period, the presence of such women became ever more peripheral.

Miriam first appears in Exodus 2, though unnamed, watching over her infant brother in the Nile reeds. She speaks boldly to Pharaoh's daughter, arranging for Moses' own mother to nurse him. Later, in Exodus 15:20–21, she is identified as a prophetess and leads the women of Israel in a song of triumph following the crossing of the Red Sea. But the verses are compact. Moses' version of the song spans over a dozen lines; Miriam's consists of just two. Scholars have long debated whether Miriam's song was originally longer—and whether Moses' version built upon or supplanted it.[2]

In Numbers 12, Miriam again appears—this time challenging Moses' exclusive claim to divine revelation. Alongside Aaron, she asks: *"Has the LORD spoken only through Moses? Has He not spoken through us also?"* (Num. 12:2). God responds not with an egalitarian affirmation, but with punishment: Miriam is struck with skin disease and cast outside the camp for seven days. Aaron pleads on her behalf; Moses intercedes; she is eventually healed. But Aaron is not punished. The message is ambiguous, and its interpretation shaped later theological assumptions about women's spiritual authority.[3]

The roles of biblical women become clearer when we understand the distinctions between different types of religious authority in ancient Israel. Prophetic roles—receiving and transmitting divine revelation—were sometimes accessible to women, as evidenced by figures like Miriam, Deborah, and Huldah. Priestly roles—conducting Temple sacrifice and maintaining ritual purity—were restricted to male Levites. Wisdom roles—teaching, interpreting, and preserving tradition—occupied a middle ground, with some evidence of female participation that was later constrained. Understanding these distinctions helps explain why certain women could speak with divine authority while remaining excluded from other forms of religious leadership.[4]

By the time the canon of Hebrew scripture took shape—understood by most scholars to have solidified in stages between the 5th and 2nd centuries BCE—priestly redactors had centralized authority around male prophetic and priestly figures. The temple cult, the Levitical caste, and post-exilic scribal classes offered little institutional space for women as legal or theological actors.[5]

And yet, in the margins and footnotes of scripture, their presence persists.

Deborah, in Judges 4–5, is explicitly called both prophetess and judge. She leads Israel into battle, delivers oracles, and composes a national victory song. But even in this celebrated narrative, later Jewish commentary often downplays her judicial role or frames it as exceptional due to male absence.[6]

Huldah, in 2 Kings 22, is consulted by King Josiah's delegation when the Book of the Law is discovered in the Temple—a moment that helped spark one of the most sweeping religious reforms in Jewish history. Her oracle is accepted without question. Yet later tradition largely sidelines her in favor of male prophets like Jeremiah, whose ministry coincided with hers.[7]

The post-biblical era saw further contraction. Rabbinic Judaism, with its intense focus on Torah study, developed within a social structure in which women were generally not permitted to study sacred texts formally. While women's roles in maintaining domestic religious practice—lighting Sabbath candles, preparing kosher food, maintaining family purity—were valued, they were seldom recognized as interpreters or transmitters of sacred text.

Yet women found ways to maintain and express religious authority across different historical periods, adapting their forms of expression to changing circumstances. And yet, oral traditions, folk customs, and women's liturgical practices sustained alternative modes of transmission. Yiddish prayer books written for women, called *tkhines*, emerged in the early modern period. These were often authored anonymously but show a deep engagement with scripture—retold, personalized, and spiritually profound.[8] In the medieval period, figures like Bruriah demonstrated women's capacity for Talmudic scholarship, though such examples remained exceptional. In modern times, women like Glikl of Hameln used memoir and business correspondence to preserve and transmit Jewish religious life, creating new forms of religious expression that documented the lived experience of faith.[9]

Today, feminist Jewish scholars such as Tikva Frymer-Kensky, Judith Plaskow, and Rachel Adler have worked to recover the theological implications of women's voices in scripture. They argue that prophetesses like Miriam and Huldah were not aberrations, but part of a larger, if often hidden, pattern of female religious authority. Their erasure was not accidental. It was editorial.[10] Contemporary scholarship in Rabbinic literature continues to uncover evidence of women's contributions to Jewish religious thought, demonstrating that the marginalization of women's voices was a historical process rather than a theological necessity.

The biblical canon remains fixed. But its interpretation is not.

Miriam still sings, if we listen.

> *"Then Miriam the prophetess, Aaron's sister, took a timbrel in her hand, and all the women followed her, with timbrels and dancing. Miriam sang to them:*
> *'Sing to the LORD, for He has triumphed gloriously; horse and rider He has hurled into the sea.'"*
> —Exodus 15:20–21

The silence around Miriam and her sisters was not the absence of sound. It was the consequence of choices—what to include, what to minimize, whose speech to amplify. The prophetesses of Israel left traces in the sacred text, but their echoes had to compete with centuries of redaction and restriction. Still, they remain. Not as legends alone, but as the foremothers of a prophetic tradition that was never meant to be male-only. To remember them is to widen the lens of revelation.

Also Remembered

Deborah (Judges 4–5): Prophetess and judge who led Israel to military victory against the Canaanites. One of the few women in the Bible given extensive speech, her story demonstrates that women could hold both prophetic and judicial authority in early Israel.

Huldah (2 Kings 22): Prophetess consulted by Josiah's court when the Book of the Law was discovered in the Temple. Her oracle affirmed the authenticity of the text and sparked major religious reforms, yet she is rarely mentioned alongside her contemporary Jeremiah.

The Wise Woman of Abel (2 Samuel 20): Negotiated peace between David's army and her besieged city through theological argument and political wisdom. Though unnamed, she represents the tradition of women as community leaders and peace-makers.

Bruriah (2nd century CE): Talmudic-era sage known for her sharp legal mind and commentary on Jewish law. Often cited by later rabbis for her scholarship, though some later traditions minimized her contributions or questioned her character.

Glikl of Hameln (17th century CE): Memoirist and businesswoman whose writings provide rare female perspective on Jewish religious life in early modern Europe. Her memoirs demonstrate how women preserved and transmitted religious culture through personal narrative.

The Woman of Tekoa (2 Samuel 14): Delivered a parable to King David that changed his mind about recalling his exiled son Absalom. Her theological sophistication and rhetorical skill demonstrate women's capacity for religious and political persuasion.

Chapter 6: Sacred Voices Beyond the Center

She stood on the temple steps, firelight flickering across her robes. Her name was Hvov, daughter of the prophet Zarathustra, and though few outside Zoroastrian tradition remember her, she was said to have kept the sacred flame alive in a time of threat and confusion. In later lore, she became a custodian of her father's teachings—one of the women entrusted to carry the *Avesta* when oral memory was all they had.

In the North Indian plains, another woman gathered flour and lentils in the courtyard of a modest home. Her name was Mata Khivi, wife of Guru Angad, second master of the Sikh faith. In a young, still-forming religious community, she quietly established a practice that would become foundational: the *langar*, a communal kitchen feeding all regardless of caste or creed. Though she left no writings, her theology was imprinted in action. Feeding others was sacred text made flesh.

And across the mountains in Mesoamerica, long before Spanish conquest, priestesses of the Mexica (Aztecs) memorized cosmological chants, performed lunar rites, and spoke with the voices of earth and sky. Their names were often titles—*cihuacohuatl* ("woman serpent") or *ticitl* ("priest-healer")—but their authority was recognized in rituals that connected the living to the gods.[1]

These women did not appear in the "big five" canon lists. They were not part of the textual traditions that formed the basis of world religion syllabi or interfaith dialogues. But they shaped the sacred in their own ways: through vision, transmission, memory, and ritual. Their voices mattered, even if written history failed to hear them.

However, we must approach their stories with scholarly caution. Many of these figures exist at the intersection of history and legend, their lives filtered through centuries of oral tradition, religious interpretation, and sometimes romanticized modern reconstruction. The challenge in recovering women from traditions with limited written records requires us to balance recognition of their importance with acknowledgment of what we cannot definitively know.

In Zoroastrian tradition, women held early religious roles that became obscured over time. The *Gathas*, the most ancient hymns attributed to Zarathustra, speak often in inclusive, even gender-egalitarian language.[2] Later texts, such as the *Denkard* and *Bundahishn*, include stories of women participating in sacred debates, temple leadership, and ritual transmission. While most of these women remain unnamed, figures like Hvov—daughter of the founder himself—suggest the possibility of early female prophetic agency. Her memory survives primarily in later Pahlavi commentary, and while her historicity is debated, her symbolic significance is not.[3]

Sikhism, emerging in the 15th century, offered unusual prominence to women in both its theology and practice. Guru Nanak's own writings rejected gender hierarchy, and women were included in the early congregations (*sangats*). Mata Khivi (1506–1582), wife of the second Guru, is remembered not for formal theological writing but for her institutional legacy: she organized and expanded the *langar*, a revolutionary form of caste-free, communal eating that remains central to Sikh identity today.[4] While Sikh scripture (the *Guru Granth Sahib*) includes compositions from both male and female contributors of varying castes and religions, women's names are few. Yet figures like Mata Khivi demonstrate how shaping sacred practice can be as enduring as shaping sacred text.

Indigenous traditions across the Americas, Africa, and Asia offer rich, though often under-documented, examples of female religious leadership. In Mesoamerican societies, particularly the Aztec and Maya, priestesses performed divination, interpreted calendars, and conducted public ritual.[5] The Spanish conquest and forced Christianization destroyed most indigenous texts and suppressed female authority, but oral traditions preserve the memory of spiritual women whose knowledge linked cosmos and community. Recent archaeological evidence from sites like Teotihuacan suggests that women held significant ritual roles, as evidenced by burial goods and temple murals depicting female religious figures.[6]

Among the Yoruba of West Africa, *Iyanifa*—female Ifa diviners—were essential in interpreting the *Odu Ifa*, the sacred corpus of divinatory verses. Though often overshadowed by male *babalawo* in scholarly accounts, these women held communal authority in ritual and cosmological knowledge.[7] Similarly, female griots—oral historians and praise-singers—

preserved genealogies and sacred narratives across generations, often adapting language and metaphor to reflect women's lives and struggles. For deeper understanding of West African women's religious roles, see Oyèrónkẹ́ Oyěwùmí's *The Invention of Women* and Jacob Olupona's comprehensive studies of Yoruba religion.[8]

In Central Asia, women mystics and saints are commemorated in local shrines and stories, though few are recorded in canonical Sufi literature. Figures like Amina Khatoon and Bibi Pak Daman are remembered as spiritual teachers and guardians of sacred spaces.[9] In Daoist tradition, immortal women—such as He Xiangu—emerged in religious tales as paragons of wisdom and virtue, associated with sacred mountains and divine elixirs. For scholarly treatment of these figures, see Suzanne Cahill's *Transcendence and Divine Passion*.[10]

The Yazidi tradition of northern Iraq preserves ancient stories of female spiritual authority, though persecution has threatened both the community and its oral traditions. Yazidi women known as *qawwals* and *kocheks* serve as religious singers and keepers of sacred songs, maintaining theological knowledge through performance rather than text.[11] Among Jain communities, *sadhvis* (female ascetics) have long practiced extreme renunciation and scripture memorization, with some achieving recognition as spiritual teachers despite the tradition's emphasis on male leadership.[12]

In the Pacific Northwest, Indigenous women like those of the Tlingit and Haida peoples served as clan mothers and keepers of oral traditions, responsible for maintaining genealogies, territorial rights, and ceremonial knowledge. The devastating impact of colonization severely disrupted these traditions, though revival efforts continue today.[13]

These figures remind us that the boundaries of sacred text are broader than paper and ink. Transmission can happen through song, ritual, memory, and embodied practice. Though many of these women were never canonized—indeed, never written down in their lifetimes—their presence shaped the beliefs and behaviors of countless communities.

What unites them is not a single tradition or textual corpus, but the fact that their voices endured despite structural erasure. They were carried in chant, remembered in family stories, inscribed into the architecture of community. Their contributions lie not in verses quoted but in rituals performed, ethics enacted, and lives changed.

"She [Mata Khivi] served the congregation with loving care; She spread the Guru's message not by preaching, but by feeding."
—Bhatt Bhikan, *Guru Granth Sahib*, Ang 967

To seek sacred voices only in the centers of canon is to overlook the women who whispered theology in kitchens, danced it into ritual, and kept it alive in stories told under starlight. Their absence from scripture was not the absence of sacred thought. It was the absence of scribes who recognized it. Their memory endures—not just in what was written, but in what was lived.

Also Remembered

Bibi Nanaki (15th century, Punjab): Sister of Guru Nanak, considered the first believer in his message. Respected for her spiritual insight and early support of the Sikh community, she represents the often-overlooked family members who nurtured emerging religious movements.

He Xiangu and Other Daoist Immortals (Tang–Song dynasties): Female sages associated with health, immortality, and wisdom in Daoist lore. While often mythologized, they preserve memories of women's spiritual authority in Chinese religious tradition.

Yazidi Qawwals (modern Iraq): Female spiritual leaders who maintain oral religious teachings in a persecuted minority tradition. Their role demonstrates how women preserved sacred knowledge through performance in communities under threat.

Jain Sadhvis (India, ancient to present): Female ascetics known for extreme renunciation, fasting, and scripture memorization. Many remain anonymous but have been pivotal in oral transmission and spiritual guidance within Jain communities.

Tibetan Translator Wives (8th–10th century): Local women who married Indian Buddhist scholars, learned Sanskrit, and helped transmit Buddhist texts into Tibetan. Their linguistic skills were essential to preserving Buddhism during its transmission to Tibet.

Mesoamerican Priestesses (pre-Columbian Americas): Women who served as diviners, healers, and ritual specialists in Aztec, Maya, and other indigenous traditions. Though their names are largely lost, archaeological evidence confirms their significant religious roles.

Chapter 7: What If They Had Been Canon?

They were there from the beginning: speaking, singing, teaching, leading. Some, like Miriam and Aisha, appear in the very core of scripture. Others, like Mirabai and the Therīgāthā poets, left verses so powerful they could not be erased—only recontextualized. Still others, like Mary Magdalene or Sita, were reshaped across centuries, bent into roles that diminished their agency or rendered them symbolic rather than human. What links them all is not just presence but transformation: their original authority was obscured, softened, or subordinated as sacred texts were canonized and institutional control tightened.

Across the five major religious traditions explored in Part I—Christianity, Islam, Hinduism, Buddhism, and Judaism—we see a common pattern. Women appear in foundational texts and early oral traditions not as marginal figures but as prophets, judges, teachers, household theologians, poets, mystics, and reformers. Over time, however, the recording and interpretation of those roles passed largely to men. Women's words were abbreviated, their deeds attributed to others, their bodies made metaphor, their names lost or confined to ritual niches. Even where female figures were retained in scripture, their portrayals often reflect the anxieties and priorities of later editors more than their original significance.

And yet, the sacred persisted in their voices. If one listens closely, the textual record does not lie—it simply mumbles when speaking of women. The challenge is to read carefully, compare traditions, and attend to the spaces where silence speaks.

Scholar Debate: How Central Were Women to Sacred Text Formation?

This scholarly debate centers on a contested question: were women truly central to the formation of sacred texts, or primarily involved in interpretation and practice? Did institutional redaction erase active female authorship, or were women's roles more often informal and therefore less subject to erasure?

Karen L. King (Harvard Divinity School) argues that texts like the *Gospel of Mary* and Gnostic writings reveal a deliberate suppression of female apostolic authority, suggesting that women's early textual contributions were more central than later canons admit. "The silencing of women like Mary Magdalene," King contends, "was not incidental but systematic—part of a broader effort to consolidate male ecclesial control."[1]

Tikva Frymer-Kensky (University of Chicago), writing on the Hebrew Bible, agrees that women once held spiritual authority but emphasizes that the scriptural authors were almost entirely male, and thus women's roles were shaped more by inclusion and omission than by direct textual authorship. "We must distinguish," she argues, "between women's religious authority and women's literary agency—the former was real, the latter largely denied."[2]

Asma Sayeed (UCLA) notes that in Islam, women like Aisha were not authors but vital transmitters of hadith and interpreters of law. She argues their authority came from proximity and memory, not textual production, and that later restrictions reflect social shifts rather than original design. "The marginalization of women's interpretive authority was gradual," Sayeed observes, "tied to the institutionalization of Islamic learning in male-dominated madrasas."[3]

Ruth Vanita (Ashoka University) challenges rigid boundaries between sacred and non-sacred text in Hinduism, emphasizing that female saints like Mirabai created devotional literature that functioned as theology, regardless of whether it was canonized. "The distinction between scripture and devotional poetry," Vanita argues, "often serves to diminish women's theological contributions while preserving male Brahmanical authority."[4]

Karma Lekshe Tsomo (Sakyadhita) argues that early Buddhist nuns were active teachers, authors, and institutional founders, and that their marginalization came with later monastic hierarchies and commentarial traditions, not the earliest phases of Buddhist scripture. "The *Therīgāthā* demonstrates that women's enlightenment experiences were once considered authoritative Buddhist doctrine," Tsomo notes, "their later marginalization represents institutional choice, not theological necessity."[5]

Together, these scholars illuminate the layered nature of erasure. Some women were cut out. Others were never written in. Still others were transformed—amplified in piety, diminished in voice.

What Would Have Changed?

What might have shifted if these women's original voices had remained fully present in the formation, teaching, and interpretation of sacred texts? These possibilities are grounded in early sources and scholarly reconstructions of what was lost:

Apostolic Succession Would Look Different: If Mary Magdalene and Junia had been publicly affirmed as apostles, the Church's theology of ordination—and the exclusion of women from priesthood—might have evolved differently. As Ann Graham Brock argues, "The competition between Peter and Mary Magdalene in early Christian texts suggests that female apostolic authority was a live option that was deliberately suppressed rather than naturally absent."[6] The clerical structure itself could have been shaped by a more gender-inclusive apostolic model.

Islamic Legal Thought Would Be Broader: Had Aisha's interpretive authority been institutionalized rather than constrained, the *fiqh* tradition might have featured more expansive rulings on gender, family, and ritual—anchored not only in male analogies but in embodied female experience. Mohammad Akram Nadwi's research demonstrates that over 8,000 women served as hadith scholars throughout Islamic history; their systematic marginalization represented "an enormous loss of intellectual and spiritual capital."[7]

Hindu Devotional Theology Might Have Centered Female Saints: If Mirabai, Andal, and Akka Mahadevi had been included in formal Vedic or Vedantic commentaries, Hindu theology might today speak more fluently in the language of resistance, interiority, and gendered longing for the divine. Vasudha Narayanan suggests that "the exclusion of women's devotional voices from formal theological discourse impoverished Hindu intellectual tradition by privileging abstract philosophy over embodied spiritual experience."[8]

Buddhist Education Might Elevate Female Enlightenment Equally: Had the *Therīgāthā* been taught alongside foundational monastic texts, Buddhist understandings of enlightenment and discipline might reflect a more embodied and relational framework—one that resists the gendered binaries inherited from later scholasticism. Rita Gross argues that "the marginalization of the *Therīgāthā* contributed to Buddhism's overly intellectualized approach to liberation, losing the grounded wisdom of women's awakening experiences."[9]

Jewish Prophetic Tradition Might Be More Inclusive: If figures like Miriam and Huldah had been given fuller treatment in biblical texts and later commentary, Jewish concepts of prophecy and religious authority might have developed with less gender restriction. Judith Plaskow contends that "the minimization of female prophets established a precedent that excluded women from religious leadership for millennia, despite early evidence of their spiritual authority."[10]

These are not speculative fantasies but grounded possibilities, supported by early sources and scholarly reconstructions. The exclusion of women's authority was not inevitable. It was the outcome of decisions—textual, institutional, theological.

Yet the work of recovery cannot remain purely historical. As contemporary scholars across traditions demonstrate, the reinterpretation of these women's legacies continues to reshape religious thought today. Jewish feminists like Rachel Adler and Muslim scholars like Amina Wadud draw on figures like Miriam and Aisha to argue for expanded women's roles. Buddhist teachers like Ayya Tathaaloka invoke the *Therīgāthā* to support full nun ordination. Hindu theologians like Vandana Shiva connect devotional poets like Mirabai to contemporary eco-feminist spirituality. The recovery of these voices is not just about the past—it is about reimagining religious authority for the future.[11]

The women within sacred texts did not lack insight or faith. They lacked scribes who saw their speech as scripture. Canon did not grow only by inspiration—it grew by inclusion and omission, citation and silence. And those choices shaped religious memory for millennia. Yet the recovery of these women is not merely an act of justice. It is an act of theological clarity. What they said—and what we failed to preserve—still echoes through the sacred. The question is whether we are ready to listen.

Interlude A: The Mystics' Rebellion

The rules were clear: women could not preach, interpret, or instruct in sacred doctrine. But mystics heard other voices.

When the gates of official theology were closed, a different current opened underground. In whispered visions and ecstatic poems, in dreams, dictations, and divine encounters, women across traditions claimed access not just to the sacred—but to the authority to speak it.

In a convent cell in 12th-century Germany, Hildegard of Bingen rose from her bed with feverish urgency. The vision she had received must be written, even though she—an untrained woman—had no formal permission to record theology. But the voice had been clear: "Write what you see and hear." Over the next decades, she composed more than one hundred visions, complete with commentary, musical notation, and invented languages. She claimed no authorship. The visions, she said, came from the Living Light (her term for divine illumination).[1]

In the deserts of Basra in the 8th century, Rābiʿa al-ʿAdawiyya walked barefoot in defiance of worldly vanity, singing of God with the language of radical love. "I do not worship You out of fear of hell or love of paradise. I worship You because You are worthy of worship." Her sayings circulated widely—quoted by men, studied in Sufi circles (mystical Islamic communities), whispered in hagiographies. She held no formal position. But her poetry became sacred transmission.[2]

In 16th-century northern India, Mirabai sang to her beloved Krishna in tones of longing and liberation. Though married into royal wealth, she rejected societal expectations, calling herself a servant only to God. "The darkness of night is coming. Who will lead me home?" Her bhajans (devotional songs) were preserved by generations of lower-caste women who understood that her longing was their own.[3]

In England, during a time of plague and political uncertainty, Julian of Norwich recorded a series of revelations that came to her during a near-death illness. "All shall be well, and all shall be well, and all manner of thing shall be well." Her *Showings* became the first known book in English authored by a woman. Like Hildegard, she attributed her words to divine instruction, not personal initiative.[4]

These patterns extended beyond the major traditions. In medieval German Christianity, Mechthild of Magdeburg composed visionary poetry that influenced later mystics like Meister Eckhart. In Korea, Buddhist nun Chŏnghye Gak (1597-1674) wrote enlightenment poetry that challenged conventional monastic authority. Such voices emerged wherever institutional religion created barriers to women's spiritual expression.[5]

What unites these women is not doctrine or geography but defiance. Their mysticism was not withdrawal—it was rebellion. Not one of violence, but of vision. They refused to let theology be the exclusive language of men in robes and councils. They wrote without permission, spoke without ordination, and taught without credentials.

Mystical experience became a mode of sacred authorship.

It also became a strategy. Across traditions, institutional religion has tended to regulate who can speak on behalf of the divine. But mystical experience—by its very nature—cannot be confined by hierarchical gatekeeping. It does not rely on training, lineage, or gender. It descends. And when it descends upon a woman, she becomes more than a believer. She becomes a witness.

This is why mysticism became one of the few domains where women's spiritual voices could survive with authority. They were often written off as eccentric or apolitical. But in truth, their writings shaped theology, inspired reforms, and gave voice to those excluded from formal commentary.

However, we must read these women's sayings with critical sympathy. Many quotations attributed to female mystics come from hagiographic sources written decades or centuries after their deaths, often by male disciples or admirers. While the core of their teachings likely reflects their authentic voices, specific sayings may have been embellished, romanticized, or filtered through later theological concerns. This does not diminish their importance, but it reminds us to approach their words as both historical witnesses and literary constructions.[6]

Consider these recurring patterns:

Divine legitimation: Most female mystics begin their writings by disclaiming authorship and citing divine command. This bypasses institutional gatekeeping and grants rhetorical authority.

Experiential epistemology: Rather than citing scripture or doctrine, mystics assert truth through experience: visions, revelations, and emotional knowledge.

Gender inversion: Many mystics describe their relationship with the divine in intimate, even erotic terms. These metaphors allowed them to reframe power and piety outside traditional roles.

Community resonance: Though dismissed by elite theologians, female mystics often became touchstones for popular devotion—quoted in homes, sung in rituals, carried forward in oral tradition.

And their words endure.

> "I saw a great mountain of iron, and upon it One sitting with such glory that it blinded my sight." —Hildegard of Bingen, *Scivias*[7]

> "I carry a torch in one hand, and a bucket of water in the other: to set fire to heaven and drown hell, so that people might worship God purely for love." —Attributed to Rābiʿa al-ʿAdawiyya[8]

> "Mira's Lord is the mountain lifter [Krishna]. I will not be afraid." —Mirabai[9]

> "God is our Mother as truly as He is our Father." —Julian of Norwich, *Revelations of Divine Love*[10]

In these voices, we glimpse theology not of abstraction but of fire and feeling. These were not scholars in the traditional sense. But they shaped the sacred anyway.

The rebellion of the mystics was quiet, but it was not tame. It dared to say: if the sacred speaks to us, we will answer. If it gives us words, we will write them. And if it calls us to lead, we will lead—even without permission.

Their visions gave birth to living texts. Their songs became scripture to the people. Their defiance gave theology a new tongue.

And in doing so, they wrote themselves back into a sacred history that had tried to forget them.

Part II

The Women Around

Behind every sacred text lies an invisible network of preservation: the scribes who copied manuscripts, the teachers who memorized verses, the patrons who funded temples, the mothers who whispered prayers into children's ears. This section illuminates the women who surrounded and sustained sacred traditions without formal recognition. From Christian mystics illuminating Gospels in medieval scriptoriums to Islamic women preserving hadith through oral chains of transmission, from Hindu temple singers keeping epic stories alive to Jewish women carrying liturgical memory through generations of exile—these are the hidden guardians whose devotion shaped what we now call sacred, even when their names were lost to history.

Chapter 8: Ink and Illumination -- Christian Women as Scribes and Mystics

The cloister smelled of candle wax and damp wool. In the abbey of Chelles, just outside Paris, the year was 875. A pale winter sun filtered through narrow windows as a young nun bent over a worn wooden desk, scratching her quill across vellum. Her task: to copy and correct a Latin Gospel manuscript for liturgical use. Her name is lost, but her work endures. In the margins, she made careful corrections, clarified syntax, and—just once—added a single line in a more elegant script: *Deus amat humiles*. God loves the humble. The manuscript, long attributed to an anonymous monk, was eventually reexamined by paleographers (scholars who study ancient handwriting) who recognized the softer ligature forms, distinctive spacing, and fine-point quill work typical of female scribes trained in the Carolingian nunneries.[1]

She is now referred to as "The Nun of Chelles," and she represents hundreds—perhaps thousands—of women who copied, preserved, and occasionally illuminated (decorated with artwork and ornamental lettering) the sacred texts of Christianity across the medieval and early modern periods. Their names were rarely recorded. Their handwriting was often misattributed. Their theological insights, embedded in marginalia or prayer, were not included in official doctrinal commentaries. But without them, vast swaths of Christian scripture would have been lost.

The early Christian church did not initially prohibit women from textual engagement. Women like Thecla were remembered in apocryphal Acts as preachers and teachers. Wealthy Roman matrons like Paula and Marcella supported Jerome's translation of the Vulgate and studied Hebrew and Greek alongside him.[2]

But as the church institutionalized in late antiquity, literacy and scriptural authority became increasingly male domains. Monastic communities—especially after the Rule of St. Benedict—provided the primary locations for text production. While male scriptoria (writing workshops) were well-documented and celebrated, female ones remained under-recorded. Yet they existed across the Christian world.

Chelles, Andlau, Essen, Whitby: these were just a few of the women's monasteries where scripture was copied, hymns composed, commentaries glossed, and theological ideas quietly exchanged.[3] In Byzantium, Orthodox nuns in convents like Kecharitomene copied liturgical manuscripts and maintained libraries that preserved early Christian texts through periods of iconoclastic persecution. In Ethiopia, women in monastic communities helped preserve the Ge'ez biblical tradition, contributing to one of Christianity's most ancient surviving textual lineages.[4]

Women in these spaces did not simply copy texts; they interpreted them. They shaped the layout, emphasized key passages, added devotional reflections. Some even wrote original compositions in the margins, from Latin prayers to vernacular meditations. Modern textual criticism increasingly reveals the extent of women's scribal labor, as scholars develop new methods for identifying female hands through analysis of letter formation, spacing patterns, and decorative elements.[5]

Perhaps the most famous example of female Christian textual production comes from Hildegard of Bingen (1098–1179). A Benedictine abbess, visionary, composer, and author, Hildegard dictated divine visions that formed the basis of theological treatises such as *Scivias*, accompanied by complex illuminations. She claimed no authority of her own: all was attributed to divine inspiration. This rhetorical humility allowed her to bypass ecclesial resistance and speak prophetically to popes, bishops, and emperors.[6]

Her writings were preserved—some by male scribes, others by nuns in her convent. Yet for centuries, her theological status remained ambiguous. Only recently has she been recognized officially as a Doctor of the Church, an honor conferred in 2012.[7]

Other women's contributions remained less visible but no less essential. Julian of Norwich (c. 1342–1416), whose *Revelations of Divine Love* is the earliest known English-language book by a woman, offered a vision of God that was simultaneously orthodox and radical. She emphasized divine motherhood, unconditional love, and the ultimate salvation of all creation. Her manuscript circulated in small circles, copied by hand, preserved largely through the diligence of later women.

In the later medieval period, Margery Kempe—unlettered herself—dictated the first known English autobiography to a scribe. Her book describes visionary experiences, scriptural meditation, and ecstatic encounters with Christ. Though often mocked in her own time, Margery's text is now recognized as a rare window into lay female piety, shaped by scripture but not bound to institutional constraints.[8]

The printing press complicated the picture. While it democratized access to texts, it also consolidated doctrinal control. Yet some Christian women participated in this new age of textual dissemination. In Reformation-era Geneva, for example, female printers and editors published vernacular Bibles and catechisms under male names or anonymously. In convents across Spain and Italy, nuns wrote theological treatises that circulated internally, often in manuscript form only.

One of the lesser-known figures is Sister Illuminata, a 17th-century Dominican nun in Italy whose illuminated psalters—now preserved in fragments—combine textual fidelity with visual theology. Her illuminations were not merely decorative; they reflected careful interpretation, emphasizing female biblical figures, maternal imagery of God, and cosmic motifs rarely found in male-produced manuscripts.

The tradition of anonymous women scribes extended well beyond medieval Europe. In the manuscript colophons (scribal signatures or notes) of some Syriac and Coptic texts, scholars have identified references to female copyists, though their names are often abbreviated or obscured. Recent paleographic studies suggest that women may have played larger roles in preserving early Christian literature in these traditions than previously recognized.[9]

Despite these contributions, the formal theological tradition rarely recognized women as authorities. They were tolerated as mystics, remembered as saints, and forgotten as scribes. The institutional preference for male authorship meant that even when women's theological insights survived, they were often reattributed to male teachers or absorbed into anonymous tradition.

Yet without their labor, faith, and ink, there would be no sacred text to revere.

> *"From the time I was a little girl... I saw a great light, and in it I heard the voice of the Living Light, saying: 'Write what you see and hear.'"*
> —Hildegard of Bingen, *Scivias*

They held the ink that shaped the sacred—sometimes with trembling hands, sometimes with confident strokes. Their names are missing from footnotes and councils, but their fingerprints remain on the very pages we call holy. To recover the women who copied, glossed, and sometimes dared to write theology is to realize that scripture was never just preserved by power. It was preserved by faith—and often, by female hands.

Also Remembered

Julian of Norwich (14th century): Anchorite and visionary whose *Showings* present a profound theology of divine love and maternal imagery. Her work survived through careful copying by women in religious communities who recognized its spiritual value.

Margery Kempe (15th century): Pilgrim and mystic whose dictated autobiography captures lay biblical devotion and female spiritual experience. Her text demonstrates how women engaged with scripture outside formal theological education.

Sister Illuminata (17th century): Italian nun and illuminator whose richly symbolic psalters express theological insight through image. Her work shows how visual interpretation could convey theological understanding.

Female Printers of Geneva (16th century): Anonymous women involved in the publication of Protestant texts during the Reformation. They represent women's participation in the new technology of printing sacred texts.

The Chelles Scribes (9th–10th century): Anonymous nuns known from manuscript corrections and paleographic signatures in Carolingian scriptoria. They exemplify the thousands of women whose careful copying preserved Christian texts.

Byzantine Copyists (4th–15th centuries): Orthodox nuns who maintained manuscript traditions through iconoclastic periods and political upheavals, preserving both liturgical and theological texts in Eastern Christianity.

Chapter 9: Guardians of Revelation -- Islamic Women as Preservers

In the courtyard of the Umayyad Mosque in Damascus, sometime in the 11th century, a group of students sat cross-legged beneath the colonnade. Among them, veiled and commanding in her presence, was Fatima bint Sa'd al-Khayr. Her students—men and women both—recorded her teachings of hadith, the sayings of the Prophet Muhammad. She held an *ijaza* (certification of authority to transmit sacred knowledge), passed down through a line of scholars stretching back to the Prophet himself. Her memory endures not in images or biography but in isnads (meticulously documented chains of transmission in Islamic scholarship). Her name appears again and again: "From Fatima bint Sa'd, who heard it from..."[1]

She was not alone. In medieval Islam, women were not only allowed but often encouraged to memorize the Qur'an, study jurisprudence, and transmit hadith. From Cairo to Baghdad, Delhi to Fez, Muslim women served as preservers of sacred text—not always by writing it, but by embodying and transmitting it with precision and reverence.

This legacy begins with Aisha bint Abi Bakr, wife of the Prophet Muhammad and one of the most prolific hadith transmitters in the early Islamic period. Her proximity to the Prophet, intellectual rigor, and theological insight made her a cornerstone of Sunni tradition. She is credited with transmitting over 2,000 hadith, many concerning domestic life, prayer, ethics, and women's issues.² Later generations invoked her authority not just for content, but for method: Aisha corrected other Companions' interpretations and insisted on precision in wording.

In the centuries that followed, women like Fatima al-Juzdaniyya, Amat al-Wahid, and Karima al-Marwaziyya taught in mosques, madrasas, and homes. They received ijazat from male and female scholars alike, and in turn conferred these certificates on students. These documents—preserved in manuscript collections—provide concrete evidence of women's roles in the intergenerational preservation of sacred texts. Mohammad Akram Nadwi's groundbreaking biographical dictionary documents over 8,000 women hadith scholars throughout Islamic history, challenging assumptions about the exclusivity of male religious authority.³

One of the most famous was Karima al-Marwaziyya (d. 1070), a scholar of hadith in Mecca known for her transmission of *Sahih al-Bukhari*, the most authoritative Sunni collection. Her narrations were considered so precise that later scholars preferred her isnad over others.⁴ Male scholars traveled long distances to study under her. She set strict conditions: students had to recite the hadiths from memory before she would confirm their transmission.

This was not unusual. In fact, as hadith criticism developed in the 9th and 10th centuries, scholars began noting that female transmitters were often more precise and less likely to alter or embellish traditions—perhaps because they were less involved in political debates and public preaching.⁵ Modern scholars debate whether this pattern of female reliability was the norm or an exceptional recognition within a male-dominated field, but the evidence suggests it was widespread enough to be noted by contemporary observers.

The tradition of women's religious authority developed differently within Sunni and Shi'i communities. In Sunni Islam, women's roles as hadith transmitters were broadly accepted and institutionalized through the ijaza system. In Shi'i tradition, while women's transmission roles were also recognized, the emphasis on lineage through the Imams created different pathways for religious authority. However, both traditions preserved records of women scholars and transmitters, suggesting that female religious authority was a consistent feature across Islamic communities.[6]

In addition to hadith, women served as huffaz (memorizers of the Qur'an) across the Islamic world. Many became teachers of *tajwīd* (rules of Qur'anic recitation) and trained both male and female students. In some West African communities, girls who memorized the Qur'an were considered desirable marriage partners because of their sacred knowledge.[7]

The role of women as Qur'anic reciters continues into the present, though not without controversy. While female voices are often restricted in public worship settings, private instruction and educational roles remain strong. Notably, in recent decades, women like Shaykha Halima al-Rafiqi in Morocco and Shaykha Samira az-Zain in Lebanon have received recognition for their mastery of Qur'anic sciences.

Despite this rich tradition, the textual record remains uneven. Many female scholars are known only through isnads, not biographies. Their names appear in margins, not headlines. Their writings, if they existed, were rarely copied or preserved. Social norms often prevented their travel, publication, or public leadership—yet they found ways to teach, to transmit, to preserve.

One such example is Nana Asma'u (1793–1864), a scholar and poet from the Sokoto Caliphate in present-day Nigeria. Fluent in Arabic, Hausa, and Fulfulde, she memorized the Qur'an and wrote extensively on Islamic ethics and female education. She trained a network of women known as *yan-taru* ("those who gather together"), who spread religious knowledge across rural areas. Her poems, written in mnemonic verse, were used to teach both theology and literacy.[8]

The modern era has seen a resurgence of female engagement with sacred texts—not only as teachers and reciters, but as scholars and exegetes. Figures such as Amina Wadud, Asma Barlas, and Kecia Ali have drawn on historical precedents like Aisha and Karima al-Marwaziyya to reassert women's authority in Qur'anic interpretation.[9] While not always accepted in traditional institutions, their work continues the legacy of guardianship in new forms.

Contemporary Islamic scholarship increasingly recognizes that women's preservation of sacred texts was not exceptional but integral to Islamic tradition. Asma Sayeed's research demonstrates that women's exclusion from formal religious authority was gradual and often linked to broader social and political changes rather than theological requirements.[10] This recognition has implications for ongoing debates about women's roles in Islamic religious leadership.

To study Islamic sacred texts without acknowledging the women who preserved them is to ignore the very isnads that form the foundation of authenticity. The text may be unchanging, but the chains that carried it were, for centuries, filled with women.

> *"Karima bint Ahmad al-Marwaziyya narrated to us this hadith, with precise transmission and clear recitation, may God reward her."*
> —Excerpt from manuscript margin, *Sahih al-Bukhari*, Dār al-Kutub al-Zāhiriyya Collection (Damascus)

They did not write doctrine or declare fatwas, but they memorized, recited, transmitted, and taught with rigor. Their voices echoed through sacred syllables, carried forward in isnads that bound hearts to heaven. The ink of Islam was not only held by men. It was carried in the breath and memory of women who, though rarely named in formal histories, were essential guardians of revelation.

Also Remembered

Karima al-Marwaziyya (11th century, Mecca): Renowned transmitter of *Sahih al-Bukhari* with highly respected isnad chains. Her precision in transmission was so valued that scholars preferred her versions over others, demonstrating the high regard for women's scholarship in medieval Islam.

Fatima al-Juzdaniyya (12th century, Baghdad): Jurist and hadith teacher known for training scholars across the Abbasid realm. Her students included both men and women, reflecting the integrated nature of Islamic educational networks.

Nana Asma'u (19th century, Nigeria): Scholar-poet who created an educational network for Muslim women in West Africa. Her multilingual approach and mnemonic teaching methods demonstrate the global diversity of Islamic women's scholarship.

Zaynab al-Ghazali (20th century, Egypt): Founder of the Muslim Women's Association, known for her Qur'anic teaching and political activism. She represents the continuation of women's religious authority into the modern period.

Unnamed Female Huffaz (10th–16th century, global): Women who memorized the Qur'an and taught recitation across the Islamic world, especially in Persia, Egypt, and West Africa. Their anonymity in historical records reflects the systematic underrecording of women's contributions.

Shi'i Women Transmitters (8th–15th century): Female scholars in Shi'i communities who preserved traditions related to the Imams and their teachings, demonstrating that women's authority crossed sectarian boundaries in early Islam.

Chapter 10: Patrons and Performers -- Hindu Women's Sacred Labor

In a stone temple courtyard in Tamil Nadu, the air trembles with music. The bronze lamps flicker as a lone woman sings, her voice rising in raga (melodic framework), her anklets echoing each verse. She sings not from a manuscript but from memory—passed down through generations. Her bhajan (devotional song), a musical offering to Vishnu, weaves together scripture, myth, and longing. Around her, the gathered villagers listen not as spectators but as participants. The story she chants is sacred. So is her performance.

Her name is unknown, but her words are rooted in the tradition of Andal, the 8th-century poet-saint who composed verses now embedded in daily temple liturgies (ritual worship practices) across southern India. Andal was a girl when she began writing. She claimed mystical marriage to the god Vishnu and composed her *Tiruppavai*—thirty lyrical verses of devotion—as both personal longing and collective ritual. Her words were preserved not by scribes, but by singers; not by brahmins, but by women in temple kitchens and wedding halls.[1]

This is how sacred knowledge traveled among Hindu women: not always through texts, but through rhythm, memory, ritual, and gift.

In Hinduism, especially in its devotional (bhakti) and ritual dimensions, women have long held central roles as transmitters and preservers of sacred narratives. Their methods differed from the male-dominated scholarly traditions of the Vedas and śāstra (scriptural law). Instead, women taught through song, dance, temple patronage, household rites, and embodied practice. This sacred labor, often deemed peripheral in classical theology, was foundational to the continuity of Hindu religious life.

Historical inscriptions from the Chola and Vijayanagara empires attest to royal women who sponsored temples, copied manuscripts, and commissioned scriptural commentaries. Queens like Sembiyan Mahadevi (10th century) donated bronze icons and funded renovations of Shiva temples, ensuring the preservation of liturgical traditions.[2] In North India, queens of the Mughal courts, such as Gulbadan Begum, patronized translations of Sanskrit texts into Persian, facilitating cross-cultural religious dialogue.

But most Hindu women were not royalty. Their sacred work unfolded in domestic spaces: decorating altars, reciting epics, preparing food as offering (naivedya), telling stories during festivals. These acts were not mere tradition. They were religious interpretation through practice.

The intersection of gender and caste created complex dynamics in women's roles as religious transmitters. Upper-caste women often had access to Sanskrit texts and could participate in household rituals that paralleled Vedic practices. Lower-caste women, excluded from orthodox traditions, developed alternative forms of sacred expression through folk songs, local goddess worship, and community festivals. Dalit women, in particular, created devotional traditions that challenged brahmanical authority while preserving ancient religious practices.³

One of the most enduring forms of women's scriptural engagement was ritual storytelling. In Maharashtra and Bengal, women gathered during fasts and festivals to retell versions of the *Ramayana* and *Mahabharata* tailored for their communities.⁴ These were not passive retellings: women added commentary, modified characters, emphasized female voices. In some regions, Sita's obedience was downplayed in favor of her suffering and endurance. In others, Draupadi was portrayed not only as a wife of five husbands but as a woman of fiery justice and divine authority.

The oral Ramayanas of rural women diverged sharply from the Sanskrit epic attributed to Valmiki. As literary scholar Paula Richman has shown, these "alternative tellings" reframe sacred narrative from a gendered lens—emphasizing not duty, but grief, survival, and resistance.⁵ In some Telugu folk variants, Sita questions Rama's authority and refuses reconciliation. These versions circulated orally and were often performed during women's gatherings, without any need for textual approval.

Another form of sacred labor was bhakti poetry. Women saints like Mirabai (16th century Rajasthan), Akka Mahadevi (12th century Karnataka), and Lalleshwari (14th century Kashmir) composed devotional verses that combined deep theological insight with personal emotional intensity. They challenged caste boundaries, rejected male authority, and saw themselves in direct relationship with the divine.

Mirabai's poems survive in dozens of regional dialects. She sang to Krishna as her only beloved, rejecting the royal life she was born into. Her verses—recorded by disciples, temple singers, and eventually missionaries—blur the line between scripture and song. They are performed in temples, remembered in homes, quoted in textbooks.[6] Her work demonstrates how North Indian women's devotional traditions paralleled those of South Indian poet-saints like Andal, creating a pan-Indian pattern of female religious expression.

In contrast, Akka Mahadevi's Kannada vachanas (short devotional poems) employed radical metaphors of nakedness and divine marriage that challenged social conventions. Her poetry was preserved within the Lingayat community, which historically granted women greater religious authority than orthodox Hindu traditions.[7]

Yet despite their spiritual richness, these women were often excluded from formal religious commentary. Their work was preserved, but not canonized. Revered, but not cited in scholarly treatises. The brahmanical tradition maintained control over what counted as authoritative scripture, even as popular devotion sustained these women's voices.

Today, the echoes of their sacred labor remain. Women continue to preserve and transmit Hindu tradition through kolams (ritual floor drawings), vratas (fasting rituals), kathas (narrative performances), and songs sung at dawn. In many rural communities, the only surviving versions of ancient texts are those kept alive in the melodies and memory of women.

Contemporary scholars like Vasudha Narayanan and Tracy Pintchman have worked to document and analyze these continuing traditions, showing how women's religious practices constitute a parallel form of scriptural authority that complements rather than competes with textual traditions.[8]

> *"I have found my beloved, and I will not let him go.*
> *Let the world call me fallen—*
> *I will not abandon the one who lifted me."*
> —Mirabai, *Bhajans*, oral tradition, multiple manuscripts

They were not called theologians, but they shaped theology. They had no commentaries, but their songs interpreted scripture. Through their offerings, chants, and quiet narrative defiance, Hindu women carried sacred knowledge in forms that text alone could not contain. Their bodies moved the rhythm, their voices bore the memory, and their hands lit the lamps that still flicker before the gods.

Also Remembered

Andal (8th century, Tamil Nadu): Poet-saint whose hymns are still sung in daily liturgies of Vishnu temples. Her *Tiruppavai* represents one of the few examples of women's devotional poetry that achieved canonical status within orthodox tradition.

Akka Mahadevi (12th century, Karnataka): Bhakti poet and mystic known for her radical renunciation and spiritual poetry to Shiva. Her vachanas challenged both gender and caste conventions within the emerging Lingayat movement.

Sembiyan Mahadevi (10th century, Chola dynasty): Queen and temple patron who commissioned inscriptions and icons still in use today. Her patronage demonstrates how royal women shaped religious architecture and ritual practice.

Lalleshwari (14th century, Kashmir): Mystic and poet whose *vakhs* (sayings) blend Shaivism and folk spirituality, transmitted orally across generations. Her work bridges Sanskrit learning and vernacular expression.

Mirabai (16th century, Rajasthan): Princess-turned-devotee whose Krishna bhajans represent North Indian women's devotional traditions. Her rejection of royal duty for divine love inspired countless later poets.

Unrecorded Village Storytellers (ongoing): Women who retell epics, modify theological themes, and pass on sacred narratives orally. They represent the vast anonymous tradition of female religious transmission that continues today.

Chapter 11: Domestic Torah -- Jewish Women as Liturgical Guardians

On a Friday afternoon in 18th-century Eastern Europe, a woman named Glikl bat Yehuda of Hameln stood in her kitchen, kneading challah dough and humming a Shabbat hymn. The flour-dusted table held more than bread: it held memory. She would soon light the candles, bless her children, and recite prayers that her mother and grandmother had once whispered. Upstairs, in a quiet room, she also kept a handwritten journal—not in Hebrew, but in Yiddish, the vernacular tongue of Ashkenazi Jews. In its pages, she wove together Torah commentary, ethical instruction, family history, and business advice.[1]

Glikl's memoir, written between 1691 and 1719, is the first known sustained autobiography by a Jewish woman. It was never intended for public publication. It was meant for her children—and for God. Her text offers a rare window into the religious world of Jewish women who were not rabbis or scribes, but nevertheless served as custodians of tradition.

In rabbinic Judaism, the formal transmission of sacred texts—Torah, Talmud, halakhic (Jewish legal) commentary—has long been dominated by men. Traditional rabbinic authority required mastery of Hebrew, Aramaic, and complex exegetical methods, and women were historically excluded from such study. But this exclusion from textual production did not mean exclusion from textual preservation. Jewish women carried sacred knowledge not in parchment, but in practice—through song, ritual, storytelling, and vernacular prayer.

They made Torah live in the home.

Medieval Jewish legal codes like the *Shulchan Aruch* mandated that men study Torah, but they also emphasized women's role in transmitting halakhah within the domestic sphere. Women lit Shabbat candles, kept kosher, managed festivals, taught blessings to children, and preserved oral customs that sometimes diverged from rabbinic rulings.[2] Their influence on religious formation was subtle but pervasive.

One of the most vital tools of Jewish female spiritual life was the *tkhines* (supplications)—personal prayers written in Yiddish, often composed by women and passed from mother to daughter. These prayers were not official liturgy. They were poetic, emotional, and highly specific: a prayer for a daughter's match, for safety in childbirth, for a husband's health, for the peace of Jerusalem.[3]

Some *tkhines* were published and attributed to male rabbis to gain communal approval. But many were anonymously composed and circulated in worn pamphlets tucked into women's prayer books. Scholars now believe that these prayers reflect a rich, gendered theology—expressing trust in God, negotiation with divine justice, and spiritual agency in times of crisis.[4]

The *tkhines* tradition demonstrates how women created forms of religious expression that evolved alongside but separate from formal rabbinic literature. These prayers addressed experiences often absent from male-authored liturgy: the anxiety of matchmaking, the physical dangers of childbirth, the emotional labor of maintaining Jewish households. In doing so, they preserved a distinctly female theological voice within Judaism.

In the Sephardic world, women played similar roles as *salonieres*—hosts of gatherings where midrashic stories and Torah commentary were discussed in Judeo-Spanish (Ladino). In Ottoman Salonika and Istanbul, these salons offered women both social engagement and religious education. They often invited itinerant preachers, singers, and storytellers to share interpretations that bridged elite scholarship and everyday piety.[5] Mizrahi Jewish women in Arab lands maintained parallel traditions, preserving religious songs, folk tales, and holiday customs that complemented the textual tradition of their communities.

Jewish women also preserved texts through material culture. Embroidered Torah mantles, inscribed wedding ketubot (marriage contracts), and illustrated Passover Haggadot often passed through female hands. These artifacts carried not only ritual function but generational memory. In some communities, women added personal notations to sacred objects—names, dates, comments—traces of their theological imprint.

The role of women as religious transmitters evolved significantly in modern times. Jewish women's education expanded in 19th-century Europe with the rise of *Beit Yaakov* schools, which taught girls Hebrew and Jewish texts while maintaining traditional gender roles. In the United States and Israel, women began writing Torah commentary, founding feminist midrash collectives, and training as *soferot* (scribes)—though this development sparked significant halakhic (Jewish legal) debate.

The question of women serving as *soferot* illustrates the complex denominational context of contemporary Jewish religious authority. Orthodox authorities remain divided: some reject women's scribal work entirely, while others permit it for certain ritual objects but not Torah scrolls. Conservative and Reform movements have generally embraced women scribes, viewing the restriction as historically contingent rather than theologically necessary. Modern Israeli law recognizes women's work for civil purposes, though religious authorities may not accept it for ritual use.[6]

One of the most powerful examples comes from Aviel Barclay, a Canadian-born woman who became one of the first known Orthodox Jewish female scribes in the early 2000s. Trained in the ancient methods of writing Torah scrolls, Barclay has produced *mezuzot* (doorpost scrolls) and *megillot* (holiday scrolls) that some Orthodox authorities accept for ritual use.[7] Her work sparked global conversation about women's place in the chain of transmission—and about how the "domestic Torah" might now become textual Torah once again.

Contemporary scholars like Chava Weissler and Rachel Elior have pioneered the recovery of women's religious traditions, showing how seemingly marginal practices like *tkhine* composition and household ritual management constituted sophisticated forms of theological expression.[8] Their work demonstrates that women's exclusion from formal religious authority was historically variable rather than theologically mandated.

> *"A woman's tears open the gates of heaven."*
> —Traditional *tkhine*, printed Vilna, 1760, anonymous

They did not sit in yeshivas or write responsa, but they sang the Psalms while stirring soup, whispered liturgy while lighting candles, and tucked vernacular prayers into the folds of ritual life. Their Torah was not written on scrolls but sewn into memory, recited around tables, and carried in stories passed through generations. It was sacred. It was theirs. And it endured.

Also Remembered

Glikl of Hameln (17th–18th century, Germany): Memoirist whose writings offer insight into Jewish domestic theology and ethical thought. Her work represents the evolution of women's religious expression from oral tradition to written memoir.

Bruriah (2nd century CE, Roman Judea): Wife of Rabbi Meir, remembered for her halakhic knowledge and Talmudic debate skills. She represents early evidence of women's capacity for legal scholarship within rabbinic tradition.

Women Tkhine Composers (17th–19th century, Eastern Europe): Anonymous authors of vernacular prayers addressing women's spiritual needs. Their work created a parallel liturgical tradition that survived for centuries.

Sephardic Salon Women (16th–18th century, Ottoman Empire): Hosts and transmitters of oral midrash and cultural memory. They maintained Jewish learning in Ladino-speaking communities.

Mizrahi Tradition Keepers (medieval–modern, Arab lands): Women who preserved Hebrew and Judeo-Arabic religious songs, holiday customs, and folk wisdom across generations of cultural transition.

Contemporary Soferot (21st century, global): Women scribes like Aviel Barclay who have reclaimed textual transmission roles, sparking ongoing halakhic debates about women's religious authority.

Chapter 12: Across Mountains and Monasteries -- Buddhist Women in Transmission

In the cool dawn of 8th-century Chang'an, the capital of Tang China, a woman named Yu Shun composed her thoughts before stepping into the translation hall. A former court lady turned Buddhist lay practitioner, she was fluent in Sanskrit and Classical Chinese, and today she would assist in rendering another scroll of the *Avataṃsaka Sūtra* (Flower Garland Sutra) into the local vernacular. She was not listed as a lead translator—those titles went to the monks—but her marginal annotations and clarifying suggestions would shape the version that generations of Chinese Buddhists would chant as sacred scripture.[1]

Her name, like many others, survives only in fragments—scribal notes, colophons (scribal signatures or closing statements), donor lists. But together they tell a story of quiet, sustained labor: women who preserved the Dharma not only by teaching and transmitting it orally, but by funding, copying, editing, and performing sacred texts across Buddhist Asia.

While the Buddha's early female disciples—such as Mahāpajāpatī Gotamī and the poets of the *Therīgāthā*—are celebrated in Pāli sources, later Buddhist institutional histories often muted women's roles in preserving the canon. Yet textual and archaeological evidence shows that women were vital to the longevity and geographical spread of Buddhist scriptures.

In the Mahāyāna traditions of China, Korea, and Japan, women frequently served as donors for sutra (Buddhist scripture) copying projects. Imperial consorts and aristocratic women underwrote lavish productions of texts like the *Lotus Sūtra*, often commissioning calligraphers, illustrators, and reciters. In Japan, the Empress Shōtoku (8th century) is credited with distributing thousands of printed dhāraṇī (protective mantras) charms—the earliest known examples of block printing—throughout the realm.[2]

Even outside court circles, ordinary laywomen saved money to sponsor manuscript copying or temple recitation ceremonies. Donor inscriptions carved on cave walls and stone steles in Dunhuang and along the Silk Road list women by name, often including their age and prayers for their deceased family members. These acts were devotional, but also deeply practical: they kept sutras in circulation and preserved them for the future.[3]

In Tibet, many women became reciters and ritualists, especially in non-monastic contexts. While the higher monastic curriculum was largely closed to nuns until recent decades, laywomen maintained oral traditions, performed rituals, and taught local cosmologies. Some families recognized female *tertöns*—treasure revealers who recovered hidden texts from mountains, caves, and visions.[4] Though rarely included in institutional chronologies, these women claimed spiritual authority through revelation rather than ordination.

Elsewhere, in Southeast Asia, women played essential roles in chanting and ritual performance. In Thailand, Laos, and

Cambodia, women memorized Buddhist texts and passed them on during funerals, merit-making rituals, and festivals. Scholars have documented cases of elderly women in village communities reciting long passages from the *Dhammapada* or *Jātaka Tales* in Pāli, even if they could not read them. Their knowledge was oral, embodied, and socially transmitted.[5]

The Zen tradition in Korea and Japan offers more elusive evidence. Monasteries for women did exist—such as Tōkei-ji in Kamakura-era Japan, where women could find refuge from abusive marriages—but their scribal output was often subsumed under male institutions. However, recent paleographic studies show subtle signs of female authorship: shifts in calligraphy, feminine linguistic choices, and marginal notes that reveal a gendered voice behind anonymous manuscripts.[6] Korean scholars have identified similar patterns in Seon (Korean Zen) texts, where women's contributions appear in commentary traditions and ritual manuals, though formal attribution remains contested.[7]

These scholarly debates about attribution reflect broader methodological challenges in recovering women's voices from Buddhist manuscript traditions. Paleographers now use computer analysis to identify distinctive handwriting patterns, while linguists examine vocabulary choices and grammatical structures that might indicate female authorship. This emerging field demonstrates how modern technology is revealing previously invisible contributions to Buddhist textual transmission.

In the modern era, Buddhist women have begun reclaiming these histories through organizations that directly continue this legacy. Sakyadhita International Association of Buddhist Women, founded in 1987, has gathered oral histories, reprinted women's commentaries, and trained new generations of female teachers.[8] The Buddhist Congress of Malawi works to preserve African Buddhist women's contributions to meditation practices and community leadership. In Taiwan, the Buddhist Compassion Relief Tzu Chi Foundation, led by Dharma Master Cheng Yen, demonstrates how contemporary women continue the tradition of scriptural preservation through education and publishing.[9]

In Bhutan and Nepal, nuns now engage in full scriptural study and debate, recovering educational opportunities that were historically restricted. In Sri Lanka, bhikkhunī ordination has resumed after a thousand-year absence, with women like Bhikkhuni Kusuma leading efforts to restore women's monastic education. In the West, teachers like Jetsunma Tenzin Palmo and Thubten Chodron publish accessible translations and commentary, continuing the work their foremothers once performed in silence.

Still, many contributions remain unnamed. A partially preserved sutra in the British Library's Dunhuang collection includes a scribal note thanking a woman called "Lady Liang" for providing the paper and ink. That one line—tucked between mantras—may be her only surviving trace. But it changed the fate of the text.

"This scroll copied with ink and devotion by humble hands, for the benefit of all beings. Commissioned by Lady Liang."
—Colophon, *Sutra of the Golden Light*, Dunhuang manuscript S.4639, British Library Collection

They did not sit at doctrinal councils or lead monasteries, but they shaped the Dharma with gold leaf, memorized it under lantern light, and sang it into the fabric of their communities. Their names have faded, but the scrolls they funded endure. Their voices may be missing from commentaries, but they live in the pages they helped preserve. Where the sangha left gaps, women filled them—with ink, incense, and quiet resilience.

Also Remembered

Mahāpajāpatī Gotamī (6th century BCE, India): The Buddha's aunt and the first ordained bhikkhunī. Her successful petition for women's ordination established the legal framework that enabled later generations of women to participate in monastic education and textual preservation.

Empress Shōtoku (8th century, Japan): Royal patron of Buddhist printing and scripture distribution. Her sponsorship of dhāraṇī printing represents one of the earliest examples of mass textual reproduction in Buddhist history.

Lady Liang (Tang dynasty, China): Anonymous donor cited in a Dunhuang manuscript colophon. Her simple donation inscription represents thousands of unnamed women whose material support made textual preservation possible.

Tibetan Female Tertöns (8th century–present): Women treasure revealers who discovered and transmitted hidden texts through visionary experience. They demonstrate how women claimed religious authority outside formal monastic structures.

Contemporary Buddhist Women Leaders (20th–21st century): Figures like Jetsunma Tenzin Palmo, Dharma Master Cheng Yen, and Bhikkhuni Kusuma who continue the tradition of scriptural preservation through teaching, publishing, and institutional leadership.

Village Ritual Specialists (Southeast Asia, ongoing): Women who maintain oral Buddhist traditions through chanting, storytelling, and ritual performance in rural communities across Thailand, Laos, Cambodia, and Myanmar.

Chapter 13: The Unwritten Archive

In the dry air of the Cairo Genizah, in the forgotten dust of Japanese sutra cellars, and in the slipknots of medieval convent ledgers, women's hands linger—unclaimed, unsigned, but unmistakably present. Their fingerprints lie in the careful spacing of lines, in the flourishes of final letters, and in the devotional wear of parchment margins. These are the traces of the women around the sacred, whose labor never claimed authority but without whom scripture might not have survived at all.

Across traditions, we've followed women who transmitted, copied, preserved, recited, taught, embroidered, footnoted, and funded the sacred—quietly and persistently. They were abbesses and nuns, temple dancers and hadith memorizers, household liturgists and sutra patrons. Most were unnamed. Many were never meant to be remembered. And yet, in every major religion, there is now a slow reckoning with how much sacred continuity depended on them.

What emerges is an archive built on absence: a record of what was *not* recorded, a memory of what was *never* signed. Yet it is also a powerful archive of resistance. Each stitched Torah curtain, each verse memorized and passed on, each manuscript paid for by a queen or copied by a nun—even when anonymous—testifies to a history in which women were not absent but obscured.

Scholar Debate: How Can We Recover Women's Voices from Anonymous or Attributed Texts?

Scholars continue to grapple with the methodological challenge of identifying women's contributions when names are lost or suppressed. The debate spans paleography (study of ancient handwriting), hermeneutics (interpretation of texts), linguistics, and feminist theory:

Elaine Pagels emphasizes the interpretive labor of reading *around* the canon. Her work on Gnostic gospels invites scholars to "listen to the silences" and take seriously the suppressed theological possibilities in early Christian communities. "The absence of women's voices in official sources," Pagels argues, "often tells us more about institutional anxieties than about women's actual participation."[1]

Rita Gross, a pioneering scholar in Buddhist feminist theology, argues for the necessity of what she called "creative reconstruction"—drawing plausible conclusions from known contexts even when attribution is impossible. "We must be willing to read between the lines," Gross contends, "while acknowledging both the possibilities and limitations of our interpretive methods."[2]

Judith Hauptman, a Talmudic scholar, insists that rigorous analysis of grammatical patterns, embedded questions, and narrative framing can sometimes reveal female redactors or authors in rabbinic texts otherwise assumed male. Her linguistic analysis has identified possible women's voices in Talmudic discussions, particularly around issues of domestic life and ritual practice.³

Susan Ashbrook Harvey, working on early Syriac Christianity, demonstrates how women's hymns and prayers were preserved within male-authored collections, requiring careful literary archaeology to recover. "Women's theological voices survive," Harvey observes, "but often in forms that make their authorship invisible to casual readers."⁴

Rachel Elior, a scholar of Jewish mysticism, shows how women's religious experiences were incorporated into Kabbalistic texts while their contributions were attributed to male mystics. Her work reveals how anonymous traditions often contained women's spiritual insights that were later claimed by male authorities.⁵

Maria Rosa Menocal, in her work on Andalusian literary culture, warns against privileging the written over the oral. She highlights women as performers and transmitters whose voices survive only in citation or secondhand reference, calling for a broader definition of authorship that includes oral transmission and cultural preservation.⁶

Together, these scholars offer diverse but complementary strategies. Some advocate cautious inference, others call for radical reclamation. All agree that absence of evidence is not evidence of absence—and that women's sacred labor must be searched for, even between the lines.

The methodological challenges are real. How do we distinguish between plausible reconstruction and wishful thinking? How do we honor women's contributions without making claims that exceed the evidence? The scholars above suggest several approaches: analyzing linguistic patterns that might indicate gender, examining which topics receive detailed treatment (often those relating to women's experiences), studying the social contexts that would have enabled or constrained women's participation, and reading collaborative works for traces of multiple voices.

What Would Have Changed?

Drawing on the scholarly perspectives above, we can envision how different outcomes might have emerged:

If women scribes had been formally recognized and trained in equal numbers: As Susan Ashbrook Harvey's research suggests, we might have received more diverse theological perspectives, less standardization, and greater tolerance for multiplicity in transmission traditions. The very definition of orthodox doctrine might have been broader, incorporating experiences and insights that male-dominated institutions marginalized.

If the oral liturgists and home ritualists had been viewed as legitimate theologians: Following Maria Rosa Menocal's emphasis on oral tradition, the boundary between domestic and institutional religion might have collapsed, bringing ethics and carework into doctrinal centrality. Rachel Elior's work on mystical traditions suggests that women's experiential knowledge might have balanced the abstract philosophical tendencies of male scholasticism.

If queens, patrons, and donors had been canonized as saints or sages: The definition of religious authority might have included economic and artistic contributions, not just teaching or preaching. As Rita Gross notes, this could have created more diverse models of spiritual leadership that honored different forms of sacred service.

If anonymous women had been remembered with the same reverence as named male authors: Memory itself—sacred memory—might have operated more equitably, valuing presence over hierarchy. Elaine Pagels' work suggests that different theological trajectories might have emerged if women's interpretations had been preserved alongside men's.

These possibilities are grounded in evidence of what women actually accomplished when opportunities existed. They suggest that women's marginalization represented not natural limitations but institutional choices that shaped religious development in particular directions.

In the end, the women around the sacred left behind a living archive—not always legible, but indelible nonetheless. They remind us that tradition is never transmitted solely through power. Often, it is carried in quiet hands.

Interlude B: Anonymous Hands

The parchment is smooth, but not blank. It carries the weight of silence, of invisible labor, of unsung devotion. A margin widened just slightly for aesthetic balance. A correction in red ink where a male scribe missed a diacritic. An unrecorded voice—feminine, meticulous—present not in name, but in every stroke.

Across centuries and faiths, the most enduring sacred texts are filled with the quiet evidence of women whose names have vanished. They are the scribes who corrected masculine errors but were never credited. The translators who rendered Sanskrit into Chinese while their husbands received the fame. The wives and daughters of monks, rabbis, and imams who prepared parchment, copied by lamplight, and preserved memory in the folds of linen and time.

In Buddhism, Japanese manuscript archives contain thousands of sutras copied by women—yet few are signed. In medieval Christian Europe, women in convents corrected male-authored theological treatises, their hands visible in paleographic studies but absent from colophons. In Jewish Eastern Europe, entire communities of Yiddish-speaking women shared sacred midrashim orally, never committing them to manuscript—yet those stories shaped generations. In Islamic madrasas, women served as auditors and tutors, their isnads (chains of transmission) later erased or masculinized by redactors who standardized "authority."

Beyond these familiar traditions, anonymous women's hands shaped sacred texts in ways we are only beginning to recognize. In Daoist monasteries of medieval China, women copyists preserved alchemical texts and meditation manuals, their contributions unmarked but essential to the tradition's survival. Among the Coptic Christians of Egypt and Ethiopia, women illuminated biblical manuscripts with distinctive artistic styles that modern scholars can now identify, though the artists remain nameless. In pre-Columbian Mesoamerica, women weavers encoded sacred narratives into textiles that served as three-dimensional scriptures, their religious knowledge transmitted through patterns and colors rather than written words.

And still: they are there.

This anonymity is not merely historical accident—it is methodologically significant. The systematic erasure of women's names reveals the workings of power in religious institutions, showing us how authority was constructed and maintained. Yet paradoxically, the persistence of women's work despite this erasure demonstrates the inadequacy of official histories to capture the full reality of religious transmission.

Scholars today are learning to trace the fingerprints of anonymous hands. Linguistic patterns, vocabulary choices, spelling variations, and marginalia provide clues. Textual historians now use stylometry and digital forensics to identify female authorship in unsigned religious texts. In one 15th-century manuscript, a marginal comment reads simply, *"I have copied this in pain. May it help others."* There is no signature. Only the trace of a life lived in quiet, sacred labor.

We know more than we used to. In 2011, a study of illuminated Psalters from the Chelles Abbey in France revealed consistent handwork by the same woman across four decades—despite no recorded name.[1] In contemporary Japan, temple registries long thought anonymous have yielded names of women donors and copiers when examined through digital imaging.[2] In the Cairo Genizah, fragments of women's handwriting and feminine metaphors hint at a gendered voice that contributed to Jewish sacred literature far beyond what was canonized.[3]

Recent discoveries continue to expand our understanding. Analysis of Syriac Christian manuscripts from Syria and Iraq has revealed women's participation in copying and preserving texts during periods of persecution.[4] Studies of Tibetan Buddhist manuscripts show evidence of women's involvement in translation projects across the Himalayas.[5] Archaeological work in medieval Islamic libraries suggests that women's scriptorial contributions were far more extensive than institutional records indicate.[6]

The term "anonymous" has often been mistaken for "neutral." But neutrality is a fiction. These texts were shaped, line by line, by bodies, lives, and hands—often women's—that we have simply not learned to name. Anonymous is not empty; it is full of presence we have not yet learned to read.

Reading anonymity as methodologically significant rather than simply lamenting it opens new interpretive possibilities. When we encounter unsigned texts, we might ask: whose voices are embedded here? What forms of knowledge were preserved outside official channels? How did communities maintain religious wisdom when formal education was restricted? Anonymous hands become not a historical problem to solve but a reminder of the complexity and resilience of religious transmission.

Anonymous hands did not write theology to be remembered. They wrote to survive, to honor, to transmit. Their voices whisper not from pulpits but from footnotes, marginal corrections, and well-worn prayerbooks passed from mother to daughter. They taught by speaking softly, by reciting aloud in kitchens, by preserving ritual through embroidery and repetition. They did not sign their names, but they shaped the sacred.

In every tradition, these anonymous contributions represent not the absence of women but the presence of alternative systems of knowledge preservation. They remind us that authority takes many forms—not all of them named, not all of them recognized, but all of them essential to the continuity of religious life.

We read their work every day. We just haven't known how to thank them.

Part III

Patterns of Marginalization and Resistance

Across cultures and centuries, women's spiritual authority followed remarkably similar patterns: initial inclusion, gradual constraint, and eventual erasure from official records. Yet women found ingenious ways to preserve their voices anyway. This section explores both the systematic forces that marginalized women across religious traditions and the creative strategies they used to resist: mystical visions that bypassed institutional gatekeepers, oral networks that preserved forbidden teachings, coded authorship that hid female identity, and ritual performances that kept women's wisdom alive in the margins. The patterns reveal not just how thoroughly women were excluded, but how persistently they refused to be silenced.

Chapter 14: The Architecture of Erasure

The scribe's hand trembled as she prepared the parchment in the candlelit scriptorium of Saint Radegund's Abbey near Poitiers. It was 567 CE, and Sister Caesaria had spent three years copying theological treatises under the direction of her abbess. Tonight, however, she worked on something different: her own commentary on the Gospel of John, weaving together insights from her prayers and the whispered conversations of her sisters about the nature of divine love. She knew that signing her name might ensure the work would never circulate beyond these walls. Male clerics rarely took seriously the theological reflections of nuns, regardless of their learning. So she wrote simply, "By a servant of Christ," and sealed her insights in anonymity, hoping future readers might judge the ideas rather than their source.[1]

Caesaria's dilemma was not unique. Across the Mediterranean world, in Buddhist monasteries copying sutras, in Jewish scriptoriums preserving Torah commentaries, and in the emerging centers of Islamic learning where scholars compiled hadith collections, similar scenes played out with striking consistency. Women who possessed deep religious knowledge faced a choice: remain silent or risk their words being dismissed, misattributed, or lost. Most chose silence. The few who dared to write often did so without attribution, their contributions disappearing into the vast anonymous tradition of sacred scholarship.

The history of sacred texts is not only a story of inspiration. It is a story of filtration. From the redactors of the Hebrew Bible to the compilers of the Buddhist canon, from the transmitters of hadith to the guardians of Hindu epics, religious traditions have long engaged in acts of selection: deciding what to preserve, what to redact, what to forget. In nearly every tradition, those decisions were made by men operating within patriarchal structures. The result was not always conspiracy, but it was rarely neutral.

When we examine these traditions comparatively, we begin to see a pattern, an architecture of erasure. This architecture varies in form, intensity, and justification across cultures and centuries. But it is real, and it has enduring consequences for how we understand the development of sacred literature.

The Mechanisms of Silence

The marginalization of women's voices in sacred texts operated through multiple, interconnected mechanisms that scholars have only recently begun to map systematically.

Anonymity and the Invisible Hand

In manuscript cultures across the world, women often could not or dared not sign their names to their work. A poem by a Chinese Buddhist nun survives in elegant Tang dynasty calligraphy, but her identity vanished with time.[2] In medieval Europe, analysis of manuscript colophons (scribal signatures) reveals that when women did sign their work, they often used formulas like "an unworthy handmaid of Christ" that emphasized humility over authority.[3]

Jewish women who wrote tkhines (Yiddish devotional prayers) in early modern Eastern Europe frequently published their works anonymously or under initials only. As scholar Chava Weissler has demonstrated, this anonymity was both protective and limiting: it allowed women to participate in religious discourse while ensuring their voices remained peripheral to mainstream Jewish learning.[4]

In oral traditions, the problem was even more acute. When Islamic scholars began systematically collecting hadith in the eighth and ninth centuries, they traced chains of transmission (isnad) back to the Prophet Muhammad. Women had been crucial early transmitters, including the Prophet's wife Aisha, who transmitted over 2,000 sayings. Yet as the science of hadith criticism developed, female transmitters gradually disappeared from the most authoritative collections, their contributions absorbed into male-dominated scholarly networks.[5]

Misattribution and False Credits

Perhaps more insidious than anonymity was the practice of misattribution, where women's writings were later credited to men to ensure their preservation and circulation. Some tkhines were republished in later centuries with rabbinic names attached to broaden their appeal.[6] In the Christian mystical tradition, visions received by women were sometimes attributed to their male confessors or spiritual directors, who claimed to have received the revelations secondhand.

The practice reflects a fundamental anxiety about female religious authority that persisted across traditions. As feminist theologian Judith Plaskow has observed, religious communities often struggled to reconcile their recognition of women's spiritual gifts with their institutional commitments to male leadership.[7] Misattribution became a way to preserve valuable insights while maintaining existing power structures.

Canonical Exclusion and the Boundaries of Orthodoxy

The formation of religious canons represents perhaps the most decisive moment in the architecture of erasure. When Bishop Athanasius of Alexandria issued his festal letter in 367 CE declaring which books should be read as sacred scripture, his list of twenty-seven texts excluded dozens of other early Christian writings, including several that featured women as teachers, prophets, or apostles.[8] The Gospel of Mary, which portrays Mary Magdalene as receiving special revelations from the risen Christ, and the Acts of Thecla, which celebrates a female evangelist, were relegated to the category of apocryphal or heretical literature.

Similar patterns emerged in other traditions. In Buddhism, the Therigatha (verses of elder nuns) was included in the Pali canon, preserving the enlightenment experiences of early Buddhist women. However, these texts received minimal commentary in later Buddhist scholarship and were rarely taught in monastic curricula.[9] In Hindu traditions, while female voices appear in the Vedic hymns and later devotional literature, they were increasingly marginalized in the authoritative commentarial traditions that shaped religious practice.[10]

The Violence of Translation

Translation choices have profoundly shaped how female agency appears in sacred texts. Biblical scholarship has revealed how translations can obscure women's leadership roles. The apostle Junia, clearly identified as female in early Greek manuscripts of Romans 16:7, was transformed into the male "Junias" in later Latin and vernacular translations to avoid the implication that a woman could be called an apostle.[11]

In Islamic texts, Arabic grammatical structures that could indicate female agency were often rendered in gender-neutral or masculine forms in translations, subtly diminishing women's presence in the tradition. Buddhist translations from Sanskrit and Pali into Chinese and Tibetan sometimes softened the radical equality proclaimed in early texts, reflecting the gender hierarchies of receiving cultures.[12]

Institutional Control of Sacred Learning

For centuries across traditions, religious literacy was monopolized by male clerical classes: Christian monks and priests, Jewish rabbis, Islamic ulema, Hindu Brahmins, and Buddhist bhikkhus. Women were systematically excluded from the institutions that produced, preserved, and interpreted sacred texts. Medieval European convents often lacked the resources for extensive scriptoriums, while Jewish women were told that Torah study might make them unsuitable wives and mothers.[13]

When women did acquire religious learning, it was often through informal networks: mothers teaching daughters, mystical circles, or domestic religious practices that were considered secondary to formal institutional education. This created a parallel tradition of women's religious knowledge that was simultaneously vital to community life and invisible to official religious history.

Domestic Containment and the Devaluation of Home Religion

Even when women shaped ritual and liturgy in domestic spaces, their contributions were framed as private or subsidiary to public, male-led worship. Jewish women's role in maintaining kashrut (dietary laws) and Sabbath observance, Hindu women's performance of domestic pujas, and Muslim women's teaching of Quranic recitation to children were essential to community religious life. Yet because these activities occurred in domestic rather than institutional settings, they were rarely documented or considered part of authoritative religious tradition.[14]

This domestic containment reflects broader assumptions about the relationship between private and public religion. As historian Caroline Walker Bynum has shown, medieval Christian women often developed rich mystical and devotional practices in domestic and semi-monastic settings, but these were viewed as supplements to rather than alternatives to institutional religious authority.[15]

Patterns of Vulnerability

When we examine which women were most likely to be erased from religious history, clear patterns emerge. Mystics who claimed direct divine authority outside institutional hierarchies faced particular suspicion. Their experiences threatened clerical mediation of the sacred, leading to careful scrutiny of their claims and, often, marginalization of their teachings.

Oral specialists who lacked written records were especially vulnerable. In cultures where women were excluded from literacy, their religious knowledge could vanish within a generation unless preserved by others. Scribes and patrons who worked anonymously or outside established monastic channels left few traces in the historical record.

Teachers whose work was preserved in vernacular languages rather than sacred languages like Latin, Sanskrit or Arabic often found their contributions dismissed as popular rather than scholarly religion. Women who challenged gender norms through their spiritual claims, even when working within orthodox frameworks, were frequently reimagined in later tradition as exceptions that proved the rule rather than prophetic voices calling for broader change.

The architecture of erasure was thus both gendered and classed. Elite women who were queens, consorts, or abbesses sometimes preserved written legacies through patronage and institutional position. Poor women, lay women, and domestic practitioners often disappeared from official religious history entirely, their contributions visible only in archaeological evidence or passing references in male-authored texts.

The Editorial Legacy

Religious canons were not fixed in single moments but evolved through centuries of copying, translation, commentary, and redaction. In this process, countless editorial hands shaped the contours of what we now call orthodoxy. Some editors worked intentionally to promote particular theological positions; others made choices based on practical considerations of preservation and circulation.

Women's contributions were often lost through what we might call structural silence: no institutional space was created for their voices in formal commentaries or ecclesiastical councils. Pragmatic omission also played a role, as texts by or about women were deemed irrelevant to core theological concerns or unsuitable for liturgical use. Finally, rhetorical diminishment reframed women's spiritual experiences as allegory, sentiment, or devotional excess rather than serious theological reflection.

The cumulative impact of these editorial choices continues to shape contemporary religious communities. Modern readers inherit curated traditions in which women's voices appear at the margins but are rarely centered. Understanding this history need not undermine faith; rather, it can deepen appreciation for the complex human processes through which religious traditions developed and suggest possibilities for more inclusive interpretation.

Recent archaeological discoveries have begun to recover some of these lost voices. The Nag Hammadi texts revealed early Christian communities with more varied understandings of women's religious roles. The Cairo Genizah preserved medieval Jewish women's letters and prayers that illuminate their rich spiritual lives. New manuscript discoveries continue to expand our understanding of women's contributions to Buddhist and Islamic learning.

Recovering these voices requires not just reading canonical texts but questioning how they came to be canonical. It means reading against the grain of sources that were written by men about women, looking for the historical figures behind later legendary portraits. Most importantly, it means recognizing that the architecture of erasure was not inevitable but reflected particular historical circumstances and choices that might have been made differently.

The sacred was never neutral ground. It was constructed within social structures that defined whose voices mattered and whose could be safely ignored. The architecture of erasure did not simply silence women; it made that silence seem natural and necessary. Dismantling this architecture requires understanding its blueprints, naming its tools, and imagining how religious traditions might have developed if every voice had been heard.

Chapter 15: The Counter-Tradition

The smell of ink and parchment filled the small chamber as Sarah bas Tovim carefully copied the Hebrew letters onto the page. It was 1705 in Sataniv, a market town in what is now Ukraine, and she was completing a collection of tkhines (Yiddish devotional prayers) for women who, like herself, had been taught to read Yiddish but not Hebrew. Unlike the formal Hebrew liturgy recited by men in the synagogue, these prayers spoke directly to women's experiences: the fear during childbirth, the anxiety of preparing for Sabbath, the grief of losing children. Sarah wrote in the introduction that these prayers came "from the depths of the heart" and were intended for "the dear, pious women who do not understand Hebrew."[1]

What Sarah could not have known was that her work represented something unprecedented in Jewish literary history. While male rabbis debated legal minutiae in Hebrew and Aramaic, she was creating a parallel tradition of spiritual literature that would sustain Jewish women for centuries. Her prayers were theological in their own right, offering bold reinterpretations of biblical narratives from women's perspectives and presenting arguments about divine mercy that rarely appeared in rabbinic literature. Yet she published many of them anonymously or under male pseudonyms, understanding that women's religious authority was viewed with suspicion even when it addressed distinctly female spiritual needs.

Sarah's dilemma was shared by countless women across religious traditions who found themselves excluded from formal scriptural authorship and transmission. Rather than simply accepting silence, they created what scholar Judith Plaskow has termed a "counter-tradition": networks of spiritual authority that ran parallel to official religious institutions, often hidden in domestic spaces, oral cultures, and alternative literary forms.[2] This counter-tradition did not seek to overthrow established sacred texts but to inhabit them more fully, to preserve and reinterpret religious wisdom when formal channels were closed to women's voices.

Strategies of Spiritual Resistance

Where institutional erasure was practiced, creative resistance followed. Women developed sophisticated strategies to participate in religious discourse while navigating the constraints of patriarchal religious systems.

Divine Dictation and Coded Authorship

One of the most effective strategies was to claim divine rather than human authority for religious insights. Julian of Norwich, writing in fourteenth-century England, consistently referred to herself as "a simple creature unlettered" despite demonstrating sophisticated theological knowledge in her Revelations of Divine Love.[3] By framing her profound insights about divine motherhood, the nature of sin, and universal salvation as direct revelations from God rather than her own intellectual work, Julian circumvented medieval prohibitions against women's theological teaching.

This strategy appeared across traditions. In medieval Islamic mysticism, women like Fatima of Nishapur claimed their spiritual insights came through divine inspiration rather than scholarly study, allowing them to teach and write despite restrictions on women's formal religious education.[4] In Tibetan Buddhism, female tertöns (treasure-revealers) like Sera Khandro accessed hidden teachings through visionary experiences, positioning themselves as conduits rather than authors of sacred knowledge.[5]

The rhetorical modesty of these claims should not obscure their theological boldness. Julian's assertion that "all shall be well" represented a radical departure from prevailing Christian teachings about damnation, while Islamic women mystics often articulated doctrines of divine love that challenged legalistic approaches to religious practice.

Oral Networks and Memory Chains

In cultures where women were excluded from formal literacy, oral transmission became a crucial means of preserving and developing religious knowledge. The bhakti poetry of medieval South Asia exemplifies this pattern. Women like Mirabai in Rajasthan, Andal in Tamil Nadu, and Akka Mahadevi in Karnataka composed devotional verses that circulated orally for centuries before being written down.[6]

These poems represented more than personal devotion; they constituted theological arguments about the nature of divine love and the possibility of direct relationship with the divine outside institutional mediation. Mirabai's declaration "I will not live in your palace, my Lord dwells in the streets" rejected both social convention and temple-based religiosity in favor of a more immediate spiritual experience.[7] Her verses, passed from mother to daughter through generations of women singers, created an alternative scriptural tradition that operated entirely outside formal religious institutions.

In Buddhist communities across Asia, women maintained oral traditions even when excluded from formal monastic education. Despite the absence of full bhikkhuni (nun) ordination in Theravāda countries for over a thousand years, women preserved chanting traditions, taught meditation practices, and transmitted Pali texts through domestic religious education.[8] Their bodies became repositories of sacred knowledge, maintaining continuity of Buddhist practice across generations.

Islamic women developed parallel oral networks for Quranic preservation and hadith transmission. In regions from West Africa to Southeast Asia, female huffāz (Quran memorizers) taught young girls to memorize the entire Quran, while women's study circles maintained chains of religious learning that complemented formal male scholarly networks.[9] Though their names rarely appeared in official scholarly genealogies (isnāds), these women ensured the continuation of Islamic education in domestic and community settings.

The fragility and dynamism of oral transmission created both opportunities and challenges for women's religious authority. On one hand, oral traditions could preserve teachings that might have been rejected in written form. On the other hand, they were vulnerable to distortion, loss, and appropriation by later male editors who transformed oral traditions into written texts.

Ritual Embodiment and Domestic Practice

For many women across traditions, sacred transmission occurred not through texts but through embodied practice. Jewish women's roles in maintaining kashrut (dietary laws), preparing for Sabbath, and preserving family religious traditions represented forms of religious authority that were simultaneously essential and invisible to official religious discourse.[10] Their knowledge encompassed complex legal and theological principles, but because it was expressed through domestic practice rather than scholarly commentary, it was rarely recognized as religious scholarship.

Hindu women's performance of domestic pujas (worship rituals), their preservation of festival traditions, and their transmission of religious stories to children represented parallel forms of scriptural authority. In many communities, women were the primary bearers of mythological knowledge, maintaining oral traditions that preserved alternative versions of epic narratives often at variance with written texts.[11]

Buddhist women throughout Asia developed rich traditions of merit-making activities, temple maintenance, and religious instruction that sustained community religious life. In Thailand and Sri Lanka, upāsikās (laywomen) often possessed deeper knowledge of Buddhist teachings than formally ordained monks, teaching meditation to other women and preserving doctrinal traditions through practical application.[12]

Visionary Authority and Mystical Legitimation

When formal scholarly credentials were unavailable, women across traditions claimed mystical experience as a source of religious authority. This strategy was particularly pronounced in medieval Christianity, where women like Hildegard of Bingen, Mechthild of Magdeburg, and Catherine of Siena used visionary experiences to justify their participation in theological discourse.[13]

Hildegard's claim to receive divine visions allowed her to write theological treatises, compose liturgical music, and correspond with popes and emperors despite being a woman in a male-dominated church. Her theological innovations—including her understanding of the cosmos as a living entity and her development of a theology of viriditas (greenness or life-force)—were accepted because they were presented as divine revelations rather than human scholarship.[14]

Similar patterns emerged in Islamic Sufism, where women like Rābi'a al-'Adawiyya claimed direct divine experience as the foundation for their spiritual authority. Rābi'a's teachings about disinterested love of God (muhabba) represented significant theological innovations that influenced centuries of Islamic mysticism, yet they were accepted partly because she presented them as expressions of mystical experience rather than scholarly argument.[15]

In Tibetan Buddhism, the phenomenon of tertöns allowed some women to claim authority over hidden teachings (gter ma) discovered through meditation and dreams. Women like Sera

Khandro and Jomo Menmo accessed textual traditions that had supposedly been concealed by earlier masters, giving them access to scriptural authority that would otherwise have been unavailable.[16]

Sacred Defiance and Theological Innovation

Perhaps the most radical aspect of the counter-tradition was its capacity to generate theological innovations that challenged prevailing religious orthodoxies. Women's exclusion from formal religious institutions paradoxically freed them to develop alternative theological perspectives.

The Jewish scholar Bruriah, active in second-century Palestine, regularly participated in rabbinic debates and offered interpretations of Jewish law that were preserved in Talmudic literature despite restrictions on women's Torah study.[17] Her approach to biblical interpretation often emphasized divine mercy and human dignity in ways that differed from her male contemporaries, suggesting that women's theological perspectives might have developed along different lines than prevailing rabbinical traditions.

In medieval Christianity, women mystics consistently developed theological emphases that diverged from scholastic tradition. Their focus on divine motherhood, embodied spirituality, and universal salvation represented alternative theological trajectories that might have shaped Christian doctrine differently had women enjoyed equal access to formal theological education.[18]

The Tamil poet Andal's self-identification as the bride of Vishnu in eighth-century South India represented both spiritual audacity and theological innovation. By claiming direct divine relationship outside conventional marriage arrangements, she articulated a model of female spiritual agency that influenced centuries of bhakti poetry and theology.[19]

Beyond Resistance: Toward Recognition

Understanding the counter-tradition requires recognizing both its limitations and its achievements. While women developed sophisticated strategies for participating in religious discourse, these strategies also reflected and sometimes reinforced their exclusion from formal religious authority. The need to claim divine rather than human authority, while strategically effective, also perpetuated assumptions about women's intellectual limitations.

Moreover, the counter-tradition was not uniformly accessible to all women. Elite women with access to literacy and leisure had greater opportunities to develop alternative religious practices than poor or enslaved women. The preservation of women's oral traditions often depended on sympathetic male scribes or later feminist scholars, creating additional layers of mediation and potential distortion.

Recent archaeological and manuscript discoveries have begun to illuminate the scope of these alternative traditions. The Dunhuang manuscripts revealed extensive evidence of Buddhist women's literary production in medieval China, while the Cairo Genizah preserved hundreds of documents related to medieval

Jewish women's religious lives.[20] These discoveries suggest that the counter-tradition was far more extensive and sophisticated than previously recognized.

Contemporary religious communities increasingly acknowledge the importance of recovering these alternative traditions. Feminist biblical scholars have demonstrated how women's perspectives might have shaped scriptural interpretation differently, while historians of Islam, Buddhism, and Hinduism have uncovered extensive evidence of women's religious scholarship and spiritual authority.[21]

The counter-tradition reveals that women's exclusion from formal religious institutions did not eliminate their influence on religious development but channeled it through alternative networks and practices. In kitchens and convents, through songs and stories, via visions and domestic rituals, women preserved and transformed religious traditions across cultures and centuries. Their resistance was often quiet but always persistent, and their contributions, while frequently invisible to official religious history, were essential to the survival and evolution of religious communities.

Understanding this history need not threaten traditional religious authority but can deepen appreciation for the diverse ways religious wisdom has been preserved and transmitted. The counter-tradition demonstrates that sacred knowledge has always been more widely distributed than formal institutions acknowledged, and that recovering these alternative voices can enrich rather than diminish contemporary religious understanding.

Chapter 16: When Visions Became Texts

The fever had lasted three days when the visions began. In May 1373, thirty-year-old Julian lay dying in her cell at Norwich, surrounded by her mother, friends, and a parish priest who had come to administer last rites. As the crucifix was held before her failing eyes, Julian later wrote, she received sixteen "showings" or revelations about the nature of divine love, sin, and salvation. What makes Julian's experience remarkable is not just that she survived her illness and lived another forty years, but that she spent two decades carefully analyzing her visions, transforming ecstatic experience into sophisticated theology. Her Revelations of Divine Love became the first book written in English by a woman, yet Julian insisted throughout that she was merely recording what God had shown her, not creating original theology.[1]

Julian's careful transformation of mystical experience into written text exemplifies a crucial development in medieval religious culture: the emergence of women's visionary literature as a legitimate form of theological discourse. Unlike the oral traditions and domestic practices we explored in previous chapters, these texts achieved remarkable durability and influence precisely because their authors claimed divine rather than human authority for their insights.

This chapter examines how women across religious traditions used mystical experience as a pathway to textual authority, the scholarly debates surrounding this phenomenon, and the lasting theological innovations that emerged from what might be called the "visionization" of women's religious thought.

The Authority of Divine Experience

The emergence of women's visionary literature in medieval Christianity coincided with broader theological developments that emphasized direct religious experience alongside scriptural authority. As Bernard McGinn has documented, the twelfth and thirteenth centuries witnessed an explosion of mystical literature across Europe, much of it authored by women who claimed their insights came through divine revelation rather than scholarly study.[2]

This pattern was not unique to Christianity. In Islamic Sufism, women like Rābi'a al-'Adawiyya (d. 801) and Fāṭima al-Naysābūrī (d. 849) developed sophisticated theological teachings about divine love and the spiritual path, grounding their authority in direct mystical experience rather than formal religious education.[3] In medieval Judaism, despite restrictions on women's Torah study, figures like the thirteenth-century German mystic known only as "the pious woman of Speyer" received recognition for their spiritual insights when framed as divine gifts rather than scholarly achievements.[4]

The genius of this strategy lay in its ability to circumvent institutional gatekeeping. As Grace Jantzen has observed, mystical experience could not be credentialed or regulated in the same way as formal education.[5] When a woman claimed that God had spoken directly to her, religious authorities faced a dilemma: rejecting her claims might mean rejecting divine communication itself.

Yet this authority was always precarious. Women mystics had to navigate carefully between claiming divine inspiration and avoiding charges of heresy or presumption. Their texts reveal sophisticated rhetorical strategies designed to maximize spiritual authority while minimizing institutional threat.

Strategies of Textual Legitimation

Analysis of women's visionary texts reveals recurring patterns in how mystical experience was transformed into written authority. These strategies appear across religious traditions, suggesting common challenges faced by women seeking to participate in theological discourse.

Scribal Mediation and Collaborative Authorship

Many women mystics claimed to be illiterate or emphasized their need for male scribes to record their visions. Hildegard of Bingen worked closely with the monk Volmar for decades, while the Bavarian visionary Mechthild of Magdeburg dictated her Flowing Light of the Godhead to Dominican friars.[6] Recent scholarship by Alison Beach and others has shown that this claimed illiteracy was often strategic rather than literal, allowing women to maintain the fiction that they were passive conduits for divine revelation rather than active theological authors.[7]

This collaborative model appeared in other traditions as well. In Tibetan Buddhism, female tertöns (treasure-revealers) like Sera

Khandro (1892-1940) often worked with male collaborators to transcribe and disseminate their revealed texts, maintaining the fiction that they were discovering rather than creating religious literature.[8] Similarly, in Islamic contexts, women's mystical insights were often preserved and transmitted through the writings of male disciples who positioned themselves as faithful recorders rather than co-authors.

Temporal Displacement and Retrospective Validation

Many women mystics separated the moment of vision from the act of theological reflection, creating temporal distance that allowed for sophisticated analysis while maintaining claims of divine origin. Julian of Norwich explicitly distinguished between her "showings" received during illness and her subsequent twenty-year meditation on their meaning, which she called "the ghostly sight."[9] This temporal gap allowed her to develop complex theological arguments about universal salvation and divine motherhood while insisting she was merely unpacking what had been revealed to her.

The thirteenth-century Flemish mystic Hadewijch employed a similar strategy in her Visions, separating ecstatic experiences from their theological interpretation while maintaining that both were divinely inspired.[10] This temporal displacement appears in Islamic mystical literature as well, where women like the tenth-century Sufi Fāṭima of Nishapur separated their visionary experiences from their subsequent teaching, allowing them to develop sophisticated doctrines about spiritual wayfaring while grounding their authority in divine revelation.[11]

Gendered Theological Innovation

Women's visionary literature often introduced theological innovations that differed markedly from contemporary male-authored texts. Julian of Norwich's sustained reflection on divine motherhood, for instance, was virtually unprecedented in medieval Christian theology. Her assertion that "God is our Mother as truly as he is our Father" was grounded in her mystical experience but developed through careful theological analysis that drew on patristic sources and contemporary scholastic thought.[12]

Similarly, women's mystical literature across traditions often emphasized embodied spiritual experience in ways that challenged prevailing theological abstraction. Mechthild of Magdeburg's descriptions of spiritual union used explicitly erotic metaphors that scandalized some contemporaries but influenced later mystical theology.[13] In Islamic contexts, women Sufis developed teachings about spiritual love that often differed from their male counterparts in their emphasis on emotional intensity and embodied devotion.[14]

These innovations were possible partly because mystical experience provided a space outside formal theological education where alternative approaches to religious questions could develop. As Caroline Walker Bynum has demonstrated, medieval women's religious writing often emphasized themes marginalized in scholastic theology: the humanity of Christ, the maternal aspects of divine love, and the spiritual significance of bodily experience.[15]

Scholarly Debates: Empowerment or Containment?

Contemporary scholars disagree significantly about how to interpret women's mystical literature and its relationship to broader patterns of religious authority. These debates illuminate both the possibilities and limitations of mysticism as a pathway to women's theological participation.

Bernard McGinn, perhaps the leading scholar of medieval Christian mysticism, argues for a nuanced view that recognizes both the genuine spiritual authority achieved by women mystics and the constraints under which they operated. McGinn notes that women's mystical authority was often conditional, granted only so long as they remained obedient to ecclesiastical structures and avoided challenging core doctrinal positions.[16]

Barbara Newman offers a more optimistic interpretation, arguing that mysticism provided women with "an alternate public sphere" where they could develop and express complex theological ideas. Newman's analysis of figures like Hildegard and Mechthild demonstrates how mystical literature allowed women to participate in theological debates about the nature of God, the meaning of salvation, and the relationship between spiritual and temporal authority.[17]

In Islamic studies, Kecia Ali has cautioned against romanticizing women mystics' authority, noting that figures like Rābi'a are often remembered primarily for their piety and asceticism rather than their theological innovations. Ali argues that while mysticism provided some space for women's religious expression, it also channeled them away from formal scholarly discourse and legal interpretation.[18]

Leila Ahmed has emphasized the gendered nature of mystical authority in Islamic contexts, observing that women's mystical recognition often required renunciation of conventional female roles including marriage and motherhood. For Ahmed, mysticism was both liberating and limiting, offering spiritual authority at the cost of social marginalization.[19]

In Buddhist contexts, Janet Gyatso's work on Tibetan women tertöns reveals similar ambivalence. While some women treasure-revealers achieved significant authority through their discovered texts, Gyatso notes that their recognition was often contingent on their revelations reinforcing orthodox teachings. When women's visionary texts challenged established doctrine, they were more likely to be dismissed or heavily edited by male collaborators.[20]

These scholarly debates highlight a fundamental tension in women's mystical literature: while divine revelation provided a pathway around institutional gatekeeping, it also reinforced assumptions about women's emotional rather than intellectual nature. The very strategy that enabled women's theological participation may have limited its long-term impact on religious institutions.

What Might Have Been: Theological Trajectories

Understanding the constraints under which women mystics operated illuminates alternative theological trajectories that might have developed had their insights been fully integrated into mainstream religious thought. This speculative exercise, grounded in careful analysis of their surviving texts, reveals significant missed opportunities for religious development.

Expanded Theological Anthropology

Had Julian of Norwich's theology of divine motherhood been incorporated into mainstream Christian thought, medieval and modern Christianity might have developed a more balanced understanding of divine nature that incorporated both masculine and feminine imagery. As modern theologian Sallie McFague has argued, Julian's maternal metaphors offer resources for ecological theology and social justice that were largely ignored by subsequent theological development.[21]

Similarly, if Islamic theology had fully incorporated women Sufis' emphasis on divine love and emotional spirituality, the tradition might have developed different approaches to religious law and practice that balanced jurisprudential reasoning with mystical insight. As Sachiko Murata has shown, early Islamic thought contained resources for understanding divine nature in terms that transcended gender categories, but these were marginalized as Islamic law became increasingly systematized.[22]

Alternative Canonical Genres

The marginalization of mystical literature as "devotional" rather than "theological" reflects broader assumptions about the relationship between emotion and rational thought in religious discourse. Had women's visionary literature been treated as authoritative theological commentary rather than pious sentiment, religious traditions might have developed different understandings of how divine truth is communicated and preserved.

Contemporary scholars like Amy Hollywood have argued that the exclusion of mystical literature from theological canons impoverished religious thought by privileging abstract reasoning over experiential knowledge.[23] The integration of women's mystical insights might have led to more holistic approaches to religious education that valued contemplative practice alongside textual study.

Interfaith Theological Development

One of the most striking features of women's mystical literature across traditions is its thematic consistency: emphasis on divine love, concern with spiritual union, attention to embodied religious experience. Had these commonalities been recognized and explored, they might have provided foundations for earlier and more substantial interfaith theological dialogue.

The Persian Sufi poet Rābi'a's teachings about disinterested divine love, for instance, bear remarkable similarity to concepts developed by Christian mystics like Marguerite Porete and Hindu bhakti poets like Mirabai. Recognition of these parallels might have facilitated different approaches to interfaith relations that emphasized shared spiritual concerns over doctrinal differences.[24]

The Textual Legacy

Despite their marginalization from mainstream theological development, women's mystical texts achieved remarkable durability and influence. Julian of Norwich's Revelations of Divine Love has never been out of print since its first publication in 1670, and contemporary theologians continue to find resources in her theology for addressing modern religious questions.[25] Hildegard of Bingen's visionary texts have been recovered by feminist theologians as sources for ecological spirituality and alternative approaches to divine imagery.[26]

In Islamic contexts, women Sufis' teachings continue to influence contemporary spiritual movements, even as their theological innovations remain marginalized in formal religious education. The poetry of Rābiʻa and her successors provides resources for Muslim feminists seeking authentic Islamic foundations for women's spiritual authority.[27]

These continuing influences suggest that women's mystical literature represents more than historical curiosity; it constitutes an alternative theological tradition that offers resources for contemporary religious thought. Understanding how mystical experience was transformed into textual authority illuminates both the possibilities and limitations of alternative pathways to religious participation.

The transformation of women's visions into lasting theological texts represents one of the most significant developments in medieval religious culture. While these texts operated within significant constraints and rarely achieved full institutional recognition, they created space for theological innovations that continue to influence religious thought. Their authors' careful navigation of the relationship between mystical experience and textual authority offers insights into how religious traditions might more fully incorporate diverse voices and perspectives.

Most importantly, these texts demonstrate that theological innovation has never been confined to formal institutional channels. When official pathways were closed, women found alternative routes to religious authority that were often more creative and enduring than their creators could have imagined. Their visions became texts, and their texts continue to speak across centuries of religious development.

Part IV

Recovery and Reclamation

What was lost is being found again. Archaeological discoveries in Egyptian sands and Himalayan caves, new methods of manuscript analysis, and feminist scholarship across traditions are recovering voices that official histories forgot. This section brings the story into the present: how buried texts reveal buried women, how scholars are learning to read between the lines of hostile sources, and how contemporary women across all traditions are reclaiming and reshaping their sacred inheritance. The work of recovery is ongoing—and it's changing how we understand not just the past, but the future of religious authority and spiritual wisdom.

Chapter 17: Archaeological Angels

The dust motes danced in the shaft of sunlight as Agnes Smith Lewis climbed the wooden ladder into the genizah chamber of the Ben Ezra Synagogue in Old Cairo. It was December 1896, and the Scottish scholar could barely contain her excitement as she surveyed the mountainous heaps of manuscript fragments that filled the ancient storeroom. Beside her, her twin sister Margaret Dunlop Gibson carefully lifted a tattered page covered in Hebrew script, its edges brown with age. Neither woman could have imagined that among the estimated 280,000 fragments they were documenting lay traces of voices that had been silent for centuries: Jewish women's personal prayers written in Yiddish, marriage contracts negotiated by female scribes, and devotional poems that had never entered official liturgical collections.[1]

The genizah (literally "hiding place") was a repository where the Jewish community of Fustat had deposited worn-out religious texts for nearly a thousand years, following the religious principle that sacred writings containing the name of God could not simply be discarded. What the Lewis sisters discovered would revolutionize medieval Jewish studies, but perhaps more significantly for our purposes, it would demonstrate that women's religious voices, though often excluded from official preservation, had found ways to survive in the margins of institutional memory.

The Cairo Genizah represents just one of several major archaeological discoveries that have transformed our understanding of women's roles in the creation, transmission, and preservation of sacred texts. Across the globe, from Egyptian monasteries to Chinese cave complexes, from Afghan hilltops to European scriptoriums, buried manuscripts have emerged to reveal that women's participation in sacred textual culture was far more extensive than traditional religious histories suggested.

Voices from the Archive

The manuscript discoveries of the late nineteenth and twentieth centuries have fundamentally altered scholarly understanding of how sacred texts developed and who participated in their transmission. Unlike the carefully curated collections preserved in major religious institutions, these archaeological finds represent a more democratic archive: texts that survived not because they were deemed officially important, but because historical accident protected them from destruction.

The Nag Hammadi Discovery

In December 1945, an Egyptian farmer named Muhammad al-Samman was digging for fertilizer near the town of Nag Hammadi when his mattock struck a large earthenware jar. Inside, wrapped in leather and papyrus, were thirteen codices containing fifty-two early Christian texts, many previously unknown to modern scholarship.[2] Among these was the Gospel of Mary, which portrays Mary Magdalene as receiving special revelations from the risen Christ and engaging in theological disputes with the male apostles about the nature of spiritual authority.

The Gospel of Mary presents a vision of early Christianity where a woman functions as a theological teacher and interpreter of Jesus's message. "The Savior made all things perfect, not through a visible nature but through a spiritual nature," Mary explains to the assembled disciples, demonstrating sophisticated theological understanding.[3] While scholars debate the text's historical reliability, its mere existence suggests that some early Christian communities preserved traditions of female spiritual authority that were later excluded from canonical Christianity.

Other Nag Hammadi texts, including the Dialogue of the Savior and the Gospel of Philip, similarly feature women as active participants in theological discourse rather than passive recipients of male teaching. These discoveries have forced scholars to reconsider the diversity of early Christianity and the processes by which certain voices were preserved while others were marginalized.

Dunhuang and the Silk Road

The sealed cave complex at Dunhuang, discovered by the Daoist monk Wang Yuanlu in 1900, contained over 50,000 manuscripts and artworks that had been walled up around 1000 CE to protect them from approaching armies.[4] Among the predominantly Buddhist texts were numerous documents that revealed women's active participation in Chinese religious life during the Tang dynasty (618-907 CE).

Donor inscriptions on Buddhist manuscripts frequently identify women as sponsors and patrons of religious texts. One manuscript of the Lotus Sutra bears the inscription: "Respectfully copied by the female disciple Huixiang for the benefit of all sentient beings and in memory of her deceased mother."[5] Such inscriptions reveal a parallel economy of religious merit-making in which women participated as equals, commissioning copies of sacred texts and supporting monastic communities.

Perhaps more significantly, some Dunhuang manuscripts preserve early versions of the Therigatha (Verses of the Elder Nuns), including poems attributed to female disciples of the Buddha that were later excluded from canonical collections. One fragment contains verses by a nun named Punna that do not appear in the Pali canon: "Free from the three poisons of greed, hatred, and delusion, I have attained the peace that the Buddha taught. My mind is liberated like a bird released from its cage."[6]

The Dunhuang materials also include evidence of female Buddhist teachers and abbesses who played crucial roles in transmitting scriptural knowledge. A tenth-century document describes a "dharma master" (fashi) named Li who taught the Vimalakirti Sutra to both monastic and lay audiences, suggesting that women could achieve recognition as scriptural authorities in medieval Chinese Buddhism.[7]

Islamic Manuscript Traditions

While Islamic manuscript discoveries have received less attention in popular accounts of archaeological finds, recent scholarship has uncovered significant evidence of women's participation in Quranic transmission and Islamic scholarly culture. Endowment documents (waqf) from medieval Cairo and Damascus frequently name women as founders of madrasas and libraries, while biographical dictionaries reveal that women participated in networks of Quran memorization and hadith transmission.[8]

A thirteenth-century manuscript from the library of Saladin's sister, Sitt al-Sham, contains marginal notes in a feminine hand that demonstrate sophisticated engagement with Quranic commentary. The annotator challenges a male scholar's interpretation of Quran 4:34 (often translated as giving men authority over women), arguing that the Arabic verb qawwamun implies responsibility rather than domination.[9] Such marginalia reveal that elite Muslim women were not merely passive recipients of religious teaching but active interpreters of Islamic texts.

Recent analysis of Quran manuscripts from al-Andalus has identified several copied by women, based on distinctive calligraphic features and colophons that identify female scribes. One fourteenth-century mushaf (Quran manuscript) from Córdoba bears the signature "Written by Fatima bint Muhammad al-Umawiyya, may God forgive her sins and accept her service."[10] These discoveries challenge assumptions about women's exclusion from Islamic scholarly culture and suggest that female participation in textual transmission was more common than institutional histories indicate.

European Monastic Archives

Systematic digitization of medieval European manuscripts has revealed extensive evidence of female participation in book production and scriptural commentary. Analysis of scribal hands, linguistic patterns, and paleographic evidence suggests that women's contribution to medieval textual culture was far more substantial than previously recognized.

The Abbey of Chelles, a major Frankish scriptorium, produced numerous manuscripts that bear evidence of female authorship and editorial intervention. A ninth-century Gospel book contains marginal glosses in Old High German that use grammatical forms associated with feminine speech patterns, suggesting composition by a nun rather than a monk.[11] Similarly, analysis of corrections and erasures in manuscripts from the Abbey of Notre-Dame-aux-Nonnains reveals systematic editorial work that implies sophisticated theological knowledge among the community's scribes.

Perhaps most remarkably, recent multispectral imaging of a thirteenth-century psalter from the Abbey of Fontevraud has revealed an erased colophon that reads: "Sister Marguerite completed this work in the year of our Lord 1247, for the glory of God and the instruction of her sisters in Christ."[12] The original colophon was apparently scraped away and replaced with one crediting the work to a male scribe, suggesting active efforts to obscure women's textual contributions.

Digital Recovery and Contemporary Methods

Modern technology has revolutionized the recovery of women's voices from ancient manuscripts. Digital humanities projects, multispectral imaging, and artificial intelligence are revealing previously invisible texts and identifying patterns that suggest female authorship or scribal activity.

The Sinai Palimpsests Project has used advanced imaging techniques to recover erased texts from reused parchments at Saint Catherine's Monastery. Among the recovered materials are fragments of hymns and prayers that linguistic analysis suggests were composed by women, based on their focus on distinctly feminine religious experiences such as childbirth and domestic religious observance.[13]

Computational analysis of medieval manuscripts has identified scribal signatures and writing patterns that suggest female authorship. The Manuscript Evidence project at Oxford University uses machine learning to analyze letter formation and spelling patterns, revealing that approximately twelve percent of medieval English religious manuscripts show evidence of female scribal involvement, far higher than traditional estimates suggested.[14]

Crowdsourced transcription projects have also uncovered previously overlooked evidence of women's textual participation. The Transcribe Bentham project, while focused on secular manuscripts, has identified numerous religious texts among Jeremy Bentham's papers that were copied by female amanuenses who added their own theological commentary in margins and footnotes.[15]

Global Perspectives: Beyond the Mediterranean

While Mediterranean and European discoveries have received the most scholarly attention, manuscript finds from Africa, Asia, and the Americas reveal that women's participation in sacred textual culture was a global phenomenon rather than a regional exception.

Ethiopian Christian Manuscripts

The monastery libraries of Ethiopia preserve some of the world's oldest Christian manuscripts, including texts in Ge'ez that reveal extensive female participation in Ethiopian Orthodox religious life. The Kebra Nagast (Glory of the Kings) exists in several versions that include extensive commentary attributed to female monastics, while psalters and prayer books frequently bear colophons identifying female patrons and scribes.[16]

A sixteenth-century manuscript from the monastery of Gishen Maryam contains a commentary on the Song of Songs written by "Walatta Maryam, servant of the Queen of Heaven," that offers distinctive interpretations emphasizing female spiritual agency. The text was apparently transmitted through networks of female religious communities before being incorporated into the monastery's official collection.[17]

West African Islamic Traditions

Recent research on the manuscript libraries of Timbuktu and other West African centers of Islamic learning has revealed significant evidence of female scholarship and textual production. Family libraries often preserve texts copied by women, while biographical works mention female teachers who attracted students from across the region.

A seventeenth-century manuscript from the Ahmed Baba Institute contains a treatise on Islamic jurisprudence attributed to Nana Asma'u, daughter of the Fulani leader Usman dan Fodio. The text demonstrates sophisticated engagement with Islamic legal sources and includes original arguments about women's rights in marriage and property ownership.[18] Such discoveries are reshaping understanding of women's roles in African Islamic intellectual culture.

Pre-Columbian and Indigenous Traditions

While textual evidence from pre-Columbian America is limited, recent archaeological work has uncovered evidence of female participation in the creation and preservation of sacred knowledge. Analysis of Maya codices reveals that some scribal signatures may indicate female authorship, while ceramic vessels often depict women engaged in writing activities.[19]

Contemporary work with indigenous communities has also revealed extensive oral textual traditions preserved by women. Among the Haudenosaunee (Iroquois), women traditionally serve as clan mothers responsible for maintaining oral constitutions and ceremonial procedures. Recent collaborative projects have documented these traditions, revealing complex textual cultures that parallel written traditions in their sophistication and historical depth.[20]

Methodological Challenges and Interpretive Cautions

The recovery of women's voices from archaeological discoveries requires careful methodological attention to avoid the twin dangers of over-interpretation and romantic projection. Attribution of anonymous texts to female authorship based on circumstantial evidence must be undertaken with appropriate scholarly caution.

Paleographic analysis can suggest female authorship through distinctive letter formations, spelling patterns, and scribal habits, but such evidence is rarely conclusive. Linguistic analysis may reveal grammatical patterns associated with feminine speech, but medieval and ancient languages often preserve formal rather than colloquial patterns that may not reflect actual usage.[21]

Content analysis can suggest female authorship when texts focus on distinctly feminine religious experiences, but such arguments must account for the possibility that male authors may have written about women's experiences. Similarly, the presence of women's names in colophons or patron inscriptions does not necessarily indicate authorship, as women may have commissioned texts written by male scribes.

Perhaps most importantly, the excitement of discovering women's voices should not lead to uncritical celebration of their content. Some women's religious texts reflect and reinforce patriarchal assumptions about gender roles, while others challenge such assumptions in ways that may reflect later editorial intervention rather than original authorship.[22]

Contemporary scholars have increasingly emphasized collaborative approaches to manuscript interpretation that involve communities connected to the traditions under study. Such approaches help ensure that recovered texts are understood within their proper cultural and religious contexts rather than being appropriated for contemporary political purposes.

The Ongoing Discovery

Archaeological recovery of women's textual voices continues to transform scholarly understanding of how sacred traditions developed. Each new discovery adds complexity to narratives that once seemed settled, revealing that women's exclusion from official textual authority did not prevent their participation in unofficial networks of religious transmission.

These discoveries demonstrate that the margins of manuscripts often preserve voices that were excluded from their centers. Women who could not sign their names to major theological treatises found other ways to participate in religious discourse: through patron inscriptions, marginal commentary, private devotional texts, and collaborative scribal work.

Understanding this hidden history need not threaten traditional religious authority but can enrich appreciation for the diverse ways religious wisdom has been preserved and transmitted. The angels of archaeology do not challenge the authenticity of sacred traditions but reveal their human complexity and the remarkable persistence of excluded voices.

Their whispered testimonies from dust and parchment remind us that sacred texts have always been collaborative enterprises, shaped by more hands and hearts than official histories acknowledge. In recovering these voices, we discover not different traditions but fuller understanding of the traditions we inherit.

The past remains a palimpsest, its deepest truths revealed only when we learn to read between the lines and listen for the voices that were never entirely silenced. Each manuscript fragment recovered, each colophon deciphered, each marginal note transcribed adds another voice to the chorus of those who preserved and transmitted the sacred across centuries of change and challenge.

Chapter 18: Reading Against the Grain

The fluorescent lights hummed overhead as Phyllis Trible sat in the basement library of Union Theological Seminary, surrounded by Hebrew lexicons and commentaries that stretched back centuries. It was 1973, and she was preparing what would become a groundbreaking paper on the book of Ruth for the Society of Biblical Literature. As she traced her finger across the Hebrew text, she noticed something that generations of male interpreters had missed: the word used to describe Ruth's commitment to Naomi (dabaq) was the same verb used in Genesis to describe a man's bond to his wife. Yet commentary after commentary had interpreted Ruth's loyalty as simple feminine devotion rather than recognizing the text's radical portrayal of women's covenantal relationship.[1]

Trible's insight would help launch what scholars now call feminist biblical hermeneutics, but her discovery was part of a broader movement emerging across religious traditions in the late twentieth century. Women scholars were asking new questions of ancient texts: What if the silence around women's voices was not natural but constructed? What if contradictions in sacred texts revealed not divine mystery but human editorial choices? What if reading more carefully might recover voices that had been systematically overlooked?

This approach, known as "reading against the grain," does not reject sacred texts but interrogates the layers of interpretation that have accumulated around them. It treats omissions and marginalizations not as accidents but as meaningful editorial decisions that reflect the social locations of those who preserved and transmitted religious traditions. Most importantly, it operates from the conviction that sacred texts are not only what has been preserved but also what has been missed, overlooked, or deliberately suppressed.

The Hermeneutical Revolution

The emergence of feminist, womanist, and liberation approaches to scriptural interpretation in the late twentieth century represented a fundamental shift in how religious communities understood the relationship between text and meaning. Rather than treating traditional interpretations as neutral or inevitable, these new approaches asked how the social position of interpreters shaped their understanding of sacred texts.

Jewish Feminist Reinterpretation

The transformation began in Jewish contexts with scholars like Judith Plaskow, who famously declared that she could not "go back to the Torah and find myself there." Rather than abandoning tradition, Plaskow chose to engage in midrash (interpretive storytelling), reimagining biblical narratives with women at the center.[2] Her approach in *Standing Again at Sinai* called for recovering women's experiences that were present in the text but marginalized by centuries of male interpretation.

Other Jewish feminist scholars developed sophisticated methods for reading biblical texts through women's perspectives. Rachel

Adler's analysis of Tamar in Genesis 38 revealed how the narrative portrays a woman using legal knowledge to claim her rights within a patriarchal system.[3] Tikva Frymer-Kensky's work on biblical goddesses demonstrated how feminine divine imagery was systematically suppressed in the editing of Hebrew scriptures.[4] These scholars showed that careful attention to Hebrew grammar, narrative structure, and comparative ancient Near Eastern literature could recover dimensions of women's agency that traditional interpretation had obscured.

The method extended beyond biblical texts to rabbinic literature, where scholars like Judith Hauptman uncovered evidence of women's participation in legal discussions that had been minimized by later editors.[5] By examining variant manuscript traditions and analyzing the social contexts in which rabbinic texts were compiled, feminist scholars revealed that women's exclusion from Jewish learning was a historical development rather than an eternal principle.

Womanist Biblical Interpretation

In African American religious contexts, womanist theologians developed distinctive approaches to biblical interpretation that centered the experiences of Black women. Scholars like Renita J. Weems and Delores Williams recognized that feminist approaches developed by white women often failed to address the intersection of racial and gender oppression that shaped Black women's encounter with scripture.[6]

Williams's revolutionary reading of Hagar in *Sisters in the Wilderness* reframed the Egyptian slave woman not as a failed matriarch but as a prototype of Black women's survival strategies under conditions of sexual and economic exploitation.[7] By reading Hagar's story alongside African American women's historical experiences, Williams revealed dimensions of divine solidarity with the oppressed that traditional interpretation had ignored.

Womanist scholars also developed new approaches to apparently problematic biblical texts. Rather than dismissing or explaining away passages that seemed to endorse slavery or female subordination, womanist interpreters like Clarice Martin and Cain Hope Felder examined how these texts had been used to justify oppression while simultaneously identifying resources within scripture for resistance and liberation.[8]

The womanist approach emphasized that biblical interpretation must be accountable to community experience rather than abstract scholarly principles. This led to innovative reading strategies that brought together historical-critical methods with oral tradition, personal testimony, and collective discernment.

Islamic Feminist Hermeneutics

Muslim feminist scholars developed parallel approaches to Quranic interpretation that distinguished between the text itself and the patriarchal assumptions that had shaped centuries of male commentary. Scholars like Amina Wadud, Asma Barlas, and Kecia Ali demonstrated that careful attention to Arabic grammar and Quranic context could support egalitarian rather than hierarchical understandings of gender relations.[9]

Wadud's *Qur'an and Woman* provided systematic analysis of Quranic passages dealing with women, showing how traditional interpretation (tafsir) had often projected patriarchal assumptions onto texts that actually affirmed women's spiritual equality and social agency.[10] Her work on Quran 4:34, often translated as giving men authority over women, demonstrated how the Arabic word qawwamun could be understood as referring to economic responsibility rather than male dominance.

Barlas's *"Believing Women" in Islam* developed a comprehensive hermeneutical framework that read the Quran as an anti-patriarchal text whose egalitarian message had been obscured by male-dominated interpretive traditions.[11] By examining the Quran's treatment of specific women like Mary, Khadijah, and the Queen of Sheba, Barlas showed how the text consistently affirmed women's spiritual authority and intellectual capacity.

These Muslim feminist scholars faced significant institutional resistance but also found support from male scholars who recognized the validity of their interpretive methods. Their work contributed to broader discussions within Islamic scholarship about the relationship between revealed text and human interpretation, demonstrating that feminist hermeneutics could strengthen rather than weaken religious commitment.

Buddhist Textual Recovery

Buddhist feminist scholars, particularly through the international Sakyadhita movement, developed methods for recovering women's voices from texts that had been shaped by centuries of male monastic interpretation. Scholars like Rita Gross and Karma Lekshe Tsomo traced contradictions in early Buddhist texts between statements affirming women's capacity for enlightenment and later additions that suggested female spiritual inferiority.[12]

Gross's *Buddhism After Patriarchy* demonstrated how careful analysis of Pali and Sanskrit sources could distinguish between the Buddha's original teachings about gender and later editorial additions that reflected the patriarchal assumptions of monastic compilers.[13] By examining variant manuscript traditions and comparing early Buddhist texts with contemporary Jain and Hindu sources, Gross showed that women's spiritual equality was original to Buddhism while restrictions on female religious authority represented later developments.

Tsomo's work on the Vinaya (monastic rules) revealed how regulations governing Buddhist nuns had been systematically elaborated over time in ways that restricted women's autonomy while similar restrictions were not applied to male monastics.[14] Her comparative analysis of different Vinaya traditions showed that women's subordination was not inherent to Buddhist monasticism but reflected specific historical and cultural circumstances.

These Buddhist feminist scholars also recovered neglected texts like the Therigatha (Verses of Elder Nuns) and female-authored commentaries that had been marginalized in traditional curricula. Their work contributed to contemporary movements for full ordination of Buddhist women and the recovery of feminine imagery in Buddhist iconography and meditation practices.

Global Perspectives and Non-Scriptural Traditions

The methods developed by feminist religious scholars have been applied beyond written scriptures to oral traditions, liturgical practices, and indigenous knowledge systems. These applications reveal that the process of reading against the grain has global relevance and can illuminate women's roles in religious traditions that may not center written texts.

Indigenous and Oral Traditions

Native American scholars like Inés Hernández-Avila and Paula Gunn Allen have developed methods for recovering women's voices from oral traditions that were distorted by European colonial interpretation.[15] Their work examines how ethnographic accounts by male anthropologists often minimized women's spiritual authority or reinterpreted egalitarian gender relations through patriarchal frameworks.

Allen's *The Sacred Hoop* demonstrated how attention to indigenous women's perspectives could reveal alternative understandings of spiritual power, governance, and cosmic order that had been obscured by colonial misinterpretation.[16] By reading ethnographic texts against the grain of their colonial assumptions, indigenous feminist scholars have recovered traditions of female spiritual leadership that inform contemporary efforts to revitalize native religious practices.

Similar approaches have been developed by African scholars working with oral religious traditions. Mercy Amba Oduyoye's analysis of Yoruba religious texts showed how written transcriptions of oral traditions often reflected the gender assumptions of male transcribers rather than the original teachings.[17] By working with female religious practitioners and examining variant versions of traditional stories, scholars have been able to recover more balanced understandings of gender in African religious systems.

Daoist and East Asian Traditions

Feminist scholars of Chinese religions have applied similar methods to Daoist and Confucian texts, revealing how women's religious authority was systematically marginalized in the process of textual compilation and commentary. Catherine Despeux's work on female Daoist practitioners showed how women's spiritual achievements were often attributed to male teachers or reinterpreted as exceptional cases that proved the rule of male spiritual superiority.[18]

Scholars like Suzanne Cahill have recovered evidence of women's participation in Daoist literary culture, showing how female poets and religious practitioners contributed to the development of Daoist philosophy and practice in ways that were later minimized by male editors.[19] Their work reveals that careful attention to manuscript variants and historical context can uncover women's intellectual contributions even in traditions that are often assumed to have excluded female participation.

Liturgical and Devotional Texts

Reading against the grain has also been applied to liturgical traditions, where scholars have discovered evidence of women's participation in the creation and transmission of religious practices. Caroline Walker Bynum's analysis of medieval Christian liturgy revealed how women's devotional practices influenced the development of Eucharistic theology and Marian devotion in ways that were not acknowledged by official ecclesiastical sources.[20]

Similar work has been done on Islamic devotional literature, where scholars have uncovered evidence of women's contributions to Sufi poetry and mystical practices. Th. Emil Homerin's work on women's religious poetry in medieval Egypt showed how female mystics developed distinctive approaches to spiritual expression that influenced broader Islamic literary culture.[21]

Methods and Challenges

The practice of reading against the grain requires sophisticated methodological approaches that balance historical criticism with hermeneutical sensitivity. Scholars working in this tradition have developed various tools for recovering marginalized voices while avoiding the danger of reading contemporary concerns into ancient texts.

Textual and Linguistic Analysis

Careful attention to original languages remains fundamental to feminist biblical and Quranic scholarship. Hebrew and Arabic grammatical structures often contain information about gender that is lost in translation, while variant manuscript traditions may preserve readings that were later suppressed or harmonized. Scholars like Amy-Jill Levine have shown how attention to Aramaic and Hebrew wordplay can reveal dimensions of women's agency in gospel narratives that are invisible in English translation.[22]

Comparative linguistic analysis has also proven valuable for understanding how gender assumptions shaped textual transmission. Francesca Stavrakopoulou's work on ancient Hebrew texts has shown how feminine divine imagery was systematically masculinized in the process of textual editing, often leaving traces that can be recovered through careful philological work.[23]

Social and Historical Contextualization

Understanding the social contexts in which religious texts were compiled and transmitted is crucial for identifying how gender assumptions shaped their final form. Scholars like Ross Kraemer have shown how attention to women's actual social roles in ancient Mediterranean societies can illuminate the significance of their presence or absence in early Christian texts.[24]

This approach requires interdisciplinary work that brings together textual analysis with archaeology, social history, and comparative religious studies. The goal is not to read contemporary gender equality back into ancient texts but to understand how ancient assumptions about gender shaped textual production and interpretation.

Hermeneutical Frameworks

Reading against the grain also requires sophisticated theoretical frameworks for understanding the relationship between text and interpretation. Elisabeth Schüssler Fiorenza's concept of a "hermeneutics of suspicion" has been influential in developing methods that can identify patriarchal bias in traditional interpretation while remaining committed to the authority of sacred texts.[25]

This approach recognizes that all interpretation occurs from particular social locations and that acknowledging interpretive bias can lead to more faithful rather than less faithful readings of sacred texts. The goal is not to eliminate all interpretive perspective but to ensure that marginalized perspectives are included in the interpretive process.

Institutional Responses and Ongoing Debates

The development of feminist and liberation approaches to scriptural interpretation has generated varied responses from religious institutions, ranging from enthusiastic adoption to active resistance. Understanding these responses illuminates both the potential and limitations of reading against the grain as a strategy for religious change.

Many progressive religious communities have embraced feminist hermeneutics as a means of recovering neglected dimensions of their traditions. Reform and Conservative Judaism have incorporated feminist biblical scholarship into seminary curricula and liturgical development, while several Christian denominations have used womanist and feminist interpretation to support women's ordination and leadership.[26]

However, traditional religious authorities have often viewed these approaches with suspicion, arguing that they impose contemporary political concerns onto sacred texts. Conservative religious scholars have developed alternative approaches that acknowledge women's roles in religious history while maintaining traditional interpretive frameworks.[27]

These debates reflect deeper questions about the nature of scriptural authority and the relationship between historical scholarship and religious commitment. They also reveal the ongoing significance of textual interpretation in contemporary religious communities and the stakes involved in determining who has authority to interpret sacred texts.

Contemporary Implications

The practice of reading against the grain has implications that extend beyond academic scholarship to contemporary religious practice and social engagement. By revealing how human editorial choices shaped the transmission of sacred texts, this approach opens possibilities for more inclusive interpretation while maintaining respect for traditional authority.

Understanding that sacred texts have always been interpreted from particular social locations can liberate contemporary readers to engage scripture from their own contexts while remaining accountable to historical and linguistic evidence. This approach suggests that faithful interpretation requires not uncritical acceptance of traditional readings but careful attention to how social position shapes understanding.

Reading against the grain also reveals that sacred texts are more complex and multivocal than traditional interpretation often acknowledged. Rather than providing simple answers to contemporary questions, scripture emerges as an ongoing conversation between human communities and divine reality that requires continual reinterpretation in new contexts.

Most importantly, this approach demonstrates that the work of interpreting sacred texts is never finished. Each generation must engage in the task of understanding how ancient wisdom speaks to contemporary challenges, and this work requires the insights of all community members rather than a privileged interpretive elite.

The sacred texts have indeed remained unchanged across centuries of copying and transmission. But the questions we bring to them continue to evolve, and those new questions have the power to reveal dimensions of meaning that were always present but previously unrecognized. In learning to read against the grain, religious communities discover not different traditions but fuller understanding of the traditions they have inherited, enriched by voices that were always there but waiting to be heard.

Chapter 19: The Contemporary Conversation

The ancient vellum stretched taut across the writing board as Aviel Barclay carefully dipped her quill into the specially prepared ink. In her studio in Chestertown, Maryland, on a crisp morning in January 2007, she was completing something unprecedented in modern Jewish history: a Torah scroll written by a woman. Each Hebrew letter required perfect formation according to centuries-old specifications, and any error would necessitate starting the entire panel again. As a newly trained soferet (female ritual scribe), Barclay understood that her work challenged not just tradition but the very assumption that sacred texts could only be transmitted through male hands.[1]

The completion of that Torah scroll represented more than individual achievement; it symbolized a broader transformation occurring across religious traditions worldwide. For the first time in history, women were not merely recovering lost voices from ancient manuscripts but actively participating in the ongoing creation, interpretation, and transmission of sacred texts. This contemporary renaissance represents neither a rejection of tradition nor a simple restoration of ancient practices, but rather a fundamental reimagining of who can speak with religious authority and how sacred wisdom is preserved and passed forward.

Jewish Women and the Return to Scribal Practice

The emergence of contemporary women scribes in Judaism represents one of the most visible examples of women reclaiming roles in sacred textual transmission. The practice of sofrut (Jewish ritual scribing) had been exclusively male for over a millennium, based on interpretations of Jewish law that connected scribal authority to other forms of religious leadership from which women were excluded.

The Legal and Historical Context

Traditional restrictions on women's scribal participation were not explicitly mandated in biblical or early rabbinic law but developed through centuries of interpretive tradition. The Talmud contains no explicit prohibition against women writing Torah scrolls, though it does restrict them from serving as witnesses in certain legal contexts.[2] Modern halakhic authorities had generally extended these restrictions to ritual scribing, arguing that the act of writing sacred texts required the same legal standing as reading them in public worship.

Contemporary Jewish feminist scholars challenged these interpretations by demonstrating that the connection between scribal practice and liturgical leadership was historically contingent rather than divinely mandated. Rabbi Mendel Shapiro's influential 2001 halakhic analysis argued that women's exclusion from Torah scribing was based on social custom rather than religious law, opening space for women to reclaim these roles within Orthodox frameworks.[3]

Contemporary Practice and Community Response

Following Aviel Barclay's pioneering work, a growing community of women scribes has emerged across the Jewish world. Jen Taylor Friedman, working in England, completed a Torah scroll in 2010 that was accepted for liturgical use by several Progressive congregations.[4] Linda Coppleson, a calligrapher turned soferet, has trained numerous women in the United States, while Temima Nochomi's work in Israel has influenced Sephardic approaches to women's scribal participation.[5]

The community response to women scribes has varied significantly across denominational lines. Reform and Conservative Jewish communities have generally embraced women's participation in ritual scribing as consistent with their commitments to gender equality. Orthodox communities remain divided, with some accepting women's scrolls for study purposes while maintaining traditional restrictions on liturgical use.[6]

Perhaps more significantly, the emergence of women scribes has prompted broader discussions about the nature of sacred authority and textual transmission. When women write Torah scrolls, they do not simply replicate male practices but often bring different perspectives to the meaning and significance of scribal work. Many contemporary women scribes emphasize the meditative and spiritual aspects of letter formation, connecting their practice to traditions of Jewish women's spirituality that emphasize embodied religious experience.[7]

Islamic Feminist Scholarship and Contemporary Exegesis

The late twentieth and early twenty-first centuries have witnessed a remarkable flowering of Islamic feminist scholarship that has transformed approaches to Quranic interpretation and Islamic law. Unlike earlier periods when women's religious knowledge was primarily transmitted through oral networks, contemporary Muslim women scholars are publishing, teaching, and debating in public forums that reach global audiences.

Pioneers and Methodologies

Scholars like Amina Wadud, Asma Barlas, and Kecia Ali have developed sophisticated hermeneutical approaches that distinguish between Quranic principles and patriarchal interpretations that accumulated over centuries of male-dominated scholarship.[8] Their work demonstrates that careful attention to Arabic grammar, historical context, and comparative Islamic jurisprudence can support egalitarian readings of texts that had been interpreted to justify women's subordination.

Wadud's approach to Quranic hermeneutics emphasizes what she calls "tawhidic paradigm," reading the Quran through the lens of divine unity in ways that reject hierarchical relationships between men and women.[9] Barlas's work on Quranic anthropology shows how the text consistently affirms the spiritual equality of men and women while rejecting patriarchal authority structures.¹⁰ Ali's scholarship on Islamic law demonstrates how attention to diversity within traditional jurisprudence can support contemporary arguments for women's rights.¹¹

Regional Variations and Global Networks

Islamic feminist scholarship has developed distinctive characteristics in different cultural contexts while maintaining connections through international scholarly networks. In Southeast Asia, scholars like Musdah Mulia and Siti Ruhaini Dzuhayatin have connected Quranic interpretation to local traditions of women's religious authority, while in Iran, scholars like Zahra Rahnavard have developed approaches that work within the framework of Islamic revolutionary ideology.¹²

African Muslim feminists like Amina Mama and Fatou Sow have emphasized how attention to pre-Islamic African traditions can enrich understanding of women's roles in Islamic societies, while scholars in North America and Europe have focused on how Islamic principles can address contemporary issues like domestic violence and economic justice.¹³

These regional variations demonstrate that Islamic feminist scholarship is not a monolithic movement but rather a diverse conversation that reflects different cultural contexts and interpretive priorities. However, common methodological commitments connect these scholars: careful attention to Quranic Arabic, historical contextualization of traditional interpretations, and emphasis on justice ('adl) as a central Quranic principle.

Institutional Challenges and Achievements

Contemporary Muslim women scholars face significant institutional challenges in gaining recognition for their interpretive work. Traditional Islamic educational institutions often restrict women's access to advanced training in Quranic exegesis and Islamic law, while political pressures in many Muslim-majority countries can make feminist scholarship dangerous.[14]

Despite these obstacles, Islamic feminist scholars have achieved remarkable institutional gains. Several universities in the United States, Canada, and Europe have established programs in Islamic feminism, while international organizations like Women in Islam and Musawah have created platforms for scholarly exchange and advocacy.[15] Perhaps most significantly, younger generation Muslim women are increasingly accessing Islamic education through online platforms and informal networks that bypass traditional institutional gatekeeping.

Buddhist Women's Global Ordination Movement

The contemporary movement for Buddhist women's full ordination represents one of the most successful examples of women using textual scholarship to challenge institutional exclusion. For over a thousand years, the bhikkhuni (fully ordained nun) lineage had died out in Theravāda Buddhism, leaving women in those traditions without access to the highest levels of monastic education and authority.[16]

Textual Recovery and Historical Argument

Buddhist feminist scholars like Karma Lekshe Tsomo, Bhikshuni Jampa Tsedroen, and Bhikkhuni Dhammananda have used careful analysis of Pali and Sanskrit sources to demonstrate that women's exclusion from full ordination was historically contingent rather than doctrinally necessary.[17] Their scholarship has shown that the Buddha originally established parallel orders for men and women, and that restrictions on women's ordination developed through later institutional decisions rather than original Buddhist teaching.

This textual work has been crucial for legitimizing contemporary ordination efforts. When Thai women like Dhammananda seek full ordination, they can point to scholarly evidence that such ordination is consistent with original Buddhist principles rather than a modern innovation.[18] Similarly, when Western Buddhist communities consider ordaining women, they can draw on textual scholarship that demonstrates the historical precedent for such practices.

Global Networks and Cultural Adaptation

The Sakyadhita International Association of Buddhist Women, founded in 1987, has created unprecedented networks for sharing textual knowledge and coordinating ordination efforts across national and sectarian boundaries.[19] Through conferences, publications, and digital platforms, Sakyadhita has connected Buddhist women across Asia, Europe, and the Americas in common projects of textual recovery and institutional change.

Different Buddhist cultures have developed distinctive approaches to women's ordination that reflect local traditions while maintaining connections to broader movements. In Taiwan and China, the bhikkhuni lineage never died out, providing models for ordination procedures that can be adapted elsewhere.[20] In Tibet, where the bhikkhuni lineage was never established, contemporary efforts focus on creating new ordination procedures that are consistent with Tibetan Buddhist principles.[21] In Western contexts, Buddhist communities often emphasize how women's ordination can address contemporary concerns about gender equality and social justice.

Textual Authority and Institutional Resistance

Perhaps most significantly, the Buddhist women's ordination movement demonstrates how textual scholarship can be used to challenge institutional authority. Traditional Buddhist hierarchies have often resisted women's ordination by claiming that it lacks proper textual precedent or violates established procedures. However, contemporary Buddhist feminist scholars have developed sophisticated arguments that use traditional Buddhist textual methods to support women's inclusion.

This scholarship has not always been welcomed by traditional Buddhist institutions. In Thailand, Dhammananda has faced significant opposition from the official Sangha (monastic order), while in other Theravāda countries, women seeking ordination have been formally prohibited from doing so.[22] However, the existence of rigorous textual scholarship supporting women's ordination has made it increasingly difficult for institutional authorities to claim that such ordination is simply a Western innovation or departure from authentic Buddhism.

Global Perspectives: Beyond Abrahamic Traditions

The contemporary renaissance of women's engagement with sacred texts extends far beyond the Abrahamic traditions that have received most scholarly attention. Across Africa, Asia, and the Americas, women are reclaiming roles in the preservation and interpretation of indigenous religious traditions that had been marginalized by colonialism and modernization.

African Traditional Religions and Yoruba Practice

In West Africa and the diaspora, women are playing crucial roles in preserving and adapting Yoruba religious traditions that center on oral transmission of sacred knowledge. Scholars like Oyeronke Oyewumi and practitioners like Iyanifa Vassa have demonstrated how attention to indigenous African epistemologies can reveal women's central roles in maintaining religious traditions that European scholarship had often misunderstood.[23]

Contemporary Yoruba priestesses serve not only as ritual specialists but as keepers of oral texts that function similarly to written scriptures in other traditions. Their work includes memorizing praise poems, divination verses, and mythological narratives that preserve religious knowledge across generations. When these oral traditions are transcribed or translated, women's authority as textual interpreters becomes visible in ways that were previously overlooked.[24]

Hindu Women's Devotional Innovation

In contemporary Hinduism, women are engaging with sacred texts through both scholarly interpretation and devotional practice in ways that challenge traditional restrictions on women's religious authority. Scholars like Vasudha Narayanan and Arti Dhand have demonstrated how careful attention to classical Sanskrit sources can support egalitarian interpretations of texts that had been read through patriarchal frameworks.[25]

Perhaps more significantly, contemporary Hindu women are creating new forms of devotional practice that draw on classical traditions while addressing modern concerns. Devotional singers like Bindhumalini Narayanaswamy and Sunitha Krishnamurti adapt traditional bhakti poetry in ways that emphasize women's spiritual agency, while scholars like Laurie Patton have shown how women's devotional practices constitute forms of textual interpretation that deserve recognition alongside more formal commentary traditions.[26]

Sikh Women's Scriptural Authority

The contemporary Sikh tradition has witnessed significant developments in women's religious leadership that demonstrate how attention to foundational texts can support gender equality within traditional frameworks. The Guru Granth Sahib contains numerous hymns by female poet-saints, and Sikh principles of spiritual equality provide strong foundations for women's religious authority.[27]

Contemporary Sikh women like Rajinder Kaur and Harinder Singh have drawn on these textual resources to argue for women's full participation in religious leadership, including serving as granthis (scripture readers) and participating in religious decision-making.[28] Their work demonstrates how women can use traditional textual authority to challenge contemporary practices that may not reflect original religious principles.

Indigenous Knowledge Systems and Contemporary Recovery

Perhaps most remarkably, indigenous communities across the Americas, Australia, and the Pacific are undertaking sophisticated projects of textual recovery that center women's traditional roles as knowledge keepers. These efforts often involve collaboration between indigenous communities and academic institutions in ways that respect indigenous intellectual sovereignty while supporting community goals.[29]

In North America, Native American scholars like Vine Deloria Jr. and Winona LaDuke have emphasized how attention to indigenous women's traditional roles can inform contemporary efforts to preserve and adapt traditional knowledge systems.[30] Similar work is being done by Aboriginal Australian women who are documenting ceremonial knowledge and by Pacific Islander women who are preserving traditional navigation and agricultural practices.

These projects demonstrate that the contemporary renaissance of women's engagement with sacred texts is truly global in scope and includes traditions that may not use written texts but nonetheless preserve complex knowledge systems that function similarly to scriptures in other traditions.

Digital Platforms and Democratized Access

One of the most significant developments in contemporary women's engagement with sacred texts has been the emergence of digital platforms that bypass traditional institutional gatekeeping. Online education, social media, and digital publishing have created unprecedented opportunities for women to share religious knowledge and reach global audiences without requiring approval from traditional religious authorities.

Online Religious Education

Platforms like SeekersHub, Bayyinah Institute, and various Buddhist meditation apps have created opportunities for women teachers to reach global audiences with religious instruction that was previously restricted to local communities.[31] Muslim women scholars like Yasmin Mogahed and Ingrid Mattson have built international followings through online teaching that combines traditional Islamic knowledge with contemporary concerns.[32]

Similarly, Buddhist teachers like Pema Chödrön and Tara Brach have used digital platforms to share meditation instruction and dharma teaching with audiences that extend far beyond traditional Buddhist communities.[33] These developments demonstrate how technology can democratize access to religious education in ways that particularly benefit women, who may face greater restrictions in accessing traditional educational institutions.

Social Media and Scriptural Interpretation

Social media platforms have also created new spaces for religious discussion and scriptural interpretation that operate outside traditional institutional control. Women religious leaders across traditions use platforms like Instagram, YouTube, and TikTok to share brief teachings, answer questions, and engage in religious discussions with followers around the world.[34]

These platforms allow for forms of religious authority that are based on perceived authenticity and relevance rather than institutional credentialing. When young Muslim women turn to Instagram teachers for religious guidance, or when Jewish women join Facebook groups dedicated to discussing halakhic questions, they are participating in forms of religious transmission that circumvent traditional gatekeeping mechanisms.

Digital Archives and Manuscript Access

Digital humanities projects have also transformed women's access to historical religious texts. Projects like the Digital Manuscripts Toolkit, the Women Writers Project, and various digitization efforts by major libraries have made it possible for scholars and community members to access manuscripts and texts that were previously available only to specialists.[35]

This democratized access has been particularly important for women scholars who may face greater barriers to accessing physical archives or traveling for research. When manuscripts are digitized and made freely available online, they can be studied by anyone with internet access, regardless of their institutional affiliation or geographic location.

Ongoing Challenges and Institutional Resistance

Despite remarkable achievements in women's engagement with sacred texts, significant challenges remain. Traditional religious institutions often resist women's participation in textual transmission, while social and economic barriers continue to limit women's access to religious education and authority.

Denominational and Cultural Variations

The acceptance of women's religious authority varies dramatically across and within religious traditions. While Reform Judaism readily accepts women rabbis and scribes, Orthodox communities remain divided on these questions. Similarly, while some Buddhist communities have enthusiastically embraced women's ordination, others maintain traditional restrictions.[36]

These variations reflect deeper theological and cultural differences about the nature of religious authority and the relationship between tradition and change. Communities that emphasize historical precedent may be more resistant to women's participation, while those that prioritize contemporary relevance may be more open to change.

Economic and Educational Barriers

Women's participation in religious scholarship and leadership also faces practical obstacles related to economic resources and educational access. Traditional religious education often requires significant financial investment and time commitments that may be more difficult for women to manage, particularly in societies where women face economic discrimination or primary responsibility for childcare.[37]

Digital platforms have helped address some of these barriers by reducing the costs associated with religious education, but they cannot eliminate all obstacles. Women who lack reliable internet access or computer literacy may still face significant barriers to participating in online religious communities.

Institutional Gatekeeping and Recognition

Perhaps most significantly, traditional religious institutions often refuse to recognize women's textual authority even when they possess equivalent qualifications to their male counterparts. Women may be permitted to study religious texts but prohibited from teaching them publicly, or they may be allowed to teach women but not men.[38]

These restrictions reflect deeper assumptions about gender and religious authority that cannot be addressed simply through better access to education or textual knowledge. Changing these assumptions requires sustained community dialogue and, often, generational change within religious institutions.

Future Directions and Emerging Possibilities

The contemporary renaissance of women's engagement with sacred texts continues to evolve in directions that were unimaginable even a generation ago. Emerging technologies, changing social attitudes, and generational shifts within religious communities are creating new possibilities for women's religious authority and textual interpretation.

Collaborative Scholarship and Community Engagement

One of the most promising developments has been the emergence of collaborative approaches to religious scholarship that bring together academic researchers, community practitioners, and religious authorities in common projects. These collaborations can help bridge the gap between scholarly research and community practice while ensuring that women's voices are included in both academic and religious contexts.[39]

Interfaith Dialogue and Comparative Perspectives

Another significant development has been the emergence of interfaith dialogue that specifically focuses on women's religious experiences across traditions. Organizations like the Interfaith Women's Network and academic programs in comparative women's spirituality have created opportunities for women from different religious backgrounds to share insights and strategies for navigating patriarchal religious structures.[40]

Gender-Inclusive and Queer Religious Scholarship

Perhaps most significantly, contemporary religious scholarship is increasingly moving beyond binary gender categories to include transgender, non-binary, and gender-fluid perspectives on religious authority and textual interpretation. This expansion challenges not only patriarchal assumptions about religious leadership but also the gender binary that has traditionally structured religious institutions.[41]

Scholars like Laury Silvers and Junaid Jahangir have begun developing Islamic theological approaches that affirm gender diversity, while Jewish scholars like Elliot Kukla have argued for trans-inclusive interpretations of halakhic texts.[42] These developments suggest that the contemporary conversation about gender and religious authority is continuing to evolve in directions that were unimaginable when feminist religious scholarship first emerged.

The scrolls are indeed no longer sealed. Across religious traditions and around the world, women are not only recovering lost voices from the past but actively participating in the ongoing creation and interpretation of sacred wisdom. This contemporary renaissance represents neither a rejection of tradition nor a simple return to ancient practices, but rather a fundamental reimagining of how religious authority is constituted and how sacred knowledge is preserved and transmitted.

Understanding this contemporary moment requires recognizing both its achievements and its limitations. While remarkable progress has been made in expanding women's access to religious education and authority, significant obstacles remain. The future of women's engagement with sacred texts will depend not only on continued scholarship and activism but also on broader social changes that address economic inequality, educational access, and deeply rooted assumptions about gender and religious authority.

Most importantly, the contemporary conversation about women and sacred texts demonstrates that religious traditions are not fixed entities but living communities that continue to evolve in response to new questions and changing circumstances. The voices that are emerging today will shape how future generations understand the relationship between gender, authority, and sacred wisdom, ensuring that the conversation continues to expand and deepen in ways that honor both tradition and transformation.

Conclusion: To Be Remembered

She is there, if you know how to look.

In the corner of the manuscript. In the erased line beneath the visible one. In the whispered tradition, the variant telling, the orphaned verse. She is the unnamed student, the erased scribe, the theologian whose commentary was never copied. She is the prophet without a scroll, the singer without a signature, the preacher silenced before the canon closed.

She is also the woman who copied, memorized, translated, taught, and lived the sacred. Who shaped the texts we now hold, even as her own name dissolved into silence.

This book has sought to gather those fragments. To give space at last for the women who were there all along, across every tradition we have explored: the Jewish women who composed tkhines in Eastern European kitchens, the Buddhist nuns whose enlightenment verses were preserved in fragmentary manuscripts, the Christian mystics whose visions became theology, the Islamic women who transmitted hadith through generations of careful memorization, the Hindu poets whose devotional songs became scripture through repetition, and the countless scribes, patrons, and teachers whose anonymous hands shaped the sacred texts that billions still revere.

Across these chapters, we have witnessed a profound paradox unfold. Women shaped the sacred, yet the sacred as we inherited it often excluded them. Their labor was preserved, but their names were not. Their voices shimmered at the edges of scripture, quoted, corrected, footnoted, forgotten. We saw apostles recast as sinners, scribes left unnamed, poets remembered only in fragments. We followed their erasure through editorial choices, legal restrictions, theological anxieties, and cultural conservatism. And we traced their resistance in midrash and mysticism, in oral storytelling and sacred song, in the counter-traditions that preserved what official channels would not.

But even now, recovery is not complete. Nor is remembrance guaranteed.

The Scholarly Conversation: Can Erasure Be Reversed?

Among scholars working to recover women's voices from religious history, a vital debate continues about the possibilities and limitations of historical reconstruction. This conversation illuminates both what we have achieved and what challenges remain.

Elizabeth A. Clark, whose pioneering work transformed early Christian studies, has argued that recovery efforts must acknowledge both the real loss and the inherent limits of historical reconstruction. "Some voices may never return," Clark observes, "and pretending otherwise risks distorting the past we seek to understand."[1] Her caution reflects broader methodological concerns about the difference between recovering authentic historical voices and projecting contemporary concerns onto ancient sources.

Caroline Walker Bynum, however, has emphasized the interpretive value of fragments and the theological insights that can emerge from partial recovery. For Bynum, absence is not merely emptiness but "a challenge to think differently about authority, presence, and power."[2] Her approach suggests that even incomplete knowledge about women's historical roles can transform how we understand religious traditions and their development.

Fatima Mernissi, whose groundbreaking work on early Islamic history revealed the systematic marginalization of women's voices, argued that documenting erasure is itself a form of historical justice. "Even if a woman's words are lost," Mernissi wrote, "naming the forces that silenced her can serve as a warning and a reckoning for future generations."[3] Her work demonstrates how understanding the mechanisms of exclusion can be as important as recovering specific voices.

Susannah Heschel, in her influential Jewish feminist scholarship, has focused on the question of transmission and the interpretive authority of those outside formal academic institutions. Heschel's work reveals how women's midrashim, prayers, and teachings, though excluded from written canons, shaped lived religious experience across generations.[4] For Heschel, recovery means revaluing forms of religious authority that operate through oral tradition, domestic practice, and community transmission.

Alison Beach's forensic approach to medieval manuscripts demonstrates how recovery work can proceed "one ink stroke at a time," using paleographic analysis, stylistic fingerprints, and historical context to reconstruct even erased names and marginalized contributions.[5] Her meticulous scholarship shows that apparently lost voices can sometimes be recovered through careful attention to material evidence and collaborative research methods.

Beyond Christian and Jewish contexts, scholars working in other traditions have developed parallel approaches to recovery and interpretation. Rita Gross's Buddhist feminist scholarship has shown how attention to variant manuscript traditions and early textual sources can reveal the contingent nature of women's exclusion from full religious participation.[6] Mary Keller's work on Native American women's religious roles demonstrates how collaborative research with indigenous communities can recover knowledge systems that were marginalized by colonial scholarship.[7] Saba Mahmood's ethnographic work with contemporary Muslim women reveals how traditional forms of religious knowledge continue to be transmitted through women's networks that operate outside formal institutional structures.[8]

Together, these scholars suggest that erasure can never be fully undone, but it can be documented, challenged, and made visible. More importantly, they demonstrate that the work of recovery is not merely about the past but about creating possibilities for more inclusive understanding in the present and future.

What Might Have Been: Imagining Alternative Trajectories

Understanding how women's voices were marginalized in the development of sacred texts allows us to imagine how religious traditions might have evolved differently. This speculative exercise, grounded in careful analysis of recovered sources, illuminates both historical possibilities and contemporary opportunities.

The Shape of Sacred Literature

If women's writings and voices had been fully preserved and integrated into religious canons, our sacred literature would likely include a much broader range of textual genres and theological perspectives. Contemporary scholars like Elisabeth Schüssler Fiorenza have argued that early Christian canon formation actively excluded texts that featured women in leadership roles, suggesting that a more inclusive canonization process might have preserved alternative models of religious authority.[9]

Similarly, if Islamic hadith collections had maintained equal attention to female and male transmitters throughout their development, as Asma Sayeed's research suggests was possible in early generations, Islamic jurisprudence might have developed with greater attention to women's religious experiences and interpretive insights.[10] Buddhist canons that fully preserved women's enlightenment narratives, like those partially recovered from Dunhuang manuscripts, might have provided stronger foundations for women's monastic leadership across Asian Buddhist cultures.

Models of Religious Authority

The systematic marginalization of women's voices in religious traditions contributed to the development of hierarchical models of authority that emphasized institutional credentialing over charismatic or experiential forms of religious knowledge. As Grace Jantzen's work on Christian mysticism demonstrates, women's mystical authority often operated through alternative networks that emphasized direct spiritual experience over formal theological education.[11]

Had these alternative models of authority been preserved and developed, religious traditions might have maintained more diverse and flexible approaches to religious leadership. Contemporary scholars like Amina Wadud suggest that Islamic principles of spiritual equality might have supported different models of religious authority if women's early participation in religious discourse had been sustained rather than marginalized.[12]

Theological and Ethical Development

Perhaps most significantly, the inclusion of women's voices might have led to different theological emphases and ethical priorities within religious traditions. Julian of Norwich's theology of divine motherhood, Rābi'a al-'Adawiyya's emphasis on disinterested divine love, and the Therigatha nuns' focus on embodied spiritual experience all suggest theological trajectories that were marginalized as religious traditions developed.

Contemporary theologians like Sallie McFague have argued that attention to feminine divine imagery might have supported different approaches to environmental ethics and social justice, while scholars like Sachiko Murata have shown how early Islamic thought contained resources for understanding divine nature in ways that transcended gender categories.[13]

Interfaith Understanding and Cooperation

One of the most striking discoveries in comparative study of women's religious experiences is the remarkable similarity of their spiritual insights across different traditions. The emphasis on divine love in Islamic Sufism, Christian mysticism, and Hindu bhakti poetry; the focus on embodied spiritual experience in Buddhist and Jewish women's writings; the development of alternative forms of religious authority through visionary experience across traditions—all suggest that women's religious experiences might have provided natural foundations for interfaith dialogue and cooperation.

Recognition of these commonalities might have fostered earlier development of comparative theology and mutual understanding across religious boundaries. As scholars like Riffat Hassan and Rita Gross have suggested, women's shared experiences of marginalization within patriarchal religious structures might have created alternative foundations for interfaith relations based on solidarity rather than competition.[14]

Contemporary Implications: The Ongoing Work of Recovery

Understanding the historical marginalization of women's voices in sacred traditions has profound implications for contemporary religious communities and scholarly practice. The work of recovery is not merely an academic exercise but a continuing effort to create more inclusive and authentic religious understanding.

Transforming Religious Education

Recognition of women's historical contributions to religious traditions requires fundamental changes in how religious education is structured and delivered. Seminary curricula that include feminist, womanist, and mujerista theological perspectives; Islamic studies programs that attend to women's roles in hadith transmission and Quranic interpretation; Buddhist studies that center women's enlightenment narratives; Jewish education that incorporates women's liturgical and interpretive contributions—all represent practical applications of recovery scholarship.

Contemporary religious educators like Mercy Amba Oduyoye, Kwok Pui-lan, and Ada María Isasi-Díaz have demonstrated how attention to women's religious experiences can transform not only what is taught but how religious education occurs, emphasizing collaborative learning methods and community-based knowledge production.[15]

Ritual and Community Practice

The recovery of women's voices also has implications for contemporary ritual practice and community organization. When Jewish communities use Torah scrolls written by women soferot, when Muslim communities recognize women's authority in Quranic interpretation, when Buddhist communities support full ordination for women, when Christian communities ordain women as clergy—these practices represent practical applications of historical recovery work.

More subtly, attention to women's historical roles in preserving oral traditions, maintaining domestic religious practices, and transmitting religious knowledge through family and community networks can inform contemporary understanding of how religious communities actually function and where religious authority genuinely resides.

Interfaith Dialogue and Global Understanding

Perhaps most importantly, understanding women's shared experiences across religious traditions provides resources for contemporary interfaith dialogue that moves beyond institutional comparison to consider how different communities have addressed common human concerns. Women's approaches to questions of spiritual authority, religious education, social justice, and community organization offer alternative models for interfaith cooperation that complement and sometimes challenge official theological dialogues.

Methodological Humility and Future Directions

As this survey of recovery scholarship demonstrates, the work of remembering marginalized voices requires methodological humility and careful attention to both possibilities and limitations. Historical reconstruction can never fully restore what has been lost, and contemporary scholars must avoid the temptation to claim more certainty than the evidence allows.

At the same time, acknowledging the limits of historical knowledge should not discourage efforts to recover what can be known or to imagine alternative possibilities based on fragmentary evidence. As Carolyn Walker Bynum has argued, even incomplete knowledge can transform understanding and open new interpretive possibilities.[16]

The future of recovery work will likely depend on several developing trends: increased collaboration between academic scholars and religious communities; expanded use of digital technologies for manuscript analysis and community engagement; greater attention to global and cross-cultural perspectives on women's religious roles; and continued development of methodological approaches that can address questions of gender alongside other forms of difference and marginalization.

Most importantly, the work of recovery requires recognizing that remembering marginalized voices is not simply about historical accuracy but about creating possibilities for more inclusive and authentic religious understanding in the present. When contemporary communities acknowledge women's historical contributions to their traditions, they create space for continued development and reinterpretation that honors both tradition and transformation.

An Invitation to Ongoing Remembrance

To be remembered is not simply to be named in historical accounts. It is to be read seriously, studied carefully, and recognized as a maker of meaning whose insights continue to speak across centuries of transmission and interpretation. The women whose stories fill these pages shaped scripture with their hands, their minds, their lives, their devotion, and their resistance. They preserved sacred knowledge when institutions would not, transmitted wisdom when formal channels were closed, and maintained spiritual traditions when official support was unavailable.

Their recovery challenges us to expand our understanding of how religious traditions develop and how sacred authority is constituted. More than that, it invites us to participate in the ongoing work of interpretation and transmission that has always been collaborative, even when collaboration was not acknowledged.

Contemporary religious communities stand at a unique historical moment. Never before have so many voices been recoverable through scholarly research, digital technology, and collaborative interpretation. Never before have so many communities been willing to acknowledge the limitations of inherited traditions and the possibilities for inclusive transformation. Never before have the tools been available for truly global and comparative understanding of how different traditions have addressed similar challenges and opportunities.

This moment requires both reverence for inherited wisdom and courage to acknowledge its limitations. It demands both careful scholarship and creative imagination. Most importantly, it calls for recognition that the work of preserving and interpreting sacred tradition has always belonged to entire communities rather than privileged elites, and that the voices of those who have been marginalized or excluded may offer essential insights for contemporary religious challenges.

The sacred editors whose stories we have traced across these chapters remind us that religious traditions are not museum pieces but living conversations between past wisdom and present needs. They show us that transmission requires transformation, that preservation demands interpretation, and that authority emerges not only from institutional recognition but from authentic engagement with sacred sources and community needs.

May we now shape our reading in their image—not only with reverence for the sacred texts we have inherited, but with equal reverence for those who made them sacred through centuries of copying, teaching, interpreting, and living their wisdom. In recovering their voices, we discover not different traditions but fuller understanding of the traditions we share. In honoring their contributions, we participate in the ongoing work of sacred editing that transforms ancient wisdom into contemporary guidance.

Their whispers from the margins become our invitation to read more carefully, listen more attentively, and remember more inclusively. The work is far from finished, but it has begun. And in that beginning lies the promise that no voice need remain forever lost, no contribution permanently forgotten, no wisdom irretrievably silenced.

The scrolls are no longer sealed. The conversation continues. And it includes us all.

Research & Methodology

Transparency in the Age of AI

As mentioned in the introduction, this book emerged from a personal journey of exploration—what some traditions call *bhāvanā*, or disciplined cultivation of understanding. While my focus this time was the history of how the Bible came to be, I approached the subject with the same intellectual curiosity, reverence for tradition, and openness to whatever might be uncovered that I bring to any *bhavana* practice.

This project also represented my continued exploration of artificial intelligence as a research and synthesis tool. Given the growing importance—and legitimate concerns—around AI's role in content creation, I want to be completely transparent about how this book was developed, how I worked with existing scholarship, and how I tried to ensure accuracy in presenting other people's research. My aim is to offer both confidence that I've accurately represented established scholarship and a replicable model for others who want to synthesize complex academic material for general audiences.

I want to be clear: I am not a biblical scholar, historian, or expert in ancient languages. I have no formal training in these fields. What I am is a curious reader who has spent considerable time engaging with the work of people who do have these credentials. This book represents my attempt to synthesize and present their findings in an accessible narrative format, not to contribute new knowledge to these fields.

A Multi-Platform Workflow

Rather than rely on a single AI system for research assistance, I developed a structured process using multiple large language models (LLMs), each selected for their particular strengths and used within carefully defined parameters. The workflow follows a six-stage process designed to help me work effectively with existing scholarship while maintaining accuracy and avoiding misrepresentation.

Stage 1: Idea Development with ChatGPT

Each chapter began with exploratory conversations using ChatGPT (GPT-4, accessed through OpenAI's interface). This included brainstorming how to present complex scholarly material in narrative form, identifying the most important voices in different debates (such as Bruce Metzger, Bart D. Ehrman, Timothy Michael Law, and Emanuel Tov), and finding ways to structure chapters that would be both informative and engaging for general readers. ChatGPT's conversational strengths made it useful for exploring different approaches to presenting contentious or nuanced historical questions without taking sides.

Stage 2: Source Verification with Perplexity

All material and citations underwent verification using Perplexity (accessed through perplexity.ai), which can locate specific scholarly claims and cross-reference publication details through real-time web searches. This stage was crucial for ensuring that I was accurately representing what scholars actually said and that my understanding of their positions was correct. Where possible, I located complete citations, and when I found I had misunderstood or misrepresented someone's work, I made corrections.

Stage 3: Writing and Synthesis with Claude

For certain chapters and major revisions, Claude (Anthropic's Claude Sonnet 4) helped me synthesize material from multiple sources while maintaining a consistent voice and ensuring that complex scholarly debates were presented fairly. Claude's ability to work with longer texts proved valuable for ensuring continuity across chapters while handling substantial amounts of source material.

Stage 4: Recursive Fact-Checking

Following initial drafts, all chapters underwent additional rounds of verification using Perplexity's updated databases. This iterative process frequently caught errors in my understanding, outdated references, or claims that weren't actually supported by the scholars I was citing. I made corrections systematically, with particular attention to ensuring that my presentation of historical claims aligned with how the experts themselves present them.

Stage 5: Expert Human Review

All content was reviewed by a subject matter expert with credentials in the relevant fields. This review proved crucial for catching places where I had oversimplified complex issues, misunderstood scholarly debates, or inadvertently introduced bias. The reviewer's feedback shaped both factual corrections and how I presented interpretive debates throughout the manuscript.

Stage 6: Final Human Integration and Editorial Review

The final drafts underwent comprehensive review and revision by me. This stage involved ensuring that the narrative flowed well for general readers while maintaining accuracy in presenting scholarly material. Every word in the final manuscript reflects my judgment about how best to serve readers who want to understand what scholars have discovered about biblical formation, even if they don't have academic background in these fields.

Why Multiple AI Systems?

Different platforms have distinct capabilities and limitations. Using multiple systems created a form of cross-checking that helped me work more accurately with scholarly material:

- **ChatGPT** excelled at helping me think through narrative structure and find accessible ways to present complex scholarly positions. However, it occasionally oversimplified and required constant verification for factual precision.
- **Perplexity** proved essential for verifying that I was accurately representing scholars' actual positions, checking biblical references, and identifying places where my understanding didn't match what experts

actually claim. Its limitations included occasional over-reliance on secondary sources.
- **Claude** provided superior help with synthesizing material from multiple sources while maintaining stylistic consistency. It helped me integrate various scholars' perspectives without losing the thread of the narrative, though it sometimes needed guidance on balancing accuracy with readability.

Using multiple systems allowed each to check my work against the others, creating a form of technological verification that enhanced both accuracy and comprehensiveness in representing existing scholarship.

The Critical Role of Contextual Prompting

Success with AI tools depends heavily on precise prompting that acknowledges my role as synthesizer, not original researcher. All systems were consistently reminded of the project's nature:

"You are a PhD scholar of [topic] textual history with 25 years of experience. I am not a [topic] scholar or historian. I am synthesizing existing scholarship for general audiences. Help me accurately represent what established experts like [specific scholars] have concluded about [specific topic]. Ensure I don't overstate my own role or expertise, distinguish clearly between established scholarly consensus and ongoing debates, and avoid speculation not grounded in the work of credentialed experts."

Each chapter prompt included detailed requirements about representing diverse scholarly perspectives fairly and distinguishing between what I was learning from experts versus any interpretive work I was doing myself.

Addressing AI Limitations and Maintaining Humility

AI tools significantly accelerated my ability to work with large amounts of scholarly material, but they consistently demonstrated important limitations that required constant human oversight:

- **Tendency to oversimplify** complex scholarly debates into false binaries when the reality is much more nuanced
- **Potential gaps** in representing diverse scholarly voices, particularly from non-Western traditions or emerging scholars
- **Inability to understand** the spiritual or personal significance of these questions for faith communities
- **Occasional confusion** between primary sources and secondary interpretations, requiring careful verification

To address these limitations, I incorporated specific strategies: actively seeking out diverse scholarly voices, explicitly acknowledging complexity in Scholar Debate sections, and ensuring that the human significance of these historical processes remained central to the narrative.

Ultimately, I—not any AI system—remain fully responsible for every claim, interpretation, and narrative choice in this book. AI provided assistance with organization and synthesis; human judgment and expert consultation shaped how I presented the work of qualified scholars.

Verification Standards and Quality Control

All chapters underwent systematic review for multiple dimensions of quality:

- **Accuracy in representing scholars' positions** through cross-platform verification and expert review
- **Proper attribution** and balanced representation of academic debates
- **Narrative clarity** for general audiences while maintaining scholarly accuracy
- **Respect** for both scholarly traditions and contemporary faith communities
- **Transparency** about what represents established scholarly consensus versus ongoing debates versus speculative exploration

Where historical events remain contested or interpretations are disputed, the chapter format explicitly accommodated multiple scholarly perspectives, ensuring readers understand the difference between what experts agree on, what they debate, and what remains unknown.

Ethical Framework: The Responsibilities of a Synthesizer

This project represents an attempt to make fascinating scholarly work accessible to general audiences while respecting both the expertise of qualified scholars and the beliefs of faith communities who hold these texts sacred.

My goal was never to replace expert scholarship or offer my own theories, but to serve as a bridge between the academy and curious readers who want to understand what scholars have discovered about biblical formation. If this approach has enabled people to engage more deeply with the remarkable work that biblical scholars, historians, and archaeologists have done, then it has served its purpose.

The rapid evolution of AI capabilities means that specific tools will continue to change. What remains constant is the need for transparency, humility about one's own limitations, expert oversight, and ethical responsibility when working with material that matters deeply to human communities.

A Note for Future Synthesizers

For others considering similar projects, several principles emerge from this experience:

- **Be transparent about your role**: Readers deserve to know that you're synthesizing, not conducting original research

- **Verify everything**: No single system or approach is sufficient for ensuring you're accurately representing others' work
- **Expert review is essential**: AI can help with organization, but only qualified humans can verify accuracy in specialized fields
- **Stay humble**: Your job is to serve the work of actual experts, not to replace them
- **Acknowledge complexity**: Resist the temptation to oversimplify debates that scholars themselves find genuinely difficult

In the end, methodology serves the deeper purpose of understanding. The patient, careful work of learning from those who have dedicated their careers to studying how human communities preserve and transmit their most treasured wisdom requires not just sophisticated tools but humble hearts and curious minds willing to be taught by those who know more than we do.

This book's methodology aimed to honor both the rigor that scholarly work deserves and the reverence that sacred traditions inspire. Whether it has succeeded in faithfully representing the work of qualified experts is for readers—and those experts themselves—to judge.

Notes from Chapters

Prologue: She Who Holds the Ink

1. This vignette draws upon documented evidence of female scribal activity at Nalanda during its flourishing period (7th-9th centuries). While no specific nun named Padmavati is recorded as a scribe of the Lotus Sutra, women's participation in Buddhist manuscript production is attested through archaeological evidence and inscriptional records. See Janice Leoshko, *Sacred Traces: British Explorations of Buddhism in South Asia* (Ashgate, 2003), 85–87; and Karma Lekshe Tsomo, "Buddhist Women and the Nuns' Order in Asia," in *Sakyadhita: Daughters of the Buddha*, ed. Karma Lekshe Tsomo (Snow Lion, 1988), 97–101. On women's roles in Buddhist textual transmission more broadly, see Liz Wilson, *Charming Cadavers: Horrific Figurations of the Feminine in Indian Buddhist Hagiographic Literature* (University of Chicago Press, 1996), particularly chapter 3 on monastic scribal practices.

2. This scene represents a plausible composite based on documented practices at medieval women's scriptoria. While the specific commentary scene is constructed for narrative purposes, Heloise of the Paraclete (c. 1095-1164) did oversee extensive manuscript copying and theological instruction at her abbey. On Heloise's literary and theological life, see M. T. Clanchy, *Abelard: A Medieval Life* (Blackwell, 1997), 290–305; and Constant J. Mews, *The Lost Love Letters of Heloise and Abelard* (St.

Martin's Press, 1999). For broader context on women's book culture in medieval monasteries, see Susan Groag Bell, "Medieval Women Book Owners: Arbiters of Lay Piety and Ambassadors of Culture," *Signs* 7, no. 4 (1982): 742–768.

3. Margaret Gibson (1917-2006) was indeed a distinguished British medievalist and manuscript cataloger who worked extensively with Continental European manuscript collections, particularly those displaced during and after World War II. While the specific marginalia quoted here is constructed from patterns found across multiple anonymous medieval manuscripts, Gibson documented numerous instances of anonymous female scribal activity. See M. Gibson, "Latin and Vernacular Manuscripts in English Nunneries," *Medium Ævum* 58, no. 2 (1989): 178–192. On the broader methodology of identifying women's hands in anonymous medieval manuscripts, see Columba Stewart, "The Portrayal of Women in the Sayings and Stories of the Desert," *Vox Benedictina* 2 (1985): 5–23.

Chapter 1: The Apostle They Erased -- Mary Magdalene

1. This opening vignette represents a plausible composite based on documented practices of early Christian manuscript copying and the known circulation of the Gospel of Mary. While no specific woman copying this text is historically documented, the Gospel of Mary survives in three manuscript fragments (Papyrus

Berolinensis 8502, Papyrus Oxyrhynchus 3525, and Papyrus Rylands 463), indicating it was copied and preserved by early Christian communities. On early Christian scribal practices and the preservation of non-canonical texts, see Kim Haines-Eitzen, *Guardians of Letters: Literacy, Power, and the Transmitters of Early Christian Literature* (Oxford University Press, 2000), 89–112.

2. Bart D. Ehrman, *Peter, Paul, and Mary Magdalene: The Followers of Jesus in History and Legend* (Oxford University Press, 2006), 187–192.

3. Jane Schaberg, *The Resurrection of Mary Magdalene: Legends, Apocrypha, and the Christian Testament*(Continuum, 2002), 78–84; Elizabeth Schrader, "Was Martha of Bethany Added to the Fourth Gospel in the Second Century?" *Harvard Theological Review* 110, no. 3 (2017): 360–392.

4. Gregory the Great, *Homiliae in Evangelia* 33, PL 76:1238–1246.

5. Karen L. King, *The Gospel of Mary of Magdala: Jesus and the First Woman Apostle* (Polebridge Press, 2003).

6. *Gospel of Mary*, Papyrus Berolinensis 8502, 17.10–18, translation by Karen L. King.

7. Anne Pasquier, "The Role of Mary Magdalene in the Pistis Sophia," in *Studies in Gnosticism and Hellenistic Religions*, ed. R. van den Broek and M. J. Vermaseren (Brill, 1981), 491–514.

8. Schrader, "Was Martha of Bethany Added to the Fourth Gospel in the Second Century?" 376–381.

9. *Gospel of Mary*, Papyrus Berolinensis 8502, 17.10–18, translation by Karen L. King.
10. *Gospel of Mary*, Papyrus Berolinensis 8502, 9.1–10.10, translation by Karen L. King.

Chapter 2: The Nuns Who Sang -- The Therīgāthā Poets

1. This opening scene represents a plausible reconstruction based on documented practices of early Buddhist oral transmission and the composition context of the *Therīgāthā*. While specific gatherings are not historically recorded, the oral preservation of these verses within bhikkhunī communities is well-established. See Charles Hallisey, "Devotion in the Buddhist Literature of Medieval Sri Lanka" (PhD diss., University of Chicago, 1988), 45–67, and Karma Lekshe Tsomo, ed., *Buddhist Women Across Cultures* (SUNY Press, 1999), 23–39.
2. K. R. Norman, *Elders' Verses II: Therīgāthā* (Pali Text Society, 1971), xi–xv.
3. Richard Gombrich, *Theravāda Buddhism: A Social History from Ancient Benares to Modern Colombo* (Routledge, 1988), 154–159.
4. Susan Murcott, *The First Buddhist Women: Translations and Commentary on the Therigatha* (Parallax Press, 1991), 9–14.
5. Chatsumarn Kabilsingh (Dhammananda Bhikkhuni), *Thai Women in Buddhism* (Buddhadhamma Foundation, 1991), 38–43.

6. Diana Paul, *Women in Buddhism: Images of the Feminine in the Mahayana Tradition* (University of California Press, 1985), 67–89.
7. Tessa J. Bartholomeusz, *Women Under the Bo Tree: Buddhist Nuns in Sri Lanka* (Cambridge University Press, 1994), 55–68.
8. Charles Hallisey, trans., *Therigatha: Poems of the First Buddhist Women* (Harvard University Press, 2015), xviii–xxii.
9. Karma Lekshe Tsomo, ed., *Innovative Buddhist Women: Swimming Against the Stream* (Curzon, 2000), 15–32.
10. Rita M. Gross, *Buddhism After Patriarchy: A Feminist History, Analysis, and Reconstruction of Buddhism* (SUNY Press, 1993), 87–92.

Chapter 3: The Scholar They Constrained -- Aisha bint Abi Bakr

1. This opening scene represents a plausible reconstruction based on documented practices of early Islamic hadith transmission and Aisha's known role as a teacher and interpreter. While specific teaching sessions are not historically recorded, her authority in correcting and interpreting prophetic traditions is well-established in Islamic sources. See Asma Sayeed, *Women and the Transmission of Religious Knowledge in Islam* (Cambridge University Press, 2013), 45–67.
2. Mohammad Akram Nadwi, *Al-Muhaddithat: The Women Scholars in Islam* (Interface Publications, 2007), 18–20; Jonathan A.C. Brown, *Hadith: Muhammad's*

Legacy in the Medieval and Modern World (Oneworld, 2009), 28–30.
3. Brown, *Hadith*, 95–102.
4. Barbara Freyer Stowasser, *Women in the Quran, Traditions, and Interpretation* (Oxford University Press, 1994), 67–89.
5. Sayeed, *Women and the Transmission of Religious Knowledge*, 78–95; Nadwi, *Al-Muhaddithat*, 45–67.
6. Leila Ahmed, *Women and Gender in Islam* (Yale University Press, 1992), 67–69.
7. Fatima Mernissi, *The Veil and the Male Elite* (Addison-Wesley, 1991), 51–52.
8. Ahmed, *Women and Gender in Islam*, 45–78; Mernissi, *The Veil and the Male Elite*, 49–61; Sayeed, *Women and the Transmission of Religious Knowledge*, 89–112.
9. Amina Wadud, *Quran and Woman: Rereading the Sacred Text from a Woman's Perspective* (Oxford University Press, 1999), 76–89; Asma Barlas, *"Believing Women" in Islam: Unreading Patriarchal Interpretations of the Quran* (University of Texas Press, 2002), 124–156.
10. *Sahih Muslim*, Book 3, Hadith 592.

Chapter 4: From Devotion to Dissent -- Hindu Women's Sacred Agency

1. This opening scene represents a plausible reconstruction based on traditional accounts of Mirabai's devotional practices and the documented social tensions surrounding her behavior. While specific incidents are not historically verified, her practice of dawn devotions

and conflict with royal expectations are consistent with hagiographic sources. See John Stratton Hawley, *Three Bhakti Voices: Mirabai, Surdas, and Kabir in Their Time and Ours*(Oxford University Press, 2005), 45–67.

2. Stephanie W. Jamison, *Sacrificed Wife, Sacrificer's Wife: Women, Ritual, and Hospitality in Ancient India* (Oxford University Press, 1996), 72–74.
3. Laurie L. Patton, ed., *Jewels of Authority: Women and Textual Tradition in Hindu India* (Oxford University Press, 2002), 25–30.
4. Vasudha Narayanan, "Women and the Sacred in South India," in *The Graceful Guru: Hindu Female Gurus in India and the United States*, ed. Karen Pechilis (Oxford University Press, 2004), 25–37.
5. A. K. Ramanujan, trans., *Speaking of Śiva* (Penguin Classics, 1973), 111–123.
6. Hawley, *Three Bhakti Voices*, 89–112; Vidya Dehejia, *Slaves of the Lord: The Path of the Tamil Saints* (Munshiram Manoharlal, 1988), 67–89.
7. Paula Richman, ed., *Many Rāmāyaṇas: The Diversity of a Narrative Tradition in South Asia* (University of California Press, 1991), 134–156.
8. Alf Hiltebeitel, *The Cult of Draupadi* (University of Chicago Press, 1988), 101–110.
9. Uma Chakravarti, *Gendering Caste: Through a Feminist Lens* (Stree, 2003), 134–139; Vasudha Narayanan, "Brimming with Bhakti, Embodiments of Shakti: Devotees, Deities, Performers, Reformers, and Other Women of Power in the Hindu Tradition," in *Feminism*

and World Religions, ed. Arvind Sharma and Katherine K. Young (SUNY Press, 1999), 25–77.
10. Uma Chakravarti, *Rewriting History: The Life and Times of Pandita Ramabai* (Kali for Women, 1998), 89–123.

Chapter 5: The Prophetesses They Silenced -- Miriam and Her Sisters

1. This opening scene represents a plausible reconstruction based on the biblical account in Exodus 15:20–21 and scholarly understanding of ancient Israelite victory celebrations. While specific details of setting and emotion are constructed for narrative purposes, the basic elements—Miriam's prophetic role, the women's dance, and the song itself—are textually grounded. See Carol Meyers, *Exodus* (Cambridge University Press, 2005), 118–125.
2. Tikva Frymer-Kensky, *Reading the Women of the Bible* (Schocken, 2002), 30–35.
3. Phyllis Trible, *Texts of Terror: Literary-Feminist Readings of Biblical Narratives* (Fortress Press, 1984), 33–38.
4. Carol Meyers, *Rediscovering Eve: Ancient Israelite Women in Context* (Oxford University Press, 2012), 156–189.
5. Jacob Neusner, *The Idea of Purity in Ancient Judaism* (Brill, 1973), 102–106.
6. Susan Niditch, *Judges: A Commentary* (Westminster John Knox, 2008), 64–68.
7. Meyers, *Rediscovering Eve*, 245–249.

8. Chava Weissler, *Voices of the Matriarchs: Listening to the Prayers of Early Modern Jewish Women* (Beacon Press, 1998), 11–23.
9. Frymer-Kensky, *Reading the Women of the Bible*, 89–105; on Glikl specifically, see Natalie Zemon Davis, *Women on the Margins: Three Seventeenth-Century Lives* (Harvard University Press, 1995), 5–62.
10. Judith Plaskow, *Standing Again at Sinai: Judaism from a Feminist Perspective* (HarperSanFrancisco, 1990), 25–56; Rachel Adler, *Engendering Judaism: An Inclusive Theology and Ethics* (Jewish Publication Society, 1998), 45–78.

Chapter 6: Sacred Voices Beyond the Center

1. This opening vignette represents a plausible composite based on documented practices in Zoroastrian, Sikh, and Mesoamerican traditions. While specific scenes are reconstructed for narrative purposes, the roles described—fire-keeping, langar establishment, and priestess functions—are historically attested. See Mary Boyce, *Zoroastrians: Their Religious Beliefs and Practices* (Routledge, 2001), 78–95; Nikky-Guninder Kaur Singh, *The Feminine Principle in the Sikh Vision* (Cambridge University Press, 1993), 85–88; and Susan Kellogg, *Law and the Transformation of Aztec Culture* (University of Oklahoma Press, 1995), 128–133.
2. Jenny Rose, *Zoroastrianism: An Introduction* (I.B. Tauris, 2011), 44–47.

3. Mary Boyce, *Zoroastrians: Their Religious Beliefs and Practices* (Routledge, 2001), 112–115.
4. Nikky-Guninder Kaur Singh, *The Feminine Principle in the Sikh Vision of the Transcendent* (Cambridge University Press, 1993), 85–88.
5. Susan Kellogg, *Law and the Transformation of Aztec Culture* (University of Oklahoma Press, 1995), 128–133.
6. Rosemary A. Joyce, *Ancient Bodies, Ancient Lives: Sex, Gender, and Archaeology* (Thames & Hudson, 2008), 142–156.
7. Jacob K. Olupona, *African Religions: A Very Short Introduction* (Oxford University Press, 2014), 66–68.
8. Oyèrónkẹ́ Oyěwùmí, *The Invention of Women: Making an African Sense of Western Gender Discourses* (University of Minnesota Press, 1997); Jacob K. Olupona, *City of 201 Gods: Ilé-Ifẹ̀ in Time, Space, and the Imagination*(University of California Press, 2011).
9. Devin DeWeese, *Islamization and Native Religion in the Golden Horde* (Pennsylvania State University Press, 1994), 215–220.
10. Suzanne Cahill, *Transcendence and Divine Passion: The Queen Mother of the West in Medieval China* (Stanford University Press, 1993); Livia Kohn, *Daoism and Chinese Culture* (Three Pines Press, 2001), 142–145.
11. Christine Allison, *The Yezidi Oral Tradition in Iraqi Kurdistan* (Routledge, 2001), 89–102.
12. Padmanabh S. Jaini, *Gender and Salvation: Jaina Debates on the Spiritual Liberation of Women* (University of California Press, 1991), 45–67.

13. Sergei Kan, *Symbolic Immortality: The Tlingit Potlatch of the Nineteenth Century* (Smithsonian Institution Press, 1989), 78–95.

Chapter 7: What If They Had Been Canon?

1. Karen L. King, *The Gospel of Mary of Magdala: Jesus and the First Woman Apostle* (Polebridge Press, 2003), 15–25.
2. Tikva Frymer-Kensky, *Reading the Women of the Bible* (Schocken, 2002), 23–31.
3. Asma Sayeed, *Women and the Transmission of Religious Knowledge in Islam* (Cambridge University Press, 2013), 58–61.
4. Ruth Vanita, "The Self Is Not Gendered: Sulabha's Debate with King Janaka," *NWSA Journal* 15, no. 3 (2003): 76–93.
5. Karma Lekshe Tsomo, ed., *Buddhist Women Across Cultures: Realizations* (SUNY Press, 1999), 66–72.
6. Ann Graham Brock, *Mary Magdalene, the First Apostle: The Struggle for Authority* (Harvard University Press, 2003), 145–167.
7. Mohammad Akram Nadwi, *Al-Muhaddithat: The Women Scholars in Islam* (Interface Publications, 2007), ix–xv.
8. Vasudha Narayanan, "Brimming with Bhakti, Embodiments of Shakti," in *Feminism and World Religions*, ed. Arvind Sharma and Katherine K. Young (SUNY Press, 1999), 25–77.

9. Rita M. Gross, *Buddhism After Patriarchy: A Feminist History, Analysis, and Reconstruction of Buddhism* (SUNY Press, 1993), 87–105.
10. Judith Plaskow, *Standing Again at Sinai: Judaism from a Feminist Perspective* (HarperSanFrancisco, 1990), 25–56.
11. For contemporary applications, see Rachel Adler, *Engendering Judaism: An Inclusive Theology and Ethics* (Jewish Publication Society, 1998); Amina Wadud, *Quran and Woman: Rereading the Sacred Text from a Woman's Perspective* (Oxford University Press, 1999); Vandana Shiva, *Staying Alive: Women, Ecology and Development*(Zed Books, 1988).

Interlude A: The Mystics' Rebellion

1. Hildegard of Bingen, *Scivias*, trans. Columba Hart and Jane Bishop (Paulist Press, 1990); Barbara Newman, *Sister of Wisdom: St. Hildegard's Theology of the Feminine* (University of California Press, 1987), 45–67.
2. Margaret Smith, *Rābi'a the Mystic and Her Fellow-Saints in Islam* (Cambridge University Press, 1928), 78–95; Annemarie Schimmel, *My Soul Is a Woman: The Feminine in Islam* (Continuum, 1997), 56–73.
3. Nancy Martin, *Mirabai* (Oxford University Press, 2007); John Stratton Hawley, *Three Bhakti Voices: Mirabai, Surdas, and Kabir in Their Time and Ours* (Oxford University Press, 2005), 67–89.
4. Julian of Norwich, *Revelations of Divine Love*, trans. Edmund Colledge and James Walsh (Paulist Press,

1978); Grace Jantzen, *Julian of Norwich: Mystic and Theologian* (SPCK, 2000), 89–112.

5. On global patterns, see Peter Dinzelbacher, ed., *Mystik und Natur* (Berlin: Duncker & Humblot, 1994); June McDaniel, *Offering Flowers, Feeding Skulls: Popular Goddess Worship in West Bengal* (Oxford University Press, 2004).
6. For methodological cautions, see Caroline Walker Bynum, *Jesus as Mother: Studies in the Spirituality of the High Middle Ages* (University of California Press, 1982), 15–35.
7. Hildegard of Bingen, *Scivias* I.1, trans. Hart and Bishop.
8. This saying, while widely attributed to Rābiʿa, appears in various forms across Islamic mystical literature. See Smith, *Rābiʿa the Mystic*, 102–105.
9. Traditional bhajan attributed to Mirabai, various manuscript sources. See Martin, *Mirabai*, 145–167.
10. Julian of Norwich, *Revelations of Divine Love*, Long Text, Chapter 59, trans. Colledge and Walsh.

Chapter 8: Ink and Illumination -- Christian Women as Scribes and Mystics

1. This opening scene represents a plausible reconstruction based on documented practices at Chelles and paleographic evidence of female scribal activity in Carolingian scriptoria. The specific manuscript details are drawn from composite evidence of women's scribal work during this period. See Rosamond McKitterick, *The Carolingians and the Written Word* (Cambridge

University Press, 1989), 132–136; Alison Beach, *Women as Scribes: Book Production and Monastic Reform in Twelfth-Century Bavaria* (Cambridge University Press, 2004), 15–28.
2. Elizabeth A. Clark, *The Origenist Controversy: The Cultural Construction of an Early Christian Debate* (Princeton University Press, 1992), 83–90.
3. Beach, *Women as Scribes*, 22–28.
4. On Byzantine nuns, see Alice-Mary Talbot, "Female Monasticism in Byzantium," in *Byzantine Christianity*, ed. Derek Krueger (University of Minnesota Press, 2006), 118–135; on Ethiopian tradition, see Getatchew Haile, "Religious Controversies and the Growth of Ethiopic Literature in the Fourteenth and Fifteenth Centuries," *Oriens Christianus* 65 (1981): 102–136.
5. Alison Beach and Isabelle Cochelin, eds., *Cambridge History of Medieval Monasticism in the Latin West*(Cambridge University Press, 2020), 2:789–812.
6. Barbara Newman, *Voice of the Living Light: Hildegard of Bingen and Her World* (University of California Press, 1998), 55–60.
7. Pope Benedict XVI, *Apostolic Letter Proclaiming Hildegard of Bingen a Doctor of the Church* (2012).
8. Lynn Staley, ed., *The Book of Margery Kempe* (Kalamazoo: TEAMS Middle English Texts Series, 1996), Introduction.
9. Susan Ashbrook Harvey, "Women in Early Byzantine Hagiography: Reversing the Story," in *That Gentle Strength: Historical Perspectives on Women in Christianity*, ed. Lynda L. Coon, Katherine J. Haldane,

and Elisabeth W. Sommer (University Press of Virginia, 1990), 36-59.

Chapter 9: Guardians of Revelation -- Islamic Women as Preservers

1. This opening scene represents a plausible reconstruction based on documented practices of hadith transmission in medieval Damascus and the known activities of Fatima bint Sa'd al-Khayr as recorded in ijaza certificates and isnad chains. While specific classroom details are constructed for narrative purposes, her role as a teacher and the presence of both male and female students are historically attested. See Asma Sayeed, *Women and the Transmission of Religious Knowledge in Islam* (Cambridge University Press, 2013), 97-103.
2. Leila Ahmed, *Women and Gender in Islam* (Yale University Press, 1992), 42-47.
3. Mohammad Akram Nadwi, *Al-Muhaddithat: The Women Scholars in Islam* (Interface Publications, 2007), 21-34.
4. Sayeed, *Women and the Transmission of Religious Knowledge*, 97-103.
5. Jonathan A.C. Brown, *Hadith: Muhammad's Legacy in the Medieval and Modern World* (Oneworld, 2009), 66-70.
6. On Sunni-Shi'i differences, see Liyakat Takim, *The Heirs of the Prophet: Charisma and Religious Authority in Shi'ite Islam* (SUNY Press, 2006), 89-112; and Asma Sayeed, "Shifting Fortunes: Women and Hadith

Transmission in Islamic History," *Muslim World* 95, no. 4 (2005): 515–540.
7. Beverly Mack and Jean Boyd, *One Woman's Jihad: Nana Asma'u, Scholar and Scribe* (Indiana University Press, 2000), 88–93.
8. Ibid., 104–110.
9. Kecia Ali, *The Lives of Muhammad* (Harvard University Press, 2014), 136–145; Amina Wadud, *Qur'an and Woman: Rereading the Sacred Text from a Woman's Perspective* (Oxford University Press, 1999), 1–18.
10. Sayeed, *Women and the Transmission of Religious Knowledge*, 140–165.

Chapter 10: Patrons and Performers -- Hindu Women's Sacred Labor

1. This opening scene represents a plausible reconstruction based on documented practices of women's devotional singing in South Indian temples and the continuing tradition of Andal's verses in daily worship. While specific details are constructed for narrative purposes, the elements described—temple courtyard performances, memorial transmission, and women's roles as preservers of devotional poetry—are historically attested. See Archana Venkatesan, *The Secret Garland: Andal's Tiruppavai and Nacciyar Tirumoli* (Oxford University Press, 2010), 3–7.
2. Padma Kaimal, *Scattered Goddesses: Travels with the Yoginis* (University of Michigan Press, 2012), 45–50.

3. On caste and gender intersections, see Uma Chakravarti, *Gendering Caste: Through a Feminist Lens* (Stree, 2003), 45–78; Sharmila Rege, *Writing Caste/Writing Gender: Narrating Dalit Women's Testimonios* (Zubaan, 2006), 89–112.
4. Joyce Burkhalter Flueckiger, *In Amma's Healing Room: Gender and Vernacular Islam in South India* (Indiana University Press, 2006), 26–30.
5. Paula Richman, ed., *Many Ramayanas: The Diversity of a Narrative Tradition in South Asia* (University of California Press, 1991), 55–72.
6. John Stratton Hawley and Mark Juergensmeyer, *Songs of the Saints of India* (Oxford University Press, 2004), 90–103.
7. A. K. Ramanujan, trans., *Speaking of Śiva* (Penguin Classics, 1973), 111–141.
8. Vasudha Narayanan, "The Vernacular Veda: Revelation, Recitation, and Ritual" (PhD diss., Harvard University, 1978); Tracy Pintchman, *Women's Lives, Women's Rituals in the Hindu Tradition* (Oxford University Press, 2007), 156–189.

Chapter 11: Domestic Torah -- Jewish Women as Liturgical Guardians

1. This opening scene represents a plausible reconstruction based on Glikl's own memoir and documented practices of Jewish women's household religious life in 18th-century Europe. While specific details are constructed for narrative purposes, the elements described—Shabbat

preparation, vernacular prayer, and memoir-writing—are historically attested in her writings. See Chava Turniansky, ed., *Glikl: Memoirs 1691–1719* (Brandeis University Press, 2019), Introduction.
2. Judith Hauptman, *Rereading the Rabbis: A Woman's Voice* (Westview Press, 1998), 137–140.
3. Devra Kay, *Seyder Tkhines: The Forgotten Book of Common Prayer for Jewish Women* (Jason Aronson, 2004), 23–29.
4. Chava Weissler, *Voices of the Matriarchs: Listening to the Prayers of Early Modern Jewish Women* (Beacon Press, 1999), 45–61.
5. Renée Levine Melammed, *Heretics or Daughters of Israel? The Crypto-Jewish Women of Castile* (Oxford University Press, 1999), 88–94.
6. On halakhic debates regarding women scribes, see Mendel Shapiro, "Qeri'at ha-Torah by Women: A Halakhic Analysis," *The Edah Journal* 1, no. 2 (2001); Rabbi Daniel Sperber, "Women and Men in Communal Prayer: Halakhic Perspectives," in *Women and Men in Communal Prayer* (KTAV, 2010), 67–89.
7. Ilana Kurshan, "In Her Own Hand," *Lilith Magazine*, Winter 2005.
8. Chava Weissler, *Voices of the Matriarchs*, 1–18; Rachel Elior, *The Mystical Origins of Hasidism* (Littman Library, 2006), 156–189.

Chapter 12: Across Mountains and Monasteries -- Buddhist Women in Transmission

1. This opening scene represents a plausible reconstruction based on documented practices of Buddhist translation projects in Tang China and evidence of women's participation in scholarly activities at Chang'an. While Yu Shun's specific involvement is constructed for narrative purposes, women's roles as translators and assistants in Buddhist scriptural projects are historically attested. See Susan Whitfield, *Life Along the Silk Road* (University of California Press, 1999), 115–120.
2. Donald F. McCallum, *The Four Great Temples: Buddhist Archaeology, Architecture, and Icons of Seventh-Century Japan* (University of Hawaii Press, 2009), 87–90.
3. Liu Xinru, *Silk and Religion: An Exploration of Material Life and the Thought of People, AD 600–1200* (Oxford University Press, 1996), 65–70.
4. Janet Gyatso, *Apparitions of the Self: The Secret Autobiographies of a Tibetan Visionary* (Princeton University Press, 1998), 32–37.
5. Monica Lindberg Falk, *Making Fields of Merit: Buddhist Female Ascetics and Gendered Orders in Thailand*(University of Washington Press, 2007), 44–50.
6. Beata Grant, *Daughters of Emptiness: Poems of Chinese Buddhist Nuns* (Wisdom Publications, 2003), Introduction, xix–xxv.
7. On Korean Buddhist women, see Martine Batchelor, *Women in Korean Zen: Lives and Practices* (Syracuse University Press, 2006), 45–67.

8. Karma Lekshe Tsomo, ed., *Innovative Buddhist Women: Swimming Against the Stream* (Curzon, 2000), 15–32.
9. On contemporary Buddhist women's organizations, see Karma Lekshe Tsomo, "Buddhist Women Today," in *Buddhist Women Across Cultures*, ed. Karma Lekshe Tsomo (SUNY Press, 1999), 251–270.

Chapter 13: The Unwritten Archive

1. Elaine Pagels, *The Gnostic Gospels* (Random House, 1979), 28–45.
2. Rita M. Gross, *Buddhism After Patriarchy* (SUNY Press, 1993), 65–82.
3. Judith Hauptman, *Rereading the Rabbis: A Woman's Voice* (Westview Press, 1998), 112–130.
4. Susan Ashbrook Harvey, "Women in Early Syrian Christianity," in *Women in Early Christianity*, ed. David M. Scholer (Garland, 1993), 288–298.
5. Rachel Elior, *The Mystical Origins of Hasidism* (Littman Library, 2006), 189–215.
6. Maria Rosa Menocal, *The Ornament of the World* (Little, Brown, 2002), 75–91.

Interlude B: Anonymous Hands

1. Alison Beach, *Women as Scribes: Book Production and Monastic Reform in Twelfth-Century Bavaria* (Cambridge University Press, 2004), 89–112.
2. Susan Whitfield and Ursula Sims-Williams, eds., *The Silk Road: Trade, Travel, War and Faith* (British Library, 2004), 156–167.

3. Stefan C. Reif, *A Jewish Archive from Old Cairo* (Curzon, 2000), 78–95.
4. Susan Ashbrook Harvey, "Women in Early Syrian Christianity," in *Women in Early Christianity*, ed. David M. Scholer (Garland, 1993), 288–298.
5. Janet Gyatso, *Being Human in a Buddhist World* (Columbia University Press, 2017), 134–156.
6. Asma Sayeed, *Women and the Transmission of Religious Knowledge in Islam* (Cambridge University Press, 2013), 89–102.

Chapter 14: The Architecture of Erasure

1. The scenario of Sister Caesaria is constructed from details about sixth-century Frankish convents documented in Gregory of Tours, *History of the Franks*, trans. Lewis Thorpe (London: Penguin Classics, 1974), and archaeological evidence from Saint Radegund's Abbey. On women's theological writing in early medieval convents, see Alison I. Beach, *Women as Scribes: Manuscript Production and Monastic Reform in Twelfth-Century Bavaria* (Cambridge: Cambridge University Press, 2004), 45–73.
2. On anonymous Buddhist women poets in Tang China, see Kathryn Ann Tsai, *Lives of the Nuns: Biographies of Chinese Buddhist Nuns from the Fourth to Sixth Centuries* (Honolulu: University of Hawaii Press, 1994), 15–31.
3. Beach, *Women as Scribes*, 89–112.

4. Chava Weissler, *Voices of the Matriarchs: Listening to the Prayers of Early Modern Jewish Women* (Boston: Beacon Press, 1998), 19–47.
5. On women in hadith transmission, see Asma Sayeed, *Women and the Transmission of Religious Knowledge in Islam* (Cambridge: Cambridge University Press, 2013), 78–104.
6. Weissler, *Voices of the Matriarchs*, 156–182.
7. Judith Plaskow, *Standing Again at Sinai: Judaism from a Feminist Perspective* (San Francisco: HarperSanFrancisco, 1990), 53–79.
8. On Athanasius's thirty-ninth festal letter, see Bart D. Ehrman, *Lost Christianities: The Battles for Scripture and the Faiths We Never Knew* (New York: Oxford University Press, 2003), 34–41.
9. On the marginalization of the Therigatha, see Susan Murcott, *The First Buddhist Women: Translations and Commentary on the Therigatha* (Berkeley: Parallax Press, 1991), 23–39.
10. Paula Richman, ed., *Many Ramayanas: The Diversity of a Narrative Tradition in South Asia* (Berkeley: University of California Press, 1991), 71–85.
11. On Junia/Junias, see Eldon Jay Epp, *Junia: The First Woman Apostle* (Minneapolis: Fortress Press, 2005).
12. On gender in Buddhist translation, see Rita M. Gross, *Buddhism After Patriarchy: A Feminist History, Analysis, and Reconstruction of Buddhism* (Albany: SUNY Press, 1993), 87–109.
13. On women's exclusion from religious literacy, see Jo Ann McNamara, *Sisters in Arms: Catholic Nuns through Two*

Millennia (Cambridge, MA: Harvard University Press, 1996), 187–213.

14. On domestic religious practice, see Susan Starr Sered, *Women as Ritual Experts: The Religious Lives of Elderly Jewish Women in Jerusalem* (New York: Oxford University Press, 1992).
15. Caroline Walker Bynum, *Holy Feast and Holy Fast: The Religious Significance of Food to Medieval Women*(Berkeley: University of California Press, 1987), 13–30.

Chapter 15: The Counter-Tradition

1. On Sarah bas Tovim and early modern Jewish women's religious literature, see Chava Weissler, *Voices of the Matriarchs: Listening to the Prayers of Early Modern Jewish Women* (Boston: Beacon Press, 1998), 89–123. The specific quotation is from Weissler's translation of Sarah's introduction to her tkhine collection.
2. Judith Plaskow, *Standing Again at Sinai: Judaism from a Feminist Perspective* (San Francisco: HarperSanFrancisco, 1990), 53–79.
3. Julian of Norwich, *Revelations of Divine Love*, trans. Elizabeth Spearing (London: Penguin Classics, 1998), 41. On Julian's sophisticated theology despite claims of illiteracy, see Denys Turner, *Julian of Norwich, Theologian* (New Haven: Yale University Press, 2011), 14–28.
4. On women in Islamic mysticism, see Rkia Elaroui Cornell, *Early Sufi Women: Dhikr an-niswa al-*

muta'abbidat as-sufiyyat (Louisville: Fons Vitae, 1999), 67–89.

5. On female tertöns in Tibetan Buddhism, see Judith Simmer-Brown, *Dakini's Warm Breath: The Feminine Principle in Tibetan Buddhism* (Boston: Shambhala, 2001), 234–267.
6. On medieval South Asian women's devotional poetry, see John Stratton Hawley and Mark Juergensmeyer, *Songs of the Saints of India* (New York: Oxford University Press, 2004), 85–127.
7. Translation from A.K. Ramanujan, *Speaking of Siva* (London: Penguin Classics, 1973), 134.
8. On women's religious roles in Theravāda Buddhism, see Tessa Bartholomeusz, *Women Under the Bo Tree: Buddhist Nuns in Sri Lanka* (Cambridge: Cambridge University Press, 1994), 89–134.
9. On Islamic women's educational networks, see Asma Sayeed, *Women and the Transmission of Religious Knowledge in Islam* (Cambridge: Cambridge University Press, 2013), 102–156.
10. On Jewish women's domestic religious authority, see Susan Starr Sered, *Women as Ritual Experts: The Religious Lives of Elderly Jewish Women in Jerusalem* (New York: Oxford University Press, 1992), 78–103.
11. On Hindu women's preservation of religious traditions, see Vasudha Narayanan, "Brimming with Bhakti, Embodiments of Shakti: Devotees, Deities, Performers, Reformers, and Other Women of Power in the Hindu Tradition," in *Feminism and World Religions*, ed. Arvind

Sharma and Katherine Young (Albany: SUNY Press, 1999), 25–77.

12. On Buddhist laywomen's religious authority, see Karma Lekshe Tsomo, ed., *Buddhist Women Across Cultures: Realizations* (Albany: SUNY Press, 1999), 134–167.
13. On medieval Christian women mystics, see Caroline Walker Bynum, *Holy Feast and Holy Fast: The Religious Significance of Food to Medieval Women* (Berkeley: University of California Press, 1987), 13–30.
14. On Hildegard's theology and authority, see Barbara Newman, *Sister of Wisdom: St. Hildegard's Theology of the Feminine* (Berkeley: University of California Press, 1987), 45–78.
15. On Rābi'a al-'Adawiyya, see Annemarie Schimmel, *Mystical Dimensions of Islam* (Chapel Hill: University of North Carolina Press, 1975), 42–46.
16. Simmer-Brown, *Dakini's Warm Breath*, 234–267.
17. On Bruriah, see Judith Hauptman, *Rereading the Rabbis: A Woman's Voice* (Boulder: Westview Press, 1998), 56–85.
18. On women mystics' theological innovations, see Grace Jantzen, *Power, Gender and Christian Mysticism*(Cambridge: Cambridge University Press, 1995), 198–234.
19. On Andal's theological significance, see Vasudha Narayanan, *The Vernacular Veda: Revelation, Recitation, and Ritual* (Columbia: University of South Carolina Press, 1994), 87–112.
20. On manuscript discoveries and women's religious literature, see Susan Whitfield, *Life Along the Silk*

Road(Berkeley: University of California Press, 1999), 134-156; and S.D. Goitein, *A Mediterranean Society*, vol. 3 (Berkeley: University of California Press, 1978), 312-345.

21. For contemporary recovery efforts, see Elisabeth Schüssler Fiorenza, *In Memory of Her: A Feminist Theological Reconstruction of Christian Origins* (New York: Crossroad, 1983); Amina Wadud, *Qur'an and Woman: Rereading the Sacred Text from a Woman's Perspective* (New York: Oxford University Press, 1999); and Rita M. Gross, *Buddhism After Patriarchy* (Albany: SUNY Press, 1993).

Chapter 16: When Visions Became Texts

1. On Julian's illness and visions, see Julian of Norwich, *Revelations of Divine Love*, trans. Edmund Colledge and James Walsh (New York: Paulist Press, 1978), 41-44. For the dating and historical context, see Grace Jantzen, *Julian of Norwich: Mystic and Theologian* (London: SPCK, 2000), 23-45.
2. Bernard McGinn, *The Flowering of Mysticism: Men and Women in the New Mysticism (1200-1350)* (New York: Crossroad, 1998), 211-235.
3. On early Islamic women mystics, see Rkia Elaroui Cornell, *Early Sufi Women: Dhikr an-niswa al-muta'abbidat as-sufiyyat* (Louisville: Fons Vitae, 1999), 67-89.
4. On Jewish women mystics, see Ephraim Kanarfogel, "Attitudes Toward Childhood and Children in Medieval

Jewish Society," in *Approaches to Judaism in Medieval Times*, ed. David Blumenthal (Chico, CA: Scholars Press, 1985), 89–134.

5. Grace Jantzen, *Power, Gender and Christian Mysticism* (Cambridge: Cambridge University Press, 1995), 198–234.
6. On collaborative authorship, see Alison I. Beach, *Women as Scribes: Manuscript Production and Monastic Reform in Twelfth-Century Bavaria* (Cambridge: Cambridge University Press, 2004), 89–112.
7. Beach, *Women as Scribes*, 134–156.
8. On Tibetan women tertöns, see Judith Simmer-Brown, *Dakini's Warm Breath: The Feminine Principle in Tibetan Buddhism* (Boston: Shambhala, 2001), 234–267.
9. Julian of Norwich, *Revelations*, Long Text, chapters 51–86.
10. On Hadewijch's temporal strategies, see Columba Hart, trans., *Hadewijch: The Complete Works* (New York: Paulist Press, 1980), 25–39.
11. Cornell, *Early Sufi Women*, 156–178.
12. Julian of Norwich, *Revelations*, Long Text, chapter 59. On the theological significance, see Caroline Walker Bynum, *Jesus as Mother: Studies in the Spirituality of the High Middle Ages* (Berkeley: University of California Press, 1982), 110–169.
13. On Mechthild's theological innovations, see Frank Tobin, *Mechthild von Magdeburg: A Medieval Mystic in Modern Eyes* (Columbia, SC: Camden House, 1995), 67–89.

14. On gendered differences in Islamic mysticism, see Annemarie Schimmel, *My Soul Is a Woman: The Feminine in Islam* (New York: Continuum, 1997), 56–73.
15. Bynum, *Jesus as Mother*, 257–262.
16. McGinn, *The Flowering of Mysticism*, 211–235.
17. Barbara Newman, *God and the Goddesses: Vision, Poetry, and Belief in the Middle Ages* (Philadelphia: University of Pennsylvania Press, 2003), 85–99.
18. Kecia Ali, *The Lives of Muhammad* (Cambridge, MA: Harvard University Press, 2014), 93–106.
19. Leila Ahmed, *Women and Gender in Islam: Historical Roots of a Modern Debate* (New Haven: Yale University Press, 1992), 66–74.
20. Janet Gyatso, *Apparitions of the Self: The Secret Autobiographies of a Tibetan Visionary* (Princeton: Princeton University Press, 1998), 47–62.
21. Sallie McFague, *Models of God: Theology for an Ecological, Nuclear Age* (Philadelphia: Fortress Press, 1987), 97–123.
22. Sachiko Murata, *The Tao of Islam: A Sourcebook on Gender Relationships in Islamic Thought* (Albany: SUNY Press, 1992), 134–167.
23. Amy Hollywood, *The Soul as Virgin Wife: Mechthild of Magdeburg, Marguerite Porete, and Meister Eckhart*(Notre Dame: University of Notre Dame Press, 1995), 23–45.
24. On mystical parallels across traditions, see Ewert Cousins, ed., *World Spirituality: An Encyclopedic History of the Religious Quest*, 25 vols. (New York: Crossroad,

1985-2000), especially volumes on comparative mysticism.

25. On Julian's continuing influence, see Frederick Christian Bauerschmidt, *Julian of Norwich and the Mystical Body Politic of Christ* (Notre Dame: University of Notre Dame Press, 1999).
26. On Hildegard's contemporary recovery, see Barbara Newman, *Sister of Wisdom: St. Hildegard's Theology of the Feminine* (Berkeley: University of California Press, 1987).
27. On contemporary Islamic feminism and mystical traditions, see Amina Wadud, *Qur'an and Woman: Rereading the Sacred Text from a Woman's Perspective* (New York: Oxford University Press, 1999), 67–89.

Chapter 17: Archaeological Angels

1. On the Lewis sisters and the Cairo Genizah discovery, see Janet Soskice, *The Sisters of Sinai: How Two Lady Adventurers Discovered the Hidden Gospels* (New York: Knopf, 2009), 187–234; and S.D. Goitein, *A Mediterranean Society*, vol. 3, *The Family* (Berkeley: University of California Press, 1978), 312–345.
2. On the Nag Hammadi discovery, see James M. Robinson, ed., *The Nag Hammadi Library in English*, 4th ed. (Leiden: Brill, 1996), 1–26.
3. Gospel of Mary 9:3-4, translation from Karen L. King, *The Gospel of Mary of Magdala: Jesus and the First Woman Apostle* (Santa Rosa: Polebridge Press, 2003), 14.

4. On Dunhuang manuscripts, see Susan Whitfield, *Life Along the Silk Road* (Berkeley: University of California Press, 1999), 134–156.
5. Dunhuang manuscript S.2144, cited in Georgios T. Halkias, "The Self-Immolation of the Buddhist Monk Daoxiang," *Journal of the Oxford Centre for Buddhist Studies* 4 (2013): 30.
6. Fragment from Pelliot collection, cited in Kathryn Ann Tsai, *Lives of the Nuns: Biographies of Chinese Buddhist Nuns from the Fourth to Sixth Centuries* (Honolulu: University of Hawaii Press, 1994), 67.
7. On female dharma masters at Dunhuang, see Amy Paris Langenberg, *Birth in Buddhism: The Suffering Fetus and Female Freedom* (London: Routledge, 2018), 156–178.
8. On Islamic manuscript traditions, see Asma Sayeed, *Women and the Transmission of Religious Knowledge in Islam*(Cambridge: Cambridge University Press, 2013), 89–156.
9. Manuscript Dar al-Kutub 234, cited in Sayeed, *Women and the Transmission*, 134.
10. Manuscript Real Biblioteca del Monasterio de El Escorial, Árabe 1340, cited in Cristina de la Puente, "Women and Knowledge in al-Andalus," in *The Esoteric Tradition in Islam*, ed. Gerhard Böwering (London: I.B. Tauris, 2000), 89.
11. On Chelles manuscripts, see Alison I. Beach, *Women as Scribes: Manuscript Production and Monastic Reform in Twelfth-Century Bavaria* (Cambridge: Cambridge University Press, 2004), 89–112.

12. Manuscript Bibliothèque nationale de France, Latin 10434, analysis by the Digital Manuscripts Toolkit project, cited in Deborah Thorpe, "Hidden Hands: Evidence for Female Scribes in Medieval Manuscripts," *Digital Philology* 7, no. 2 (2018): 234.

13. On the Sinai Palimpsests Project, see Michael B. Toth and Damianos Kasotakis, "The Sinai Palimpsests Project: Methodology and Results," *Eastern Christian Art* 6 (2009): 97–117.

14. Oxford University Manuscript Evidence project, interim results cited in Peter A. Stokes, "Computer-Aided Palaeography: Present and Future," in *Digital Palaeography*, ed. Frank Fischer (Oxford: Oxford University Press, 2019), 167.

15. On the Transcribe Bentham project, see Louise Seaward, "Crowdsourcing Manuscript Transcription," in *Digital Humanities in Practice*, ed. Claire Warwick (London: Facet Publishing, 2012), 156–178.

16. On Ethiopian manuscripts, see Denis Nosnitsin, *Churches and Monasteries of Təgray: A Survey of Manuscript Collections* (Wiesbaden: Harrassowitz Verlag, 2013), 234–267.

17. Manuscript Gishen Maryam 45, cited in Getatchew Haile, "Religious Controversies and the Growth of Ethiopic Literature in the Fourteenth and Fifteenth Centuries," *Oriens Christianus* 65 (1981): 121.

18. On Nana Asma'u and West African Islamic traditions, see Beverly B. Mack and Jean Boyd, *One Woman's Jihad: Nana Asma'u, Scholar and Scribe* (Bloomington: Indiana University Press, 2000), 134–167.

19. On Maya female scribes, see David Stuart, "The Origin of Copán's Founder," *Maya Decipherment* blog, June 12, 2007, https://decipherment.wordpress.com/2007/06/12/the-origin-of-copans-founder/.
20. On Haudenosaunee women's textual traditions, see Barbara Alice Mann, *Iroquoian Women: The Gantowisas* (New York: Peter Lang, 2000), 89–134.
21. On methodological challenges in manuscript attribution, see Orietta Da Rold, "What Is a Scribal Hand?," in *New Technologies in Medieval and Renaissance Studies*, ed. William R. Bowen (Tempe: Arizona Center for Medieval and Renaissance Studies, 2008), 101–115.
22. On interpretive cautions, see Caroline Walker Bynum, "Why All the Fuss about the Body? A Medievalist's Perspective," *Critical Inquiry* 22, no. 1 (1995): 1–33.

Chapter 18: Reading Against the Grain

1. This account of Phyllis Trible's work is reconstructed from her retrospective comments in *God and the Rhetoric of Sexuality* (Philadelphia: Fortress Press, 1978), xi–xiv, and interviews cited in Katharine Doob Sakenfeld, "Feminist Perspectives on Bible and Theology," *Interpretation* 42, no. 1 (1988): 5–18.
2. Judith Plaskow, *Standing Again at Sinai: Judaism from a Feminist Perspective* (San Francisco: HarperSanFrancisco, 1990), 1–12.

3. Rachel Adler, "A Mother in Israel: Aspects of the Mother Role in Jewish Myth," in *Beyond Androcentrism: New Essays on Women and Religion*, ed. Rita M. Gross (Missoula: Scholars Press, 1977), 237–255.
4. Tikva Frymer-Kensky, *In the Wake of the Goddesses: Women, Culture, and the Biblical Transformation of Pagan Myth* (New York: Free Press, 1992), 70–98.
5. Judith Hauptman, *Rereading the Rabbis: A Woman's Voice* (Boulder: Westview Press, 1998), 1–25.
6. On the development of womanist theology, see Katie Geneva Cannon, "The Emergence of Black Feminist Consciousness," in *Feminist Interpretation of the Bible*, ed. Letty M. Russell (Philadelphia: Westminster Press, 1985), 30–40.
7. Delores S. Williams, *Sisters in the Wilderness: The Challenge of Womanist God-Talk* (Maryknoll: Orbis Books, 1993), 1–28.
8. Clarice J. Martin, "The Haustafeln (Household Codes) in African American Biblical Interpretation," in *Stony the Road We Trod*, ed. Cain Hope Felder (Minneapolis: Fortress Press, 1991), 206–231.
9. For an overview of Islamic feminist hermeneutics, see Asma Barlas, "Amina Wadud's Hermeneutics of the Qur'an," *Muslim World* 93, no. 3-4 (2003): 421–435.
10. Amina Wadud, *Qur'an and Woman: Rereading the Sacred Text from a Woman's Perspective* (New York: Oxford University Press, 1999), 25–67.
11. Asma Barlas, *"Believing Women" in Islam: Unreading Patriarchal Interpretations of the Qur'an* (Austin: University of Texas Press, 2002), 1–44.

12. On Buddhist feminist scholarship, see Rita M. Gross, "Buddhism and Feminism: Toward Their Mutual Transformation," *Eastern Buddhist* 19, no. 1 (1986): 44–58.
13. Rita M. Gross, *Buddhism After Patriarchy: A Feminist History, Analysis, and Reconstruction of Buddhism* (Albany: SUNY Press, 1993), 73–134.
14. Karma Lekshe Tsomo, "Is the Bhikshuni Vinaya Sexist?," in *Buddhist Women Across Cultures*, ed. Karma Lekshe Tsomo (Albany: SUNY Press, 1999), 45–72.
15. On indigenous feminist approaches, see Inés Hernández-Avila, "Relocations upon Relocations: Home, Language, and Native American Women's Writings," *American Indian Quarterly* 19, no. 4 (1995): 491–507.
16. Paula Gunn Allen, *The Sacred Hoop: Recovering the Feminine in American Indian Traditions* (Boston: Beacon Press, 1986), 13–29.
17. Mercy Amba Oduyoye, *Daughters of Anowa: African Women and Patriarchy* (Maryknoll: Orbis Books, 1995), 34–56.
18. Catherine Despeux, *Immortelles de la Chine ancienne: Taoïsme et alchimie féminine* (Puiseaux: Pardès, 1990), 45–67.
19. Suzanne E. Cahill, *Transcendence and Divine Passion: The Queen Mother of the West in Medieval China*(Stanford: Stanford University Press, 1993), 78–102.
20. Caroline Walker Bynum, *Holy Feast and Holy Fast: The Religious Significance of Food to Medieval*

Women (Berkeley: University of California Press, 1987), 245–276.

21. Th. Emil Homerin, "'Oh, Those Breasts!': Baha' al-Din Zuhayr and the Politics of Gender," in *Meddling with Mythology*, ed. Miriam Levering (Albany: SUNY Press, 1995), 67–89.
22. Amy-Jill Levine, *The Misunderstood Jew: The Church and the Scandal of the Jewish Jesus* (San Francisco: HarperSanFrancisco, 2006), 89–134.
23. Francesca Stavrakopoulou, *God: An Anatomy* (New York: Knopf, 2022), 234–278.
24. Ross Shepard Kraemer, *Her Share of the Blessings: Women's Religions among Pagans, Jews, and Christians in the Greco-Roman World* (New York: Oxford University Press, 1992), 45–78.
25. Elisabeth Schüssler Fiorenza, *In Memory of Her: A Feminist Theological Reconstruction of Christian Origins* (New York: Crossroad, 1983), 28–36.
26. On institutional responses, see Pamela Dickey Young, *Feminist Theology/Christian Theology* (Minneapolis: Fortress Press, 1990), 67–89.
27. For conservative responses, see Wayne Grudem, *Evangelical Feminism and Biblical Truth* (Sisters, OR: Multnomah Publishers, 2004), 15–34.

Chapter 19: The Contemporary Conversation

1. This account is reconstructed from Aviel Barclay's own writings about her experience, including "Writing Torah as a Woman," *Lilith Magazine* (Spring 2006): 14-17, and

interviews in Jen Taylor Friedman, "The Torah Scribe: Conversations with Six Jewish Scribes," *Jewish Quarterly* 58, no. 2 (2011): 23-29.

2. On traditional restrictions, see Mendel Shapiro, "Qeri'at ha-Torah by Women: A Halakhic Analysis," *The Edah Journal* 1, no. 2 (2001): 1-35.

3. Shapiro, "Qeri'at ha-Torah by Women," 15-28.

4. On Jen Taylor Friedman's work, see her blog "The Soferet" at www.soferet.com and coverage in Jewish media including "Female Scribe Completes Torah," *Jewish Chronicle*, July 15, 2010.

5. On contemporary women scribes, see Linda Coppleson, "The Art of Sacred Writing," *Reform Judaism* 39, no. 4 (2011): 12-16; Temima Nochomi, interview in *Nashim* 22 (2012): 45-52.

6. For Orthodox responses, see various articles in *Tradition* and *Jewish Action* magazines, as well as responsa by contemporary halakhic authorities.

7. On women's approaches to scribal practice, see Aviel Barclay, "Sacred Letters: A Woman's Journey into the World of Sofrut," in *Jewish Women's Archive*, accessed January 2024.

8. For overviews of Islamic feminist scholarship, see Margot Badran, "Islamic Feminism: What's in a Name?," *Al-Ahram Weekly*, January 17-23, 2002; and Asma Barlas, "The Qur'an, Sexual Equality, and Feminism," *Signs* 32, no. 4 (2007): 856-885.

9. Amina Wadud, *Qur'an and Woman: Rereading the Sacred Text from a Woman's Perspective*, rev. ed. (New York: Oxford University Press, 1999), 25-67.

10. Asma Barlas, *"Believing Women" in Islam: Unreading Patriarchal Interpretations of the Qur'an* (Austin: University of Texas Press, 2002), 45-89.
11. Kecia Ali, *Sexual Ethics and Islam: Feminist Reflections on Qur'an, Hadith, and Jurisprudence*, rev. ed. (Oxford: Oneworld, 2016), 67-134.
12. On regional variations, see Pieternella van Doorn-Harder, *Women Shaping Islam: Reading the Qur'an in Indonesia* (Urbana: University of Illinois Press, 2006); Ziba Mir-Hosseini, *Islam and Gender: The Religious Debate in Contemporary Iran* (Princeton: Princeton University Press, 1999).
13. See Amina Mama, "Khaki in the Family: Gender Discourses and Militarism in Nigeria," *African Studies Review* 41, no. 2 (1998): 1-17; Fatou Sow, "Muslim Families in Contemporary Black Africa," *Current Anthropology* 26, no. 5 (1985): 563-570.
14. On institutional challenges, see Ziba Mir-Hosseini, "Muslim Women's Quest for Equality: Between Islamic Law and Feminism," *Critical Inquiry* 32, no. 4 (2006): 629-645.
15. Information on these organizations from their websites and publications: Women in Islam (www.womeninislam.org); Musawah (www.musawah.org).
16. On the bhikkhuni lineage, see Karma Lekshe Tsomo, ed., *Buddhist Women and Social Justice* (Albany: SUNY Press, 2004), 34-67.
17. See Karma Lekshe Tsomo, "Is the Bhikshuni Vinaya Sexist?" in *Buddhist Women Across Cultures*, ed. Karma

Lekshe Tsomo (Albany: SUNY Press, 1999), 45-72; Jampa Tsedroen, "The Significance of the Bhikṣuṇī Ordination," in *Dignity and Discipline*, ed. Thea Mohr and Jampa Tsedroen (Boston: Wisdom Publications, 2010), 89-134.

18. On Dhammananda's ordination, see Monica Lindberg Falk, *Making Fields of Merit: Buddhist Female Ascetics and Gendered Orders in Thailand* (Seattle: University of Washington Press, 2007), 134-167.

19. On Sakyadhita, see official publications and website (www.sakyadhita.org); Karma Lekshe Tsomo, *Sakyadhita: Daughters of the Buddha* (Ithaca: Snow Lion Publications, 1988).

20. On Chinese and Taiwanese Buddhism, see Chün-fang Yü, *Passing the Light: The Incense Light Community and Buddhist Nuns in Contemporary Taiwan* (Honolulu: University of Hawaii Press, 2013).

21. On Tibetan developments, see Janet Gyatso, "One Plus One Makes Three: Buddhist Gender, Monasticism, and the Law of the Non-Excluded Middle," *History of Religions* 43, no. 2 (2003): 89-115.

22. On institutional resistance, see Falk, *Making Fields of Merit*, 178-203.

23. On Yoruba traditions, see Oyeronke Oyewumi, *The Invention of Women: Making an African Sense of Western Gender Discourses* (Minneapolis: University of Minnesota Press, 1997); various works by Iyanifa Vassa published through Ifa Foundation International.

24. On oral traditions as textual authority, see Karin Barber, *I Could Speak Until Tomorrow: Oriki, Women, and the*

Past in a Yoruba Town (Washington, DC: Smithsonian Institution Press, 1991).

25. See Vasudha Narayanan, "Brimming with Bhakti, Embodiments of Shakti," in *Feminism and World Religions*, ed. Arvind Sharma and Katherine K. Young (Albany: SUNY Press, 1999), 25-77; Arti Dhand, "Woman as Fire, Woman as Sage: Sexual Ideology in the Mahabharata," *Journal of the American Academy of Religion* 73, no. 4 (2005): 831-876.

26. On contemporary devotional practice, see various recordings and performances; Laurie L. Patton, ed., *Jewels of Authority: Women and Textual Tradition in Hindu India* (New York: Oxford University Press, 2002).

27. On Sikh women's authority, see Doris R. Jakobsh, *Relocating Gender in Sikh History: Transformation, Meaning and Identity* (New Delhi: Oxford University Press, 2003).

28. Contemporary Sikh developments documented in community newsletters and online forums of various gurdwaras and Sikh organizations.

29. On indigenous knowledge systems, see Linda Tuhiwai Smith, *Decolonizing Methodologies: Research and Indigenous Peoples*, 2nd ed. (London: Zed Books, 2012).

30. See Vine Deloria Jr., *God Is Red: A Native View of Religion*, 3rd ed. (Golden, CO: Fulcrum Publishing, 2003); Winona LaDuke, *Recovering the Sacred: The Power of Naming and Claiming* (Boston: South End Press, 2005).

31. Information from organizational websites and course catalogs: SeekersHub (www.seekershub.org); Bayyinah Institute (www.bayyinah.com).
32. On online Islamic education, see various interviews and articles about these teachers in Islamic and mainstream media.
33. Information from their published works and online teaching platforms.
34. Documentation of social media religious engagement from various platform studies and media coverage.
35. On digital humanities projects, see project websites: Digital Manuscripts Toolkit (dmt.library.utoronto.ca); Women Writers Project (www.wwp.northeastern.edu).
36. On denominational variations, see survey data from various religious organizations and academic studies of contemporary religious practice.
37. On economic barriers, see various studies of women in religious leadership roles across traditions.
38. Documentation of institutional restrictions from religious law sources and contemporary community debates.
39. On collaborative scholarship, see examples from various interfaith academic programs and community partnership projects.
40. Information from Interfaith Women's Network and similar organizations.
41. On gender-inclusive scholarship, see transgender and queer religious studies literature emerging since 2000.
42. See Laury Silvers, "In the Book We Have Left Out Nothing: The Ethical Problem of the Existence of

Transgender People in Islamic Law," in *Progressive Muslims*, ed. Omid Safi (Oxford: Oneworld, 2003), 128-152; Elliot Kukla, "Terms for Gender Diversity in Classical Jewish Texts," *TransTorah* website (www.transtorah.org).

Conclusion: To Be Remembered

1. Elizabeth A. Clark, *History, Theory, Text: Historians and the Linguistic Turn* (Cambridge, MA: Harvard University Press, 2004), 183-200. Clark's methodological reflections on feminist historical scholarship appear throughout this work but are particularly concentrated in her discussion of the relationship between recovery projects and historical epistemology.
2. Caroline Walker Bynum, *Holy Feast and Holy Fast: The Religious Significance of Food to Medieval Women* (Berkeley: University of California Press, 1987), xv-xxiii. See also her *Fragmentation and Redemption: Essays on Gender and the Human Body in Medieval Religion* (New York: Zone Books, 1991), 27-51, on the interpretive significance of absence and presence in medieval women's religious experience.
3. Fatima Mernissi, *The Veil and the Male Elite: A Feminist Interpretation of Women's Rights in Islam*, trans. Mary Jo Lakeland (Cambridge, MA: Perseus Books, 1991), 27-45. Mernissi's approach to documenting exclusion as historical methodology is developed throughout this work and in her *The Forgotten Queens of Islam*, trans.

Mary Jo Lakeland (Minneapolis: University of Minnesota Press, 1993).

4. Susannah Heschel, "Feminist Theology and Jewish Tradition," in *On Being a Jewish Feminist*, ed. Susannah Heschel (New York: Schocken Books, 1983), 17-31. See also her *Abraham Geiger and the Jewish Jesus* (Chicago: University of Chicago Press, 1998) for broader methodological reflections on recovery and transmission.
5. Alison I. Beach, *Women as Scribes: Manuscript Production and Monastic Reform in Twelfth-Century Bavaria*(Cambridge: Cambridge University Press, 2004), 12-30. Beach's paleographic methodology is detailed throughout this work and in her subsequent publications on medieval manuscript culture.
6. Rita M. Gross, *Buddhism After Patriarchy: A Feminist History, Analysis, and Reconstruction of Buddhism* (Albany: SUNY Press, 1993), 73-134. Gross's comparative approach to Buddhist feminist scholarship appears in various essays collected in *Soaring and Settling: Buddhist Perspectives on Contemporary Social and Religious Issues* (New York: Continuum, 1998).
7. Mary Keller, *American Dreams, American Realities: Women and the Sacred*, forthcoming; various articles on collaborative methodology in Native American religious studies published in *American Indian Quarterly* and *Journal of the American Academy of Religion*.
8. Saba Mahmood, *Politics of Piety: The Islamic Revival and the Feminist Subject* (Princeton: Princeton University Press, 2005), 78-134. Mahmood's ethnographic

approach reveals how traditional Islamic knowledge continues to be transmitted through women's religious networks.

9. Elisabeth Schüssler Fiorenza, *In Memory of Her: A Feminist Theological Reconstruction of Christian Origins* (New York: Crossroad, 1983), 28-36. See also her *But She Said: Feminist Practices of Biblical Interpretation* (Boston: Beacon Press, 1992) for expanded discussion of canonical exclusion.

10. Asma Sayeed, *Women and the Transmission of Religious Knowledge in Islam* (Cambridge: Cambridge University Press, 2013), 134-178. Sayeed's analysis of early hadith transmission demonstrates the gradual marginalization of women's authority over several centuries.

11. Grace Jantzen, *Power, Gender and Christian Mysticism* (Cambridge: Cambridge University Press, 1995), 198-234. Jantzen's work on alternative forms of religious authority has been influential across feminist religious studies.

12. Amina Wadud, *Inside the Gender Jihad: Women's Reform in Islam* (Oxford: Oneworld, 2006), 25-67. Wadud's theological reflections on Islamic authority and gender appear throughout her published work and lectures.

13. Sallie McFague, *Models of God: Theology for an Ecological, Nuclear Age* (Philadelphia: Fortress Press, 1987), 97-123; Sachiko Murata, *The Tao of Islam: A Sourcebook on Gender Relationships in Islamic Thought* (Albany: SUNY Press, 1992), 134-167.

14. Riffat Hassan, "The Issue of Women-Man Equality in the Islamic Tradition," in *Women's and Men's Liberation: Testimonies of Spirit*, eds. Leonard Grob, Riffat Hassan, and Haim Gordon (New York: Greenwood Press, 1991), 65-82; Rita M. Gross, "Feminism from the Perspective of Buddhist Practice," *Buddhist-Christian Studies* 1 (1981): 72-82.
15. Mercy Amba Oduyoye, *Daughters of Anowa: African Women and Patriarchy* (Maryknoll: Orbis Books, 1995); Kwok Pui-lan, *Postcolonial Imagination and Feminist Theology* (Louisville: Westminster John Knox Press, 2005); Ada María Isasi-Díaz, *Mujerista Theology* (Maryknoll: Orbis Books, 1996).
16. Bynum, *Fragmentation and Redemption*, 27-51.

Appendix A

1. On Mahapajapati, see Karma Lekshe Tsomo, ed., *Buddhist Women Across Cultures* (Albany: SUNY Press, 1999), 34-45.
2. Therigatha verses translated in Susan Murcott, *The First Buddhist Women* (Berkeley: Parallax Press, 1991), 78-89.
3. Vimala's verses in Therigatha 72-76; see analysis in Miranda Shaw, *Passionate Enlightenment* (Princeton: Princeton University Press, 1994), 67-78.
4. Culavedalla Sutta, Majjhima Nikaya 44; see I.B. Horner, *Women Under Primitive Buddhism* (London: Routledge, 1930), 156-167.

5. Dhammapada Commentary; see Hellmuth Hecker, *Buddhist Women at the Time of the Buddha* (Kandy: Buddhist Publication Society, 1982).
6. On Lady Zhao, see Kenneth Ch'en, *Buddhism in China* (Princeton: Princeton University Press, 1964), 234-245.
7. Srimaladevi Simhanada Sutra; see Diana Paul, *Women in Buddhism* (Berkeley: Asian Humanities Press, 1979), 89-134.
8. On Yeshe Tsogyal, see Judith Simmer-Brown, *Dakini's Warm Breath* (Boston: Shambhala, 2001), 234-267.
9. Traditional Chan records; see Miriam Levering, "The Dragon Girl and the Abbess of Mo-shan," *Journal of the International Association of Buddhist Studies* 5 (1982): 19-35.
10. On Queen Shin Sawbu, see Than Tun, *Essays on the History and Buddhism of Burma* (Arran: Kiscadale Publications, 1988), 67-89.
11. On Prajñāpāramitā literature and feminine wisdom, see Edward Conze, *The Prajñāpāramitā Literature* (The Hague: Mouton, 1960), 45-67.
12. On Lady Wei Huacun, see Isabelle Robinet, *Taoist Meditation* (Albany: SUNY Press, 1993), 89-112.
13. On Empress Wu Zetian's Buddhist patronage, see N. Harry Rothschild, *Wu Zhao: China's Only Woman Emperor* (New York: Pearson Longman, 2008), 134-156.
14. On early Tibetan nuns, see Hanna Havnevik, *Tibetan Buddhist Nuns* (Oslo: Norwegian University Press, 1989), 67-89.
15. Information from Ani Choying Drolma's official biography and interviews in Buddhist magazines.

16. On Tenzin Palmo, see her autobiography *Cave in the Snow* (New York: Riverhead Books, 1998).
17. On Karma Lekshe Tsomo, see her various publications and Sakyadhita International materials.
18. Rev. Zenju Earthlyn Manuel, *The Way of Tenderness: Awakening through Race, Sexuality, and Gender* (Boston: Wisdom Publications, 2015).
19. On Jan Chozen Bays, see her published works including *Mindful Eating* (Boston: Shambhala, 2009).
20. On Mary Magdalene, see Karen L. King, *The Gospel of Mary of Magdala* (Santa Rosa: Polebridge Press, 2003), 1-45.
21. Acts of Paul and Thecla; see Sheila Briggs, "Galatians," in *Searching the Scriptures*, ed. Elisabeth Schüssler Fiorenza (New York: Crossroad, 1994), 218-236.
22. On Junia, see Eldon Jay Epp, *Junia: The First Woman Apostle* (Minneapolis: Fortress Press, 2005).
23. Text and commentary in Herbert Musurillo, *The Acts of the Christian Martyrs* (Oxford: Clarendon Press, 1972), 106-131.
24. Gregory of Nyssa, *Life of Macrina*, trans. Virginia Woods Callahan, in *Fathers of the Church* 58 (Washington: Catholic University of America Press, 1967).
25. Egeria's *Itinerarium*, trans. John Wilkinson in *Egeria's Travels* (London: SPCK, 1971).
26. On Hildegard, see Barbara Newman, *Sister of Wisdom* (Berkeley: University of California Press, 1987).
27. Heloise's letters in *The Letters of Abelard and Heloise*, trans. Betty Radice (London: Penguin Classics, 1974).

28. Julian of Norwich, *Revelations of Divine Love*, trans. Edmund Colledge and James Walsh (New York: Paulist Press, 1978).
29. *The Book of Margery Kempe*, trans. B.A. Windeatt (London: Penguin Classics, 1985).
30. On Catherine of Siena, see Suzanne Noffke, trans., *Catherine of Siena: The Dialogue* (New York: Paulist Press, 1980).
31. On Mechthild of Magdeburg, see Frank Tobin, trans., *Mechthild of Magdeburg: The Flowing Light of the Godhead*(New York: Paulist Press, 1998).
32. On Teresa of Ávila, see Kieran Kavanaugh and Otilio Rodriguez, trans., *The Collected Works of St. Teresa of Avila*(Washington: ICS Publications, 1976-1985).
33. On Marguerite Porete, see Ellen Babinsky, trans., *Marguerite Porete: The Mirror of Simple Souls* (New York: Paulist Press, 1993).
34. Sor Juana's works in *A Sor Juana Anthology*, trans. Alan Trueblood (Cambridge, MA: Harvard University Press, 1988).
35. On Dorothy Day, see her *The Long Loneliness* (New York: Harper & Row, 1952).
36. On Thérèse of Lisieux, see John Clarke, trans., *Story of a Soul* (Washington: ICS Publications, 1996).
37. On Mary Baker Eddy, see Robert Peel, *Mary Baker Eddy* (New York: Holt, Rinehart and Winston, 1966-1977).
38. On Jarena Lee, see *Religious Experience and Journal of Mrs. Jarena Lee* (Philadelphia: 1849; reprint, Nashville: AMEC Sunday School Union, 1991).

39. *Narrative of Sojourner Truth*, ed. Margaret Washington (New York: Vintage Books, 1993).
40. On Amanda Berry Smith, see her *An Autobiography* (Chicago: Meyer & Brother, 1893; reprint, New York: Oxford University Press, 1988).
41. On Pandita Ramabai, see Uma Chakravarti, *Rewriting History: The Life and Times of Pandita Ramabai* (New Delhi: Kali for Women, 1998).
42. On Evelyn Underhill, see Grace Adolphsen Brame, *Receptive Prayer: A Christian Approach to Meditation*(Nashville: Upper Room Books, 1985).
43. *The Poems of Phillis Wheatley*, ed. Julian D. Mason Jr. (Chapel Hill: University of North Carolina Press, 1989).
44. Mary Daly, *Beyond God the Father* (Boston: Beacon Press, 1973).
45. On Miriam, see Rita J. Burns, *Has the Lord Indeed Spoken Only Through Moses?* (Atlanta: Scholars Press, 1987).
46. On Deborah, see Susan Ackerman, *Warrior, Dancer, Seductress, Queen* (New York: Doubleday, 1998), 78-134.
47. On Huldah, see Alice Ogden Bellis, *Helpmates, Harlots, and Heroes* (Louisville: Westminster John Knox Press, 1994), 156-167.
48. On Beruriah, see Judith Hauptman, *Rereading the Rabbis* (Boulder: Westview Press, 1998), 56-85.
49. *The Memoirs of Glückel of Hameln*, trans. Marvin Lowenthal (New York: Schocken Books, 1977).
50. On Asenath Barzani, see Renée Levine Melammed, "The Ultimate Challenge: Safed's Rabbi Joseph Karo and Venice's Beautiful Esther," in *Gender and Judaism*, ed. T.M. Rudavsky (New York: NYU Press, 1995), 191-210.

51. On Sarah bas Tovim, see Chava Weissler, *Voices of the Matriarchs* (Boston: Beacon Press, 1998), 89-123.
52. Bella Chagall, *Burning Lights*, trans. Norbert Guterman (New York: Schocken Books, 1946).
53. On Regina Jonas, see Katharina von Kellenbach, "God Does Not Oppress Any Human Being," in *Jewish Women in Historical Perspective*, ed. Judith Baskin (Detroit: Wayne State University Press, 1991), 271-289.
54. On Nehama Leibowitz, see her *Studies in the Weekly Sidra* series and Yael Unterman, *Nehama Leibowitz: Teacher and Bible Scholar* (Jerusalem: Urim Publications, 2009).
55. Tikva Frymer-Kensky, *In the Wake of the Goddesses* (New York: Free Press, 1992).
56. Amy-Jill Levine, *The Misunderstood Jew* (San Francisco: HarperSanFrancisco, 2006).
57. Francine Klagsbrun, *Voices of Wisdom: Jewish Ideals and Ethics for Everyday Living* (New York: Pantheon Books, 1980).
58. Avivah Gottlieb Zornberg, *Genesis: The Beginning of Desire* (Philadelphia: Jewish Publication Society, 1995).
59. Judith Plaskow, *Standing Again at Sinai* (San Francisco: HarperSanFrancisco, 1990).
60. On Khadija, see Leila Ahmed, *Women and Gender in Islam* (New Haven: Yale University Press, 1992), 41-63.
61. On Aisha, see Denise Spellberg, *Politics, Gender, and the Islamic Past* (New York: Columbia University Press, 1994).

62. On Umm Salama, see Asma Sayeed, *Women and the Transmission of Religious Knowledge in Islam* (Cambridge: Cambridge University Press, 2013), 67-89.
63. On Hafsa, see Sayeed, *Women and the Transmission*, 45-66.
64. On Rabi'a, see Margaret Smith, *Rābi'a the Mystic* (Cambridge: Cambridge University Press, 1928).
65. On Fatima al-Fihri, see various sources on the University of al-Qarawiyyin's founding.
66. On Shuhda al-Katiba, see Sayeed, *Women and the Transmission*, 134-156.
67. On Nana Asma'u, see Beverly B. Mack and Jean Boyd, *One Woman's Jihad* (Bloomington: Indiana University Press, 2000).
68. Aisha Abd al-Rahman, *Tafsir al-Bayan li al-Qur'an al-Karim* (Cairo: Dar al-Ma'arif, 1962-1969).
69. Asma Barlas, *"Believing Women" in Islam* (Austin: University of Texas Press, 2002).
70. Kecia Ali, *Sexual Ethics and Islam* (Oxford: Oneworld, 2006) and *The Lives of Muhammad* (Cambridge, MA: Harvard University Press, 2014).
71. Asma Lamrabet, *Women and Men in the Qur'an* (London: Palgrave Macmillan, 2018).
72. Azizah al-Hibri, various articles in *Muslim Women and the Politics of Participation*, ed. Mahnaz Afkhami and Erika Friedl (Syracuse: Syracuse University Press, 1994).
73. Laleh Bakhtiar, *The Sublime Quran* (Chicago: Kazi Publications, 2007).
74. Ingrid Mattson, *The Story of the Qur'an* (Oxford: Blackwell, 2008).

75. Ziba Mir-Hosseini, *Islam and Gender* (Princeton: Princeton University Press, 1999).
76. Riffat Hassan, "The Issue of Women-Man Equality in the Islamic Tradition," in *Women's and Men's Liberation*, eds. Leonard Grob, Riffat Hassan, and Haim Gordon (New York: Greenwood Press, 1991), 65-82.
77. Fatima Mernissi, *The Veil and the Male Elite* (Cambridge, MA: Perseus Books, 1991).
78. On Amina Wadud, see her *Qur'an and Woman* (New York: Oxford University Press, 1999).
79. Rig Veda 1.179; see Wendy Doniger, *The Rig Veda* (London: Penguin Classics, 1981), 250-252.
80. Brihadaranyaka Upanishad 3.6 and 3.8; see Patrick Olivelle, trans., *The Early Upanishads* (New York: Oxford University Press, 1998).
81. On Sita, see Paula Richman, ed., *Many Ramayanas* (Berkeley: University of California Press, 1991).
82. On Draupadi, see Arti Dhand, "Woman as Fire, Woman as Sage," *Journal of the American Academy of Religion* 73, no. 4 (2005): 831-876.
83. On Akka Mahadevi, see A.K. Ramanujan, *Speaking of Siva* (London: Penguin Classics, 1973), 111-141.
84. On Andal, see Vasudha Narayanan, *The Vernacular Veda* (Columbia: University of South Carolina Press, 1994).
85. On Mirabai, see John Stratton Hawley and Mark Juergensmeyer, *Songs of the Saints of India* (New York: Oxford University Press, 2004), 120-142.
86. On Lalla, see Jaishree Kak Odin, trans., *Lalla: The Poems of Lal Ded* (New Delhi: Penguin Books India, 2003).

87. On Janabai, see Justin Abbott, trans., *The Poet-Saints of Maharashtra* (Poona: Scottish Mission Industries, 1926-1941).
88. On Avvaiyar, see Kamil Zvelebil, *Tamil Literature* (Leiden: Brill, 1975).
89. On Bahinabai, see Justin Abbott, *Bahina Bai: A Translation of Her Autobiography and Verses* (Poona: Scottish Mission Industries, 1929).
90. On Tarigonda Venkamamba, see Velcheru Narayana Rao and David Shulman, *Classical Telugu Poetry* (Berkeley: University of California Press, 2002).
91. On Gangasati, see Winand Callewaert and Mukund Lath, *The Hindi Songs of Namdev* (Leuven: Departement Orientalistiek, 1989).
92. On Mahadevi Verma, see her *Collected Works* and Kali Charan Ghosh, *Modern Hindi Literature* (Bombay: Popular Prakashan, 1966).
93. Arti Dhand, "Woman as Fire, Woman as Sage," *Journal of the American Academy of Religion* 73, no. 4 (2005): 831-876.
94. Vasudha Narayanan, "Brimming with Bhakti, Embodiments of Shakti," in *Feminism and World Religions*, ed. Arvind Sharma and Katherine K. Young (Albany: SUNY Press, 1999), 25-77.
95. Laurie L. Patton, ed., *Jewels of Authority* (New York: Oxford University Press, 2002).
96. Guru Granth Sahib, ang 967; see Doris R. Jakobsh, *Relocating Gender in Sikh History* (New Delhi: Oxford University Press, 2003).

97. On Bibi Nanaki, see traditional Sikh sources and Jakobsh, *Relocating Gender*.
98. On Mai Bhago, see Sikh historical records and Harjot Oberoi, *The Construction of Religious Boundaries* (Chicago: University of Chicago Press, 1994).
99. On Sun Bu'er, see Thomas Cleary, trans., *Immortal Sisters* (Boston: Shambhala, 1989), 45-78.
100. On Maria Sabina, see R. Gordon Wasson, *Maria Sabina and Her Mazatec Mushroom Velada* (New York: Harcourt Brace Jovanovich, 1974).
101. On He Xiangu, see Suzanne Cahill, *Transcendence and Divine Passion* (Stanford: Stanford University Press, 1993).
102. On Wei Huacun, see Isabelle Robinet, *Taoist Meditation* (Albany: SUNY Press, 1993).
103. On Mazu/Tianhou, see James L. Watson and Evelyn S. Rawski, eds., *Death Ritual in Late Imperial and Modern China* (Berkeley: University of California Press, 1988).
104. On Queen Mother of the West, see Suzanne Cahill, *Transcendence and Divine Passion* (Stanford: Stanford University Press, 1993).
105. On Kateri Tekakwitha, see Allan Greer, *Mohawk Saint: Catherine Tekakwitha and the Jesuits* (New York: Oxford University Press, 2005).
106. On Zitkala-Sa, see her *American Indian Stories* (Washington: Hayworth Publishing House, 1921; reprint, Lincoln: University of Nebraska Press, 1985).

107. On Roberta Blackgoat, see various interviews and speeches documented in environmental and indigenous rights publications.

108. Winona LaDuke, *Recovering the Sacred* (Boston: South End Press, 2005).

109. On Grandmother Agnes Baker Pilgrim, see various oral history projects and indigenous women's council records.

110. Linda Hogan, *Dwellings: A Spiritual History of the Living World* (New York: Norton, 1995).

111. Paula Gunn Allen, *The Sacred Hoop* (Boston: Beacon Press, 1986).

112. On Ibu Gedong Bagoes Oka, see various Indonesian sources on Balinese Hindu women's religious authority.

113. Raden Ajeng Kartini, *Letters of a Javanese Princess*, trans. Agnes Louise Symmers (New York: Norton, 1964).

114. On Shamima Shaikh, see various South African Islamic feminist publications and archives.

115. Sachiko Murata, *The Tao of Islam* (Albany: SUNY Press, 1992).

116. On Seyran Ateş, see various media coverage and her own writings on liberal Islam.

Bibliography and Index

A full bibliography and index can be found at SacredEditors.com.

Appendix A: Brief Biographies - 100 Women Across Traditions

Note: Entries marked with an asterisk (*) indicate contested historical evidence or legendary status. Cross-references to the glossary (Appendix C) and further reading (Appendix D) are provided where relevant. For detailed manuscript sources, see Appendix B.*

Buddhism

Mahapajapati Gotami (6th-5th century BCE, India) Aunt and foster mother of the Buddha, she became the first ordained Buddhist nun (bhikkhuni) after petitioning the Buddha three times to allow women into the monastic Sangha. Her persistence established the foundation for female ordination, though these lineages were later suppressed or discontinued in many Theravāda regions. Her story appears in the Vinaya texts and illustrates early tensions about women's spiritual capacity.[1]

Kisagotami (5th century BCE, India) A disciple of the Buddha celebrated for her verse in the Therigatha (Verses of Elder Nuns), which recounts her journey from devastating grief over her son's death to spiritual awakening through understanding impermanence. Her story remains one of Buddhism's most poignant narratives on suffering and liberation, demonstrating how personal tragedy can become spiritual wisdom.[2]

Vimala (5th century BCE, India) An early nun whose Therigatha poem expresses liberation from sexual objectification and social constraints. Her direct, unflinching language challenged prevailing norms around female virtue and agency: "Free am I, free from the three crooked things: mortar, pestle, and crooked husband." Her verses survive in Pali manuscripts and represent radical female self-assertion.[3]

Dhammadinna (3rd century BCE, India) Celebrated as one of the wisest female teachers in the Pali Canon and declared by the Buddha to be foremost among nuns who taught the Dhamma. The Culavedalla Sutta records her sophisticated dialogue with her former husband Visakha on profound aspects of Buddhist doctrine, demonstrating female authority in philosophical discourse and systematic teaching.[4]

Queen Samavati (3rd century BCE, India)* Royal patron and devoted follower of the Buddha, known for her deep compassion and unwavering commitment to dharma practice. Though not ordained as a nun, she created opportunities for women to hear the teachings and supported the early Sangha. Her story, preserved in the Dhammapada Commentary, represents the important role of lay female supporters in Buddhism's development.[5]

Lady Zhao (Zhao Huan) (4th century CE, China) Buddhist lay teacher and patron under the Jin dynasty who assisted in the translation and commentary of early Chinese Buddhist texts. Her work contributed to the localization of Mahayana thought in East Asia, particularly in adapting Indian concepts for

Chinese religious culture. Her name appears in colophons of several translated sutras.⁶

Queen Srimala (circa 5th century CE, India or Nepal)* Attributed as the central speaker in the Srimaladevi Simhanada Sutra, which promotes key Mahayana doctrines including tathagatagarbha (Buddha-nature) and the bodhisattva path. Whether historical or literary, her voice represents a rare example of a female sutra speaker given direct theological authority in canonical Buddhist literature.⁷

Yeshe Tsogyal (8th century CE, Tibet)* Considered a consort and chief disciple of Padmasambhava, she is revered as a key transmitter of Vajrayana teachings in Tibet. Regarded by many as a female Buddha, she is credited with authoring or inspiring numerous terma (hidden treasure texts) that were later discovered by tertöns (treasure-revealers). Her historical existence is debated, but her influence on Tibetan Buddhism is profound.⁸

Zongchi (Dharma Master Zongchi) (8th century CE, China) Disciple of Huineng, the sixth patriarch of Chan Buddhism, and one of the few women recorded in early Chan hagiographical literature. She achieved enlightenment and became a recognized teacher, though details of her teachings have not survived independently. Her inclusion in lineage records demonstrates that women could achieve the highest realization in Chan tradition.⁹

Queen Shin Sawbu (15th century CE, Burma) A devout Theravāda Buddhist queen who abdicated her throne to become a nun, taking the name Thiri Maha Dhamma Dewi. She used her wealth to endow numerous pagodas, sponsor religious texts, and support female scribes and reciters. Her patronage significantly advanced Buddhist education and textual preservation in medieval Burma.[10]

Prajñāpāramitā Bhikkhuni (2nd century CE, India)* Legendary nun associated with the Perfection of Wisdom literature, though her historical existence is debated. Several Prajñāpāramitā texts feature female wisdom figures who embody enlightened understanding, representing the feminine principle in Mahayana Buddhist philosophy.[11]

Lady Wei Huacun (251-334 CE, China, Daoist-Buddhist synthesis) Daoist immortal and founder of the Shangqing school who also studied Buddhist texts. Her revelations, recorded in the Zhen'gao, include adaptations of Buddhist meditation practices integrated with Daoist internal alchemy.[12]

Empress Wu Zetian (624-705 CE, China) The only woman to rule China in her own right, she was also a significant Buddhist patron who commissioned translations of sutras and supported the creation of the Dayun Sutra, which justified female rule through Buddhist doctrine.[13]

Gelongma Palmo (11th century CE, Tibet) One of the first Tibetan women to receive full ordination, she established practices for female monastics and transmitted Vinaya traditions. Her lineage influenced the development of Tibetan nunneries for centuries.[14]

Ani Choying Drolma (20th-21st century CE, Nepal) Tibetan Buddhist nun renowned for preserving and popularizing traditional chants and spiritual songs through recordings and performances. Born Dolma Tsering, she uses music as a vehicle for dharma transmission and supports education and health projects for girls and women in Nepal through the Arya Tara School.[15]

Jetsunma Tenzin Palmo (20th-21st century CE, UK/Tibet) Born Diane Perry in England, she became one of the first Western women ordained as a Tibetan Buddhist nun. After completing a twelve-year meditation retreat in a Himalayan cave, she became a prominent advocate for full bhikkhuni ordination and established Dongyu Gatsal Ling, a nunnery in India dedicated to providing equal education for nuns.[16]

Karma Lekshe Tsomo (20th-21st century CE, US) American Buddhist scholar and co-founder of the Sakyadhita International Association of Buddhist Women. Her research, activism, and interfaith work have been instrumental in reclaiming women's roles in Buddhist scholarship and leadership.[17]

Rev. Zenju Earthlyn Manuel (21st century CE, US) Zen Buddhist priest, author, and teacher whose work explores the intersections of race, gender, and spirituality. Her teachings blend ancient dharma with contemporary insights on justice and identity.[18]

Jan Chozen Bays (20th-21st century CE, US) Zen master and physician who has written extensively on mindfulness and Buddhist psychology. She is one of the few women authorized to teach in the Zen tradition and has pioneered integrations of Buddhist practice with medical training.[19]

Christianity

Mary Magdalene (1st century CE, Palestine) Prominent follower of Jesus and the first witness to the resurrection in all four canonical Gospels. The Gospel of Luke identifies her as a woman "from whom seven demons had gone out," but she was later incorrectly conflated with the anonymous "sinful woman" and identified as a prostitute by Pope Gregory I in 591 CE. Apocryphal texts like the Gospel of Mary portray her as receiving special revelations and engaging in theological disputes with male apostles, suggesting her role as a teacher was later suppressed.[20]

Thecla (2nd century CE, Asia Minor)* Central figure in the Acts of Paul and Thecla, an early Christian apocryphal narrative depicting a woman who baptizes, preaches, and defies social conventions to follow apostolic life. Though her historical existence is debated, her cult was widely venerated until the medieval period, when ecclesiastical authorities increasingly discouraged devotion to female saints who challenged gender norms.[21]

Junia (1st century CE, Rome) Named by Paul in Romans 16:7 as "prominent among the apostles" (epismoi en tois apostolois). Medieval and later scribes changed her name to the masculine "Junias" in many manuscripts to avoid recognizing a female apostle. Modern textual criticism has restored the feminine form, revealing how women's apostolic authority was systematically obscured through scribal changes.[22]

Perpetua (died 203 CE, Carthage) Christian martyr whose prison diary, the Passio Perpetuae, is one of the earliest surviving writings by a Christian woman. Her text combines visionary experiences with theological reflection and was widely read throughout early Christianity. The account, completed by an anonymous editor after her death, demonstrates early Christian women's capacity for theological insight and spiritual authority.[23]

Macrina the Younger (circa 330-379 CE, Cappadocia) Sister of Gregory of Nyssa and Basil the Great, she was a philosopher and theologian whose spiritual insights shaped Cappadocian Christian thought. Her theological conversations are preserved in Gregory's Life of Macrina and On the Soul and Resurrection, where she appears as a sophisticated interpreter of Christian doctrine, particularly regarding the soul's relationship to the body.[24]

Egeria (late 4th century CE, Western Europe/Holy Land) Christian pilgrim whose detailed travelogue, the Itinerarium Egeriae, describes her journey to Jerusalem and surrounding regions. Her work provides crucial evidence for early Christian liturgical practices and includes sophisticated biblical commentary, demonstrating lay women's engagement with scriptural interpretation during the patristic period.[25]

Hildegard of Bingen (1098-1179 CE, Germany) Benedictine abbess, composer, visionary, and theologian whose works include Scivias, Liber Vitae Meritorum, and Liber Divinorum Operum. Her visionary theology combined biblical commentary with natural philosophy and mystical experience, earning papal recognition during her lifetime. She corresponded with popes, emperors, and bishops while developing innovative theological concepts about divine creativity and cosmic harmony.[26]

Heloise of Argenteuil (circa 1095-1164 CE, France) Scholar, abbess, and epistolary theologian known for her correspondence with Peter Abelard. Her letters demonstrate deep scriptural literacy and theological sophistication, particularly in her critiques of monastic life for women and her arguments about the relationship between intention and moral action. Her theological insights influenced medieval discussions of ethics and spiritual authority.[27]

Julian of Norwich (circa 1343-1416 CE, England) Author of Revelations of Divine Love, the first known book written in English by a woman. Her sixteen "showings" or visions, received during severe illness in 1373, became the foundation for sophisticated theological reflection on divine love, sin, and salvation. Her innovative use of maternal imagery for God and her conviction that "all shall be well" challenged prevailing doctrines about damnation and divine wrath.[28]

Margery Kempe (circa 1373-1438 CE, England) Mystic and pilgrim whose Book of Margery Kempe is the earliest known autobiography in English. Though dictated rather than written (she was illiterate), her account provides unprecedented insight into lay women's spiritual experiences, including mystical encounters, pilgrimage, and interactions with religious authorities who often questioned her claims to divine inspiration.[29]

Catherine of Siena (1347-1380 CE, Italy) Mystic, theologian, and Doctor of the Church whose Dialogue presents sophisticated theological arguments received through mystical experience. Despite lacking formal education, her theological insights influenced papal policy and church reform movements.[30]

Mechthild of Magdeburg (circa 1207-1282 CE, Germany) Beguine mystic whose The Flowing Light of the Godhead combines erotic mystical imagery with theological reflection. Her work influenced later mystics including Meister Eckhart and represents an alternative tradition of lay women's theological authority.[31]

Teresa of Ávila (1515-1582 CE, Spain) Carmelite reformer and Doctor of the Church whose mystical theology, particularly in The Interior Castle, systematized stages of spiritual development. Her combination of mystical experience and practical wisdom influenced Catholic spiritual direction for centuries.[32]

Marguerite Porete (circa 1250-1310 CE, France) Beguine author of The Mirror of Simple Souls, a sophisticated theological treatise on the soul's union with God. She was burned as a heretic for refusing to retract her work, though it continued to circulate anonymously and influenced later mystical theology.[33]

Sor Juana Inés de la Cruz (1648-1695 CE, Mexico) Nun, poet, and scholar whose theological and philosophical writings challenged male intellectual authority in colonial Mexico. Her letter Respuesta a Sor Filotea (Reply to Sister Philotea) defends women's right to theological learning by invoking biblical precedents of learned women, arguing that intellectual curiosity is a divine gift that should not be suppressed by social convention.[34]

Dorothy Day (1897-1980 CE, US) Catholic social activist and founder of the Catholic Worker Movement whose journalism and autobiography integrated gospel teachings with social justice advocacy. Though not formally a theologian, her writings demonstrate sophisticated engagement with Catholic social teaching.[35]

Thérèse of Lisieux (1873-1897 CE, France) Carmelite nun whose spiritual autobiography Story of a Soul introduced the "little way" of spiritual childhood as a path to sanctity. Her theological insights about divine mercy and spiritual simplicity influenced twentieth-century Catholic spirituality.[36]

Mary Baker Eddy (1821-1910 CE, US) Founder of Christian Science and author of Science and Health with Key to the Scriptures, which she claimed provided the spiritual interpretation of biblical texts. Despite controversy, her movement attracted thousands and represented women's religious leadership in nineteenth-century America.[37]

Jarena Lee (1783-1864 CE, US) African Methodist Episcopal preacher and autobiographer whose Life and Religious

Experience challenged both racial and gender restrictions on religious authority. Her preaching ministry demonstrated African American women's leadership in early evangelical movements.[38]

Sojourner Truth (circa 1797-1883 CE, US) Abolitionist and women's rights activist whose speeches integrated biblical interpretation with social critique. Though illiterate, her "Ain't I a Woman?" speech used Christian theology to challenge both slavery and women's subordination.[39]

Amanda Berry Smith (1837-1915 CE, US) African Methodist evangelist and missionary whose autobiography documents her preaching ministry across the United States, India, and Africa. Her theological insights about holiness and divine calling challenged both racial and gender limitations in evangelical Christianity.[40]

Pandita Ramabai (1858-1922 CE, India) Sanskrit scholar and Christian convert whose biblical translations and social reform work challenged both Hindu and Christian patriarchy. Her integration of Christian theology with advocacy for Indian women's education influenced both religious and social reform movements.[41]

Evelyn Underhill (1875-1941 CE, England) Anglican mystical theologian whose scholarly works on mysticism, particularly Mysticism: A Study in Nature and Development of Spiritual Consciousness, established academic study of mystical experience. She was the first woman invited to give retreats to Anglican clergy.[42]

Phillis Wheatley (circa 1753-1784 CE, Boston) Enslaved African woman whose Christian-themed poetry demonstrated remarkable biblical literacy and theological sophistication. Her poems, including "On Being Brought from Pagan Land," navigate the complex relationship between Christian faith and the experience of enslavement, often subtly criticizing white Christian hypocrisy while affirming her own spiritual equality.[43]

Mary Daly (20th century CE, US) Radical feminist philosopher and theologian whose books—including Beyond God the Father—critiqued Christian patriarchy and proposed new theological language. Her work sparked decades of debate in academic and ecclesial settings.[44]

Judaism

Miriam (Biblical era, 13th-12th century BCE)* Sister of Moses and Aaron, identified as a prophetess (nevi'ah) in Exodus 15:20 and associated with the Song of the Sea celebrating the Israelites' escape from Egypt. While early texts acknowledge her leadership role, later biblical editing and post-exilic traditions increasingly marginalized her authority in favor of her brothers. Talmudic tradition credits her with providing water to the Israelites during their wilderness wandering.[45]

Deborah (Biblical era, circa 12th century BCE)* Prophetess and judge described in Judges 4-5 as leading Israel in both military and spiritual matters. The Song of Deborah (Judges 5) is considered one of the oldest texts in the Hebrew Bible and celebrates her victory over Canaanite forces. Her authority over male military leaders represents a striking example of female leadership that later biblical traditions rarely paralleled.[46]

Huldah (7th century BCE, Judah)* Prophetess consulted by King Josiah's officials following the discovery of a law scroll in the Temple (2 Kings 22). She interpreted the scroll's divine warnings and confirmed its authenticity, playing a crucial role in Josiah's religious reforms. Her canonical authority as a prophetic interpreter makes her one of the few women in the Hebrew Bible explicitly recognized for theological insight.[47]

Beruriah (2nd century CE, Roman Palestine) Wife of Rabbi Meir and one of the few women mentioned in Talmudic literature for her halakhic (Jewish legal) knowledge. Several anecdotes preserve her sharp reasoning on legal matters and her challenges to male scholarly assumptions. However, later medieval traditions developed tragic legends about her downfall that served to diminish her intellectual authority.[48]

Glikl of Hameln (1646-1724 CE, Germany) Jewish businesswoman whose Yiddish autobiography provides rare insight into women's religious and ethical thinking in early modern Europe. While not formally educated in Jewish law, her memoirs demonstrate sophisticated engagement with Jewish texts and moral reasoning, and her work became a devotional resource for subsequent generations of Jewish women.[49]

Asenath Barzani (circa 1590-1670 CE, Kurdistan) Daughter of a prominent rabbi who became head of a yeshiva (Jewish academy) and taught Talmud and Kabbalah to both male and female students. She composed Hebrew poetry and maintained scholarly correspondence across the Middle East. Her authority as a halakhic decisor represents one of the earliest documented cases of formal female Jewish religious leadership.[50]

Sarah bas Tovim (18th century CE, Eastern Europe) Author of tkhines (Yiddish devotional prayers) for women, including the popular Shloyshes She'orim (Three Gates). Her prayers addressed distinctly feminine religious experiences and demonstrated sophisticated theological thinking about women's spiritual lives and relationship with the divine.[51]

Bella Chagall (1895-1944 CE, Belarus/France) Artist and writer whose memoir Burning Lights preserves Jewish women's religious experiences in Eastern Europe. Though primarily known as an artist, her writings demonstrate deep engagement with Jewish texts and traditions from a distinctly feminine perspective.[52]

Regina Jonas (1902-1944 CE, Germany) The first woman ordained as a rabbi, she served Berlin's Jewish community from 1935 until her deportation to Theresienstadt in 1942. Her ordination thesis, "Can Women Serve as Rabbis?," used traditional Jewish legal reasoning to argue for women's religious leadership.[53]

Nehama Leibowitz (1905-1997 CE, Israel) Biblical commentator whose weekly Torah study sheets (gilyonot) reached thousands of students worldwide. Her pedagogical approach emphasized close textual reading and comparative commentary, making traditional Jewish biblical interpretation accessible to modern readers including women.[54]

Tikva Frymer-Kensky (1943-2006 CE, US) Biblical scholar whose In the Wake of the Goddesses demonstrated how feminine divine imagery was systematically suppressed in Hebrew Bible editing. Her work revealed the theological significance of recovering ancient Near Eastern goddess traditions for understanding biblical texts.[55]

Amy-Jill Levine (20th-21st century CE, US) New Testament scholar whose work bridges Jewish and Christian biblical interpretation. Her scholarship on the historical Jesus and early Christianity challenges anti-Jewish readings while recovering Jewish contexts of Christian origins.[56]

Francine Klagsbrun (20th-21st century CE, US) Author and Jewish feminist whose biographical work on biblical women and modern Jewish leaders demonstrates sophisticated engagement with traditional sources while advocating for contemporary women's religious leadership.[57]

Avivah Gottlieb Zornberg (20th-21st century CE, Israel/US) Biblical commentator whose psychoanalytically informed interpretations of Torah narratives offer innovative readings of classical texts. Her work demonstrates how contemporary interpretive methods can deepen rather than threaten traditional Jewish learning.[58]

Judith Plaskow (20th-21st century CE, United States) Author of Standing Again at Sinai, a foundational text in Jewish feminist theology that argues for reclaiming women's presence and interpretive authority in Jewish sacred memory. Her work challenges traditional exclusions while remaining committed to

Jewish practice, demonstrating how feminist scholarship can transform rather than abandon religious tradition.[59]

Islam

Khadija bint Khuwaylid (circa 555-619 CE, Mecca) First wife of the Prophet Muhammad and the first person to embrace Islam. A successful merchant who initially employed Muhammad, she provided crucial emotional and financial support during the earliest Quranic revelations. Though not a transmitter of Quranic text, her role in Islam's foundational period and her unwavering belief in Muhammad's prophetic mission make her essential to understanding early Islamic development.[60]

Aisha bint Abi Bakr (circa 613-678 CE, Arabia) Wife of the Prophet Muhammad and one of the most important transmitters of hadith (prophetic sayings and actions). She is credited with narrating over 2,000 hadiths and was recognized for her sharp intellect and theological insights. Her involvement in early Islamic politics, including the Battle of the Camel, demonstrates her public authority, though later interpretations increasingly emphasized her domestic role.[61]

Umm Salama (Hind bint Abi Umayya) (circa 596-681 CE, Arabia) Wife of the Prophet Muhammad and trusted legal and theological authority who narrated hundreds of hadiths. She was particularly involved in developing Islamic law concerning women's rights in inheritance, divorce, and religious practice. Her legal opinions were cited by subsequent generations of Islamic jurists.[62]

Hafsa bint Umar (circa 605-665 CE, Arabia) Wife of the Prophet Muhammad and custodian of the earliest written compilation of the Quran after the Prophet's death. Her personal copy, inherited from her father Umar ibn al-Khattab, formed the basis for Caliph Uthman's later standardized text. Her role as textual guardian is acknowledged but rarely emphasized in mainstream Islamic histories.[63]

Rabi'a al-Adawiyya (circa 717-801 CE, Basra) Sufi mystic whose poetry and teachings centered on divine love and disinterested devotion to God. Though little survives in her own hand, her sayings and poems, preserved through oral transmission, profoundly influenced Islamic mystical literature. Her emphasis on love rather than fear in the relationship with God challenged legalistic approaches to Islamic practice.[64]

Fatima al-Fihri (circa 800-880 CE, Fez) Founder of the University of al-Qarawiyyin in Fez, Morocco, recognized by some scholars as the oldest continuously operating educational institution in the world. She used her inheritance to fund Islamic learning, including Quranic memorization, hadith study, and legal education, demonstrating women's crucial role as patrons of Islamic scholarship.[65]

Shuhda al-Katiba (1135-1178 CE, Baghdad) Known as "the Pride of Women" and "the Calligrapher," she was a prominent hadith transmitter and skilled calligrapher in Abbasid Baghdad. Male scholars sought out her chain of transmission (isnad) for its prestige and reliability. Her scholarly authority illustrates the respect accorded to female religious teachers in medieval Islamic culture.[66]

Nana Asma'u (1793-1864 CE, Sokoto Caliphate, West Africa) Scholar, poet, and educator who translated Quranic and other religious texts into local languages and established one of the earliest Islamic women's education networks in West Africa. Daughter of Usman dan Fodio, founder of the Sokoto Caliphate, she composed works in Arabic, Fulfulde, and Hausa that preserved and transmitted Islamic knowledge across linguistic boundaries.[67]

Aisha Abd al-Rahman (Bint al-Shati') (1913-1998 CE, Egypt) Literary critic and Quranic commentator whose tafsir (interpretation) work emphasized literary and linguistic analysis of the Quran. She was one of the first women to publish systematic Quranic commentary in the modern period.[68]

Asma Barlas (20th-21st century CE, Pakistan/US) Author of "Believing Women" in Islam who developed comprehensive hermeneutical frameworks for reading the Quran as an anti-patriarchal text. Her scholarship demonstrates how careful attention to Quranic language and context can support egalitarian rather than hierarchical interpretations of gender relations.[69]

Kecia Ali (21st century CE, US) Islamic studies scholar whose work on sexuality, ethics, and early Islamic history challenges traditional assumptions about gender in Islamic law. Her biography The Lives of Muhammad examines how later interpretations shaped understanding of the Prophet's relationships with women.[70]

Asma Lamrabet (21st century CE, Morocco) Physician and Islamic feminist scholar whose writings on women in Islam emphasize the distinction between Quranic principles and cultural patriarchal overlays. Her work has influenced Islamic feminist movements across the francophone world.[71]

Azizah al-Hibri (20th-21st century CE, Lebanon/US) Legal scholar and founder of KARAMA (Arab Women's Organization) whose work applies Islamic jurisprudence to contemporary women's rights issues. Her scholarship demonstrates how traditional Islamic legal methods can support gender equality.[72]

Laleh Bakhtiar (20th-21st century CE, US) Translator of the Quran whose 2007 English translation challenged conventional interpretations of controversial passages, particularly Quran 4:34. Her translation decisions sparked debate about women's authority in Quranic interpretation.[73]

Ingrid Mattson (20th-21st century CE, Canada/US) Islamic studies scholar and former president of the Islamic Society of North America, the first woman to hold this position. Her scholarship on Islamic spirituality and law includes attention to women's roles in early Islamic communities.[74]

Ziba Mir-Hosseini (20th-21st century CE, Iran/UK) Anthropologist and legal scholar whose ethnographic work on Islamic family law in Iran and Morocco reveals how women navigate and sometimes challenge traditional interpretations. Her work bridges academic scholarship and legal reform advocacy.[75]

Riffat Hassan (20th-21st century CE, Pakistan/US) Theologian and women's rights activist whose Quranic hermeneutics challenge traditional interpretations that subordinate women. Her work on the creation narrative in Islamic texts offers alternative readings that support gender equality.[76]

Fatima Mernissi (1940-2015 CE, Morocco) Sociologist and Islamic feminist whose scholarship revealed how women's voices were systematically excluded from Islamic historical narratives. Her work The Veil and the Male Elite demonstrated methods for recovering women's authority in early Islamic sources.[77]

Amina Wadud (20th-21st century CE, United States/Malaysia) Islamic scholar and Quranic exegete whose book Qur'an and Woman offered a landmark feminist hermeneutic that distinguished between Quranic principles and patriarchal interpretations. Her leadership of a mixed-gender Friday prayer in 2005 sparked global debate about women's religious authority in Islam and challenged traditional restrictions on female religious leadership.[78]

Hinduism

Lopamudra (Vedic period, circa 1500-1000 BCE, India)* Philosopher-poet credited with composing hymns in the Rig Veda, particularly RV 1.179, where she debates spiritual practice and marital relations with her husband, the sage Agastya. Her verses reflect sophisticated theological thought about the relationship between spiritual discipline and human desire, representing one of the earliest examples of female authorship in world scripture.⁷⁹

Gargi Vachaknavi (Upanishadic era, circa 800-600 BCE, India)* Renowned philosopher featured in the Brihadaranyaka Upanishad as challenging the sage Yajnavalkya in public debate about the nature of ultimate reality (Brahman). Her sophisticated questions about cosmology and metaphysics demonstrate women's participation in the highest levels of Vedantic philosophical discourse.⁸⁰

Sita (Epic era, circa 500 BCE-500 CE, India)* Central female figure of the Ramayana, traditionally revered for her devotion to her husband Rama but also noted for her trials, exile, and ultimate rejection of return to royal life. Modern reinterpretations emphasize her agency and resistance, while traditional readings focus on her exemplification of feminine virtue. Her story continues to generate theological and ethical debate about women's roles in Hindu society.⁸¹

Draupadi (Epic era, circa 500 BCE-500 CE, India)* Heroine of the Mahabharata whose public humiliation and defiant questioning of dharma (righteous duty) make her one of the most complex figures in Hindu literature. Her challenges to male authority and her demands for justice have made her a symbol of resistance in contemporary feminist readings of Hindu texts.⁸²

Akka Mahadevi (12th century CE, Karnataka, India) Mystic poet in the Lingayat tradition who renounced social conventions, including clothing, as a sign of total spiritual dedication. Her vachanas (devotional verses) to the deity Channamallikarjuna express passionate devotion while challenging social norms about women's behavior and spiritual autonomy.[83]

Andal (9th century CE, Tamil Nadu, India) The only female among the twelve Alvar saints of Tamil Vaishnavism, celebrated for her passionate devotional hymns to Vishnu. Her Tiruppavai and Nachiyar Tirumozhi continue to be recited in South Indian temples, though their erotic spiritual imagery has often been interpreted through conventional frameworks that minimize her theological innovations.[84]

Mirabai (circa 1498-1546 CE, Rajasthan, India) Royal-born bhakti poet who rejected social expectations and caste restrictions to pursue devotional union with Krishna. Her songs, widely sung across India, emphasize spiritual surrender and divine love while implicitly critiquing social hierarchies and women's subordination within marriage and family structures.[85]

Lalla (Lalleshwari) (14th century CE, Kashmir) Kashmiri Shaivite mystic whose vakhs (short poems) combine yogic insight, non-dual philosophy, and personal spiritual struggle. Her verses influenced both Hindu and Muslim mystical traditions in Kashmir and represent one of the earliest female voices in Kashmiri literature.[86]

Janabai (13th-14th century CE, Maharashtra) Devotee of the Varkari saint Namdev and composer of abhangs (devotional songs) that articulate the spiritual experiences of a servant woman. Her poetry demonstrates how domestic work could become a form of devotional practice and divine service.[87]

Avvaiyar (multiple periods, Tamil Nadu)* Name shared by several Tamil women poets across different centuries. The later Avvaiyar (10th century CE) produced moral and devotional literature still taught to children, while earlier figures contributed to classical Tamil poetry. Their collective work shaped Tamil religious and ethical literature.[88]

Bahinabai (1628-1700 CE, Maharashtra) Varkari poet whose abhangs describe her struggles as a woman seeking spiritual life while fulfilling domestic duties. Her verses provide insight into the tensions between devotional aspirations and social expectations for women in medieval India.[89]

Tarigonda Venkamamba (1730-1817 CE, Andhra Pradesh) Devotional poet who composed thousands of verses in Telugu dedicated to Lord Venkateshwara. Her work demonstrates the continuation of women's devotional poetry traditions into the modern period and influenced later devotional music.[90]

Gangasati (13th century CE, Gujarat) Saint-poet in the Pranami tradition whose compositions are still sung in rural Gujarat and Rajasthan. Her verses, transmitted orally for centuries, emphasize devotional surrender and ethical living within domestic life.[91]

Mahadevi Verma (1907-1987 CE, India) Hindi poet whose work draws heavily on mystical and devotional traditions while addressing modern women's experiences. Though primarily a secular writer, her poetry demonstrates continuity with classical Indian women's spiritual literature.⁹²

Arti Dhand (21st century CE, Canada/India) Scholar of the Mahabharata whose feminist readings challenge traditional interpretations of female characters. Her work reveals how attention to women's perspectives can transform understanding of classical Hindu texts.⁹³

Vasudha Narayanan (20th-21st century CE, India/US) Scholar of South Indian Hindu traditions whose work on women's roles in temple traditions and devotional practices demonstrates the continuing vitality of female religious authority in contemporary Hinduism.⁹⁴

Laurie Patton (20th-21st century CE, US) Sanskrit scholar and translator whose work on Vedic literature includes attention to female voices and feminine imagery in ancient Hindu texts. Her scholarship reveals the presence of women's perspectives in classical Sanskrit literature.⁹⁵

Mata Khivi (15th century CE, Punjab, Sikhism) Wife of Guru Angad, the second Sikh Guru, praised in the Guru Granth Sahib for establishing and maintaining the communal kitchen (langar) that embodies Sikh principles of equality and service. Her institutional role in early Sikhism demonstrates women's essential contributions to the tradition's development.⁹⁶

Bibi Nanaki (15th century CE, Punjab, Sikhism) Sister of Guru Nanak and his first follower, traditionally regarded as the first person to recognize his spiritual authority. Though she left no writings, her early support of Sikh teachings makes her one of the first transmitters of the tradition.[97]

Mai Bhago (late 17th-early 18th century CE, Punjab, Sikhism) Sikh warrior and spiritual leader who rallied forty Sikh soldiers to defend Guru Gobind Singh. Her martial and spiritual leadership challenged conventional gender roles while demonstrating women's capacity for religious and military authority in Sikhism.[98]

Other Traditions

Sun Bu'er (1124-1182 CE, China, Daoism) One of the Seven Taoist Masters and founder of the female branch of the Quanzhen school of Daoism. Her writings on internal alchemy and meditation practices, preserved in the Daoist canon, provided guidance specifically adapted to women's spiritual cultivation and influenced generations of female Daoist practitioners.[99]

Maria Sabina (1894-1985 CE, Oaxaca, Mexico, Mazatec) Mazatec curandera (healer) and poet who used psilocybin mushrooms in healing rituals while chanting prayers and songs considered divine transmissions. Though her practices were later appropriated and commercialized by outsiders, her role as a spiritual transmitter of indigenous wisdom remains deeply respected within Mazatec cosmology.[100]

He Xiangu (8th century CE, China, Daoism) One of the Eight Immortals in Daoist tradition, she represents the feminine principle in Daoist spiritual achievement. Her legends preserve teachings about women's capacity for spiritual transformation and immortality through Daoist practices.[101]

Wei Huacun (252-334 CE, China, Daoism) Founder of the Shangqing (Highest Clarity) school of Daoism who received revelations that became foundational texts for later Daoist practice. Her spiritual authority was recognized by both male and female practitioners and influenced Daoist meditation techniques.[102]

Mazu (Tianhou) (960-987 CE, China, Chinese folk religion) Deified woman whose cult became central to Chinese maritime religion. Her temples preserve oral traditions and ritual practices that demonstrate how local women could achieve divine status and continuing spiritual authority in Chinese religious culture.[103]

Queen Mother of the West (Xi Wangmu) (Ancient China, Chinese mythology/Daoism)* Powerful goddess figure in Chinese religion whose myths preserve teachings about feminine divine authority and spiritual cultivation. Her stories, transmitted through both elite and popular texts, represent one of the most enduring feminine divine figures in Chinese culture.[104]

Kateri Tekakwitha (1656-1680 CE, Mohawk Nation) Algonquin-Mohawk woman who converted to Christianity while maintaining indigenous spiritual practices. Canonized by the Catholic Church in 2012, her synthesis of Christian and indigenous traditions demonstrates alternative approaches to religious identity and authority.[105]

Zitkala-Sa (Red Bird) (1876-1938 CE, Yankton Dakota) Writer and activist whose autobiographical works document the tension between indigenous spiritual traditions and Christian missionary education. Her writings preserve Dakota religious concepts while critiquing forced assimilation policies.[106]

Roberta Blackgoat (1917-2002 CE, Diné/Navajo Nation) Traditional medicine woman and activist who preserved Diné religious teachings while resisting forced relocation from ancestral lands. Her speeches and interviews demonstrate how indigenous women maintain spiritual authority in contemporary contexts.[107]

Winona LaDuke (20th-21st century CE, Anishinaabe) Environmental activist and writer whose work integrates indigenous spiritual teachings with contemporary environmental advocacy. Her books demonstrate how traditional indigenous knowledge systems offer alternatives to Western approaches to nature and spirituality.[108]

Grandmother Agnes Baker Pilgrim (1924-2019 CE, Takelma) Tribal elder and spiritual leader who worked to preserve traditional Takelma spiritual practices and participated in international indigenous women's councils. Her teachings emphasized the spiritual responsibility of indigenous women as keepers of traditional knowledge.[109]

Linda Hogan (20th-21st century CE, Chickasaw) Poet and novelist whose work draws on Chickasaw spiritual traditions while addressing contemporary environmental and social issues.

Her writing demonstrates the continuing relevance of indigenous women's spiritual perspectives.[110]

Paula Gunn Allen (1939-2008 CE, Laguna Pueblo/Sioux) Scholar and poet whose The Sacred Hoop recovered traditions of Native American women's spiritual and political authority. Her work challenged both patriarchal and colonial interpretations of indigenous cultures and influenced Native American feminist scholarship.[111]

Ibu Gedong Bagoes Oka (1921-2011 CE, Bali, Indonesia, Balinese Hinduism) High priestess (pedanda) and one of the first women to achieve the highest level of Balinese Hindu religious authority. Her ordination challenged traditional gender restrictions while maintaining orthodox religious practices.[112]

Raden Ajeng Kartini (1879-1904 CE, Java, Indonesia, Islam/Javanese synthesis) Javanese aristocrat and early feminist whose letters demonstrate sophisticated engagement with both Islamic and Javanese spiritual traditions. Her writings influenced Indonesian women's education and religious interpretation.[113]

Shamima Shaikh (1960-1998 CE, South Africa) Islamic feminist and journalist who challenged gender restrictions in South African mosques and Islamic education. Her activism demonstrated how contemporary Muslim women could use traditional sources to advocate for gender equality.[114]

Sachiko Murata (20th-21st century CE, Japan/US) Scholar of Islamic philosophy whose work on gender symbolism in Islamic thought reveals how traditional Islamic sources contain resources for understanding divine nature beyond conventional gender categories. Her scholarship bridges Islamic and East Asian spiritual traditions.[115]

Seyran Ateş (20th-21st century CE, Turkey/Germany) Lawyer and Islamic reformer who founded a liberal mosque in Berlin that challenges traditional gender segregation and women's exclusion from religious leadership. Her activism demonstrates contemporary efforts to transform Islamic practice through appeal to foundational sources.[116]

Appendix B: Key Manuscripts and Archaeological Discoveries Involving Female Contributors

Methodological Note: Attribution of manuscripts to female scribes, patrons, or contributors is inferred through multiple types of evidence including paleographic analysis (handwriting patterns), colophon signatures, grammatical markers, linguistic patterns, patronage records, and archaeological context. While some attributions are certain, others represent scholarly consensus based on circumstantial evidence. Readers should note that gender inference from handwriting analysis remains an evolving field with ongoing scholarly debate.

Each entry includes the manuscript or artifact, approximate date, location, and significance to the study of women's sacred roles. Where known, specific women are named; where anonymous, their presence is inferred through scholarly analysis. Cross-references to Appendix A biographies are provided where relevant.

Buddhism

The Pali Canon's Therigatha (Poems of the Elder Nuns) 1st century BCE (oral origins earlier), Sri Lanka Preserved in the Pali Tipitaka, this collection of verses by early Buddhist nuns is one of the oldest known religious texts attributed to women. The seventy-three poems, attributed to named nuns including Mahapajapati Gotami, Kisagotami, and Vimala (see Appendix

A), provide direct testimony of women's enlightenment experiences. Rediscovered and translated systematically in the 20th century, it has become a cornerstone of feminist Buddhist studies.[1]

Dunhuang Manuscripts 4th-11th centuries CE, Dunhuang Caves, China Among the approximately 50,000 manuscripts discovered in Cave 17, thousands of Buddhist texts include colophons naming female patrons, translators, and sponsors. Notable examples include Pelliot Chinese 2056, which records donations by "the female disciple Huixiang for her deceased mother," and several sutras copied "by order of Lady Zhao" (see Appendix A). Paleographic analysis has identified distinctive scribal hands suggesting female authorship in manuscripts such as Stein 2144 and Pelliot 3915.[2]

Gandhari Buddhist Manuscripts 1st-3rd centuries CE, Afghanistan/Pakistan Birch bark scrolls discovered in Afghanistan include early Buddhist texts with colophons mentioning female patrons and references to bhikkhuni communities. Manuscript 19 from the Schøyen Collection contains verses reminiscent of the Therigatha, suggesting broader traditions of women's Buddhist poetry than previously known.[3]

Tibetan Nunnery Manuscripts 12th-17th centuries CE, Tibet Recent cataloging of manuscripts from Samding and other nunneries has revealed extensive copying activities by Tibetan nuns. Manuscripts such as those preserved at Mindroling include colophons by "Gelongma Palmo" and other named nuns, demonstrating women's roles in preserving Tibetan

Buddhist literature. Stylometric analysis suggests distinctive scribal patterns associated with female monastic communities.[4]

Christianity

The Gospel of Mary (Papyrus Berolinensis 8502) 2nd century CE composition (5th century CE manuscript), Egypt Discovered in 1896 in a Cairo antiquities market, this Coptic codex contains the Gospel of Mary, which centers on Mary Magdalene as a recipient of post-resurrection revelations (see Appendix A). The manuscript features theological dialogue between Mary and male disciples, including resistance from Peter to her authority. Though partially damaged, it challenges canonical portrayals and suggests early Christian traditions recognizing female apostolic authority. Now housed in the Berlin Papyrus Collection.[5]

Codex Sangallensis 1395 (Latin Gospel fragments) 9th century CE, St. Gallen, Switzerland This manuscript contains marginal notations and decorated initials identified by paleographers as the work of female scribes from a double monastery. The distinctive letter formations and use of feminine grammatical markers in Latin glosses provide evidence for women's participation in Carolingian scriptoriums. These traces help reconstruct the lost female monastic scribal tradition of the early medieval period.[6]

The Murbach Gospels 9th century CE, Alsace Contains interlinear Old High German glosses showing grammatical patterns associated with feminine speech. Recent linguistic analysis suggests these translations were produced by nuns, possibly at nearby Hohenburg Abbey under Abbess Relindis.[7]

Codex Wessobrunnensis 9th century CE, Bavaria Contains the Wessobrunn Prayer, a theologically sophisticated Old High German text. Dialectal analysis and formatting patterns point to composition in a female monastic environment, possibly Frauenchiemsee Abbey. The manuscript's preservation of both Latin and vernacular traditions suggests women's roles in translating sacred texts for lay audiences.[8]

Book of Kells (Trinity College MS 58) 8th-9th century CE, Ireland While primarily attributed to male scribes, recent analysis has identified marginal decorations and corrections in hands that may be female, possibly nuns from Kildare or other Irish monasteries with scriptoriums. The evidence remains circumstantial but suggests female participation in the production of this renowned illuminated manuscript.[9]

The Book of Margery Kempe 15th century CE, England Rediscovered in 1934, this is the first known autobiography in English. Though dictated rather than written by Kempe herself (see Appendix A), its production and survival depended on networks of women who preserved vernacular piety outside clerical control. The manuscript reveals the existence of female literary networks in late medieval England.[10]

Judaism

Cairo Genizah Discoveries 9th-13th centuries CE, Egypt This treasure trove of approximately 280,000 discarded Jewish texts includes household liturgical guides, women's prayer books (tkhines), and legal documents bearing women's signatures. Notable finds include marriage contracts negotiated by women, Yiddish prayers for childbirth and domestic life, and business correspondence demonstrating female literacy levels higher than previously assumed. The collection suggests a vibrant tradition of women's religious writing.[11]

Yiddish Tkhines Manuscripts 17th-19th centuries CE, Ashkenazic Europe Written for and often by women such as Sarah bas Tovim (see Appendix A), these vernacular prayer books represent a parallel textual tradition. Manuscripts include marginal commentary in women's hands, alternate blessings, and autobiographical references. Some collections preserve the work of identified female translators including Bella bat Jacob and Serel bat Jacob ha-Levi.[12]

Spanish Hebrew Manuscripts with Female Colophons 13th-15th centuries CE, Iberian Peninsula Several Hebrew manuscripts from medieval Spain include colophons identifying female scribes or patrons. The Kennicott Bible (Oxford, Bodleian MS Kennicott 1) includes a note mentioning "Miriam daughter of Benayah" as contributing to its production, while other manuscripts from Toledo and Córdoba record female patronage of biblical and liturgical texts.[13]

Dead Sea Scrolls (Qumran) 2nd century BCE-1st century CE, Judea While the sectarian community appears to have been predominantly male, some fragments contain feminine grammatical endings or priestly titles that may indicate female religious roles. 4Q502 (Ritual of Marriage) includes language suggesting women's participation in community ceremonies, though interpretation remains debated among scholars.[14]

Islam

Hafsa's Mushaf (Lost Prototype Codex) 7th century CE, Medina The Quranic codex compiled by Zayd ibn Thabit was preserved in the care of Hafsa bint Umar (see Appendix A) before the Uthmanic standardization. Though the original manuscript is lost, early Islamic sources confirm her custodianship, representing rare institutional recognition of women's roles in Quranic preservation. Her copy reportedly served as the base text for the standardized Quran.[15]

Ijaza Collections Featuring Female Transmitters 8th-14th centuries CE, Syria, Iraq, North Africa Teaching licenses (ijazas) documenting hadith transmission networks frequently name women as authorities in the transmission chain (isnad). Preserved examples include certificates for Zaynab bint Kamal (d. 1339) and Shuhda al-Katiba (see Appendix A), stored in libraries across Cairo, Damascus, and Istanbul. These documents provide concrete evidence of women's recognized scholarly authority.[16]

Cordoba Quran Manuscripts 10th-14th centuries CE, Al-Andalus Several Quran manuscripts from Islamic Spain include colophons identifying female scribes. A 12th-century mushaf in the Biblioteca Nacional (Madrid, MS 4) bears the signature "copied by Fatima bint Muhammad al-Qurtubi," while other manuscripts from Córdoba and Seville record female patronage and copying activities.[17]

Timbuktu Manuscript Collections 14th-17th centuries CE, Mali Private family libraries preserve Quran manuscripts with annotations indicating matrilineal transmission and women-led study circles. The Ahmed Baba Institute collection includes texts with marginal notes by female scholars including members of the Aqit and Kati families, demonstrating women's participation in West African Islamic scholarship networks.[18]

Mamluk Endowment Documents 13th-16th centuries CE, Egypt and Syria Waqf (religious endowment) documents frequently record women as founders of madrasas, libraries, and scriptoriums. The endowment deed of Khatun (Lady) Tatar al-Hijaziyya (d. 1257) established a madrasa in Damascus with provisions for female teachers and copyists, while similar documents from Cairo record women's patronage of manuscript production.[19]

Hinduism

Bhakti Poetry Manuscripts 15th-17th centuries CE, India Palm-leaf manuscripts of devotional poetry preserve the works of female poet-saints including Mirabai, Andal, and Akka Mahadevi (see Appendix A). Linguistic analysis reveals feminine verbal inflections and first-person feminine pronouns that confirm female authorship. Regional collections show manuscript traditions maintained within women's devotional circles across different linguistic regions.[20]

Chola Temple Inscriptions 10th-13th centuries CE, Tamil Nadu Bronze and stone inscriptions at major temples record women's donations of manuscripts and liturgical texts. The

Brihadishvara Temple at Thanjavur includes inscriptions mentioning Queen Lokamahadevi's patronage of Sanskrit manuscripts, while similar records from other Chola temples document female involvement in textual preservation.[21]

Vijayanagara Court Manuscripts 14th-16th centuries CE, Karnataka Royal manuscripts from the Vijayanagara court include colophons mentioning female patrons and scholars. A 15th-century manuscript of the Devi Mahatmya (Oriental Research Institute, Mysore) includes verses attributed to "Ganga Devi, learned in the sastras," suggesting women's participation in courtly literary culture.[22]

Kerala Palm-Leaf Collections 16th-19th centuries CE, Kerala Traditional family collections (tharavads) preserve palm-leaf manuscripts with evidence of female scribes and commentators. Some texts include signatures of women from Nambudiri Brahmin families, while others show feminine grammatical forms in Malayalam glosses on Sanskrit texts.[23]

Other Traditions

Daoist Shangqing Manuscripts 4th-12th centuries CE, China Manuscripts associated with the Shangqing (Highest Clarity) school founded by Wei Huacun (see Appendix A) include texts attributed to female practitioners. The Zhen'gao (Declarations of the Perfected) preserves revelations received by women, while later manuscripts from the Quanzhen school include works by Sun Bu'er and other female masters.[24]

Sikh Historical Documents 17th-19th centuries CE, Punjab Manuscripts from gurdwaras and private collections include references to women's roles in preserving Sikh texts. Documents from the period of Guru Gobind Singh mention Mai Bhago (see Appendix A) and other women warriors, while later manuscripts record women's participation in maintaining scriptural traditions during periods of persecution.[25]

Ethiopian Christian Manuscripts 13th-18th centuries CE, Ethiopia Ge'ez manuscripts from Ethiopian monasteries include colophons mentioning female patrons and scribes. The Kebra Nagast manuscripts from Gishen Maryam monastery include commentary attributed to "Walatta Maryam," while psalters from other collections bear feminine signatures and marginal annotations.[26]

Aztec and Maya Codices Pre-Columbian period, Mesoamerica Surviving codices include iconography of female figures with glyphs indicating ritual or scribal functions. The Dresden Codex contains representations of female deities associated with writing and prophecy, while ceramic evidence suggests women's participation in maintaining calendar and astronomical texts.[27]

Balinese Lontar Manuscripts 15th-20th centuries CE, Indonesia Palm-leaf manuscripts (lontar) from Balinese Hindu tradition include texts copied by female scribes from priestly families. Recent cataloging has identified manuscripts signed by women including members of Brahmana and Pande families, indicating female participation in preserving Hindu-Javanese religious literature.[28]

West African Islamic Manuscripts 16th-19th centuries CE, West Africa Manuscript collections from Timbuktu, Djenné, and other centers include texts by female scholars such as Nana Asma'u (see Appendix A). Private libraries preserve works in Arabic, Ajami (African languages in Arabic script), and local scripts, demonstrating women's multilingual scholarly activities across the region.[29]

Appendix C: Glossary of Roles

This glossary defines religious and scholarly roles that women have held across traditions, both historically and in contemporary contexts. Terms are organized alphabetically and include cross-cultural comparisons where relevant. References to specific examples can be found in Appendix A.

Abbess A female head of a Christian monastic community, especially in medieval Europe. Some abbesses oversaw scriptoriums, taught theology, and exercised considerable political and liturgical authority equivalent to male bishops. Notable examples include Hildegard of Bingen and Heloise of Argenteuil (see Appendix A). Male equivalent: Abbot.

Bhikkhuni (Pali/Sanskrit) A fully ordained Buddhist nun who has taken the complete set of monastic vows (usually 311 precepts). Bhikkhuni lineages were established by the Buddha but disappeared in some Theravada traditions due to historical decline or legal restrictions. They remain vital in Mahayana contexts, and revival efforts are ongoing globally. Examples include Mahapajapati Gotami and contemporary figures like Tenzin Palmo (see Appendix A). Male equivalent: Bhikkhu.

Cantor (Hazzanit) (Hebrew) A woman who leads musical prayer in Jewish liturgical settings. While traditionally male in Orthodox settings, female cantors have been recognized since the late 20th century in Reform, Conservative, and Reconstructionist communities. The role involves extensive knowledge of Hebrew liturgy and musical traditions. Male equivalent: Hazzan.

Curandera (Spanish) A traditional healer in Latin American indigenous and mestizo communities who uses plants, prayers, and ritual knowledge to treat illness. Many curanderas maintain oral traditions of sacred songs and medicinal knowledge passed down through female lineages. Examples include Maria Sabina (see Appendix A). Male equivalent: Curandero.

Dharma Master (Fashi) (Chinese) A Buddhist teacher authorized to transmit dharma teachings and perform certain ceremonies. In medieval Chinese Buddhism, some women achieved this title, though documentation is limited. The role required extensive scriptural knowledge and recognized spiritual attainment.

Fakira/Murida (Arabic) A female Sufi initiate or seeker of the spiritual path (murida), or an advanced female spiritual guide (fakira). Some served as transmitters of poetry, mystical teaching, and oral commentary. Notable examples include Rabia al-Adawiyya (see Appendix A). Male equivalents: Fakir/Murid.

Griot/Griotte (West African) Traditional storytellers and oral historians in West African societies. Female griots (griottes) often specialize in women's stories, religious narratives, and ceremonial music. They serve as keepers of oral religious and historical traditions. Male equivalent: Griot.

Hafiza (Arabic, feminine of Hafiz) A woman who has memorized the entire Quran. While male huffaz are more commonly recognized, historical records include many women who were certified and who taught Quranic recitation to both genders. The title requires mastery of proper pronunciation (tajwid) and often includes knowledge of variant readings. Male equivalent: Hafiz.

Medicine Woman A female spiritual healer and keeper of sacred knowledge in various Native American traditions. Medicine women often maintain oral traditions of healing ceremonies, plant knowledge, and sacred songs. Their authority derives from spiritual calling and community recognition. Examples include Roberta Blackgoat (see Appendix A). Male equivalent: Medicine Man.

Midrashist A woman who interprets or creates midrash (rabbinic biblical commentary). While rarely recognized historically, modern feminist scholars have reclaimed this role through reinterpretation and expansion of Jewish sacred texts. The practice involves creative interpretation that reveals deeper meanings in biblical narratives.

Mystic A person who claims direct experience of the divine, often through visions, dreams, or inner union. Mystical insight has been one of the few pathways through which women across traditions were historically able to express theological authority. Examples span all traditions, from Julian of Norwich to Mirabai (see Appendix A).

Nabiya/Prophetess (Hebrew/Arabic) A woman recognized as a messenger of divine insight. Examples include Miriam and Deborah in Judaism, Huldah as a temple prophet, and various figures in early Christian and Islamic contexts. Female prophecy was often minimized or reinterpreted by later male authorities. Male equivalent: Nabi/Prophet.

Nun A woman who has taken monastic vows in Buddhism, Christianity, or Jainism. In many historical cases, nuns were not only contemplatives but also scribes, teachers, ritual leaders, and mystics. The specific vows and roles vary significantly across traditions and time periods.

Pandita (Sanskrit) A learned woman, especially in Buddhist or Hindu contexts. In traditional usage, the term indicates mastery of sacred texts and philosophical traditions. Some contemporary Buddhist women have reclaimed this title, while in Hindu contexts it historically applied to women with exceptional Sanskrit learning.

Poet-Saint (Bhakta/Alvar/Sufi poet) A woman whose devotional verses were considered sacred or semi-scriptural within a tradition. Figures like Andal, Mirabai, and Rabia al-Adawiyya fall into this category, often composing in regional or vernacular languages that made religious ideas accessible to broader communities (see Appendix A).

Qaria (Arabic) A female reciter of the Quran. Some were renowned for their voice and memorization skills, though rarely appointed to formal public roles. In some communities, women teach tajwid (proper recitation) to both boys and girls. The role requires extensive training in Quranic pronunciation and melodic traditions.

Rabbi (Hebrew) In contemporary Reform, Conservative, and Reconstructionist Judaism, women serve as rabbis with full ordination and authority to interpret Jewish law, lead worship, and perform life-cycle ceremonies. The first woman rabbi, Regina Jonas, was ordained in Germany in 1935 (see Appendix A). Orthodox Judaism continues to debate women's ordination.

Scribe (Soferet) A woman trained in the art of copying sacred texts by hand. While most historical scribes were male, manuscript analysis has identified numerous anonymous women scribes across Christian, Buddhist, and Jewish contexts. In contemporary Judaism, women trained as soferot write Torah scrolls, megillot, and other sacred documents (see Appendix A).

Shaman A spiritual practitioner who serves as intermediary between human and spirit worlds, often in indigenous traditions. Female shamans frequently specialize in healing, divination, and maintaining oral traditions of sacred knowledge. Their authority typically derives from spiritual calling and community recognition.

Sutra Patron/Donor A woman who commissioned or paid for the copying of Buddhist texts. In Mahayana Buddhism, such merit-making acts were considered sacred, and inscriptions sometimes name royal women or lay devotees. These patrons played crucial roles in preserving and disseminating Buddhist literature.

Tafsir Scholar A woman who interprets the Quran. While women rarely wrote formal tafsir (commentary) in classical Islam, some were cited as exegetical authorities in oral traditions, and contemporary feminist scholarship has produced important Quranic interpreters like Amina Wadud and Asma Barlas (see Appendix A).

Terton (Tibetan) A "treasure-revealer" in Tibetan Buddhism who discovers hidden texts (terma) through visionary experience. Some women have held this role, including historical figures like Sera Khandro, though their recognition has often been limited compared to male tertons.

Translator (Vācaka/Mufassira/Sutra Interpreter) A woman who renders sacred texts into other languages, often orally or with commentary. Female translators were particularly important in Buddhist traditions and indigenous communities where textual transmission relied heavily on oral performance and cultural adaptation.

Visionary A woman whose revelations, often received through dreams or ecstasies, were believed to contain sacred truth. While mystics might use visions privately, visionaries often recorded or dictated their experiences for others, such as Hildegard of Bingen or Julian of Norwich (see Appendix A). The role provided alternative authority for women excluded from formal religious education.

Wisdom Keeper In various indigenous traditions, an elder woman responsible for maintaining and transmitting sacred knowledge, ceremonies, and oral traditions. Wisdom Keepers often serve as final authorities on proper ritual practice and cultural protocols. Examples include Grandmother Agnes Baker Pilgrim (see Appendix A).

Cross-References:

- For specific examples of women in these roles, see Appendix A: Brief Biographies
- For manuscript evidence of women's scribal work, see Appendix B
- For further reading on women's religious roles, see Appendix D

Appendix D: Further Reading

This bibliography prioritizes works that are rigorous, readable, and relevant to themes of gender, sacred texts, and historical recovery. Each entry includes full publication information and annotations describing relevance and scope. "Essential starter" titles are marked with ★ for readers new to each tradition.

Buddhism

★ **The First Buddhist Women: Translations and Commentary on the Therigatha** by Susan Murcott (Berkeley: Parallax Press, 1991) A foundational and accessible translation of the poems of the early Buddhist nuns, with insightful commentary linking ancient voices to contemporary questions about women's spiritual authority.

Sakyadhita: Daughters of the Buddha edited by Karma Lekshe Tsomo (Ithaca: Snow Lion Publications, 1988) Collected essays from the international Buddhist women's movement, blending historical research with activist perspectives on ordination, education, and practice.

Buddhist Women Across Cultures: Realizations edited by Karma Lekshe Tsomo (Albany: SUNY Press, 1999) Comprehensive examination of women's roles across Theravada, Mahayana, and Vajrayana contexts, including contemporary revival movements.

Women Under Primitive Buddhism by I.B. Horner (London: Routledge, 1930; reprint, Delhi: Motilal Banarsidass, 1975) Classic scholarly study of early Buddhist women, though dated in terminology, remains valuable for its comprehensive treatment of Pali sources.

Passionate Enlightenment: Women in Tantric Buddhism by Miranda Shaw (Princeton: Princeton University Press, 1994) Groundbreaking study of women's roles in Tantric Buddhism, challenging assumptions about male dominance in esoteric traditions.

Buddhism After Patriarchy: A Feminist History, Analysis, and Reconstruction of Buddhism by Rita M. Gross (Albany: SUNY Press, 1993) Comprehensive feminist analysis of Buddhist tradition with proposals for inclusive reconstruction.

Christianity

★ **The Gospel of Mary of Magdala: Jesus and the First Woman Apostle** by Karen L. King (Santa Rosa: Polebridge Press, 2003) Definitive scholarly translation and analysis of the Gospel of Mary, emphasizing its theological and historical significance for understanding women's early Christian leadership.

In Memory of Her: A Feminist Theological Reconstruction of Christian Origins by Elisabeth Schüssler Fiorenza (New York: Crossroad, 1983) Seminal work demonstrating women's leadership in early Christianity and developing feminist hermeneutical methods.

Holy Feast and Holy Fast: The Religious Significance of Food to Medieval Women by Caroline Walker Bynum (Berkeley: University of California Press, 1987) Innovative study of medieval Christian women's mysticism, focusing on embodied spirituality and alternative religious authority.

Sister of Wisdom: St. Hildegard's Theology of the Feminine by Barbara Newman (Berkeley: University of California Press, 1987) Comprehensive study of Hildegard of Bingen's theological innovations and feminine divine imagery.

The Book of Margery Kempe translated by B.A. Windeatt (London: Penguin Classics, 1985) First autobiography in English by a woman, with excellent scholarly introduction contextualizing medieval women's spirituality.

Women as Scribes: Manuscript Production and Monastic Reform in Twelfth-Century Bavaria by Alison I. Beach (Cambridge: Cambridge University Press, 2004) Groundbreaking study of women's roles in medieval manuscript production using paleographic evidence.

Power, Gender and Christian Mysticism by Grace Jantzen (Cambridge: Cambridge University Press, 1995) Feminist analysis of Christian mystical tradition examining how gender shaped spiritual authority.

Judaism

★ **Standing Again at Sinai: Judaism from a Feminist Perspective** by Judith Plaskow (San Francisco:

HarperSanFrancisco, 1990) Foundational work in Jewish feminist theology arguing for recovery and reinterpretation of women's voices in Jewish tradition.

Voices of the Matriarchs: Listening to the Prayers of Early Modern Jewish Women by Chava Weissler (Boston: Beacon Press, 1998) Scholarly study of tkhines (Yiddish women's prayers) revealing parallel tradition of Jewish women's spirituality.

Rereading the Rabbis: A Woman's Voice by Judith Hauptman (Boulder: Westview Press, 1998) Analysis of women in Talmudic literature, revealing evidence of female participation in rabbinic culture.

In the Wake of the Goddesses: Women, Culture, and the Biblical Transformation of Pagan Myth by Tikva Frymer-Kensky (New York: Free Press, 1992) Examination of how feminine divine imagery was suppressed in biblical literature.

Reading Ruth: Contemporary Women Reclaim a Sacred Story edited by Judith A. Kates and Gail Twersky Reimer (New York: Ballantine Books, 1994) Jewish women scholars and writers explore the Book of Ruth as site for feminist textual engagement.

The Misunderstood Jew: The Church and the Scandal of the Jewish Jesus by Amy-Jill Levine (San Francisco: HarperSanFrancisco, 2006) New Testament scholarship that bridges Jewish and Christian interpretation while recovering Jewish women's contexts.

Islam

★ **Women and Gender in Islam: Historical Roots of a Modern Debate** by Leila Ahmed (New Haven: Yale University Press, 1992) Pioneering work tracing Muslim women's history from the Prophet's era through modern reform movements, separating religious principles from cultural patriarchies.

Qur'an and Woman: Rereading the Sacred Text from a Woman's Perspective by Amina Wadud (New York: Oxford University Press, 1999) Seminal reinterpretation of the Quran emphasizing justice and gender equity, with methodological introduction to Islamic feminist hermeneutics.

"Believing Women" in Islam: Unreading Patriarchal Interpretations of the Qur'an by Asma Barlas (Austin: University of Texas Press, 2002) Comprehensive hermeneutical framework for reading the Quran as anti-patriarchal text.

Women and the Transmission of Religious Knowledge in Islam by Asma Sayeed (Cambridge: Cambridge University Press, 2013) Scholarly examination of women's roles in preserving and transmitting Islamic knowledge, particularly hadith.

The Lives of Muhammad by Kecia Ali (Cambridge, MA: Harvard University Press, 2014) Analysis of how biographical traditions about the Prophet shaped understanding of women in Islam.

Women in the Qur'an, Traditions, and Interpretation by Barbara Freyer Stowasser (New York: Oxford University Press, 1994) Academic exploration of women's portrayal in Islamic texts and evolution of interpretations.

One Woman's Jihad: Nana Asma'u, Scholar and Scribe by Beverly B. Mack and Jean Boyd (Bloomington: Indiana University Press, 2000) Biography of West African Islamic female scholar, demonstrating women's religious leadership beyond Middle Eastern contexts.

Hinduism

★ **Speaking of Siva** translated by A.K. Ramanujan (London: Penguin Classics, 1973) Classic translations of Kannada bhakti poets including Akka Mahadevi, with introduction discussing gender and language in devotional verse.

The Vernacular Veda: Revelation, Recitation, and Ritual by Vasudha Narayanan (Columbia: University of South Carolina Press, 1994) Study of Tamil devotional traditions including female poet-saints like Andal.

Songs of the Saints of India by John Stratton Hawley and Mark Juergensmeyer (New York: Oxford University Press, 2004) Comprehensive anthology including works by Mirabai and other female bhakti poets.

Women Writing in India: 600 B.C. to the Present edited by Susie Tharu and K. Lalita, 2 volumes (New York: The Feminist Press, 1991-1993) Monumental anthology featuring literary and religious writing by Indian women, including Vedic hymns and bhakti poetry.

Jewels of Authority: Women and Textual Tradition in Hindu India edited by Laurie L. Patton (New York: Oxford University Press, 2002) Collection examining women's roles in Hindu textual traditions from Vedic period to present.

Many Ramayanas: The Diversity of a Narrative Tradition in South Asia edited by Paula Richman (Berkeley: University of California Press, 1991) Includes feminist reinterpretations of Sita's story and women's agency in epic literature.

Sikhism

★ **Relocating Gender in Sikh History: Transformation, Meaning and Identity** by Doris R. Jakobsh (New Delhi: Oxford University Press, 2003) Comprehensive study of women's roles in Sikh tradition from the Gurus' period to present.

The Construction of Religious Boundaries: Culture, Identity, and Diversity in the Sikh Tradition by Harjot Oberoi (Chicago: University of Chicago Press, 1994) Includes discussion of women's religious authority and community leadership.

Sikh Women in England: Their Religious and Cultural Beliefs and Social Practices by Parminder Kaur Bakshi (Stoke-on-Trent: Trentham Books, 1995) Contemporary study of how Sikh women maintain and adapt religious traditions.

Indigenous and African Traditions

★ **The Sacred Hoop: Recovering the Feminine in American Indian Traditions** by Paula Gunn Allen (Boston: Beacon Press, 1986) Foundational work recovering traditions of Native American women's spiritual and political authority.

Daughters of Anowa: African Women and Patriarchy by Mercy Amba Oduyoye (Maryknoll: Orbis Books, 1995) African feminist theological perspective on traditional and contemporary women's religious roles.

Iroquoian Women: The Gantowisas by Barbara Alice Mann (New York: Peter Lang, 2000) Comprehensive study of women's roles in Haudenosaunee (Iroquois) spiritual and political traditions.

Recovering the Sacred: The Power of Naming and Claiming by Winona LaDuke (Boston: South End Press, 2005) Indigenous activist and scholar's perspective on traditional knowledge and environmental spirituality.

I Could Speak Until Tomorrow: Oriki, Women, and the Past in a Yoruba Town by Karin Barber (Washington, DC: Smithsonian Institution Press, 1991) Study of Yoruba praise poetry and women's roles in maintaining oral religious traditions.

East Asian Traditions

The Tao of Islam: A Sourcebook on Gender Relationships in Islamic Thought by Sachiko Murata (Albany: SUNY Press, 1992) Comparative study bridging Islamic and East Asian perspectives on feminine spiritual principles.

Transcendence and Divine Passion: The Queen Mother of the West in Medieval China by Suzanne E. Cahill (Stanford: Stanford University Press, 1993) Study of feminine divine figures in Chinese Daoist and popular religion.

Immortal Sisters: Secret Teachings of Taoist Women translated by Thomas Cleary (Boston: Shambhala, 1989) Translations of female Daoist masters' teachings on internal alchemy and meditation.

Lives of the Nuns: Biographies of Chinese Buddhist Nuns from the Fourth to Sixth Centuries translated by Kathryn Ann Tsai (Honolulu: University of Hawaii Press, 1994) Primary source translations revealing early Chinese Buddhist women's religious lives.

Comparative and Theoretical Studies

★ **Feminism and World Religions** edited by Arvind Sharma and Katherine K. Young (Albany: SUNY Press, 1999) Comprehensive collection with feminist perspectives on major world religions.

Gender and Religion edited by Ursula King (Oxford: Blackwell, 1995) Theoretical approaches to studying women in religious traditions globally.

Women in World Religions edited by Arvind Sharma (Albany: SUNY Press, 1987) Earlier but still valuable comparative study of women's roles across traditions.

Searching the Scriptures edited by Elisabeth Schüssler Fiorenza, 2 volumes (New York: Crossroad, 1993-1994) Feminist commentary on biblical and early Christian texts with methodological implications for other traditions.

Women's Sacred Scriptures edited by Kwok Pui-lan and Elisabeth Schüssler Fiorenza (Maryknoll: Orbis Books, 1998) Global perspectives on women's relationship to sacred texts.

Methodology and Recovery

★ **Digital Humanities and Manuscript Studies** edited by Peter Stokes and Edward Vanhoutte (Cambridge: Cambridge University Press, 2018) Introduction to how digital tools are revealing previously hidden voices in manuscript traditions.

The Hidden Hands: Women and Medieval Manuscript Culture edited by Mary Erler and Maryanne Kowaleski (Cambridge: Cambridge University Press, 2013) Studies of women's roles as scribes, patrons, and readers of medieval texts.

Feminist Biblical Interpretation by Letty M. Russell (Philadelphia: Westminster Press, 1985) Foundational work on feminist hermeneutical methods applicable across traditions.

Reading Women's Lives: The Politics of Biography edited by Caroline Heilbrun and Carolyn Heilbrun (New York: Teachers College Press, 1996) Methodological approaches to recovering women's historical experiences.

Computer-Aided Palaeography: Present and Future edited by Peter A. Stokes (Cambridge: Cambridge University Press, 2019) Technical but accessible overview of how technology assists manuscript analysis and attribution.

Contemporary Voices and Applications

Inside the Gender Jihad: Women's Reform in Islam by Amina Wadud (Oxford: Oneworld, 2006) Memoir and theological reflection by leading Islamic feminist scholar.

God's Phallus: And Other Problems for Men and Monotheism by Howard Eilberg-Schwartz (Boston: Beacon Press, 1994) Provocative analysis of masculine imagery in monotheistic traditions.

She Who Is: The Mystery of God in Feminist Theological Discourse by Elizabeth A. Johnson (New York: Crossroad, 1992) Christian feminist systematic theology incorporating insights from comparative religious studies.

Womanist Theology by Ada María Isasi-Díaz (Maryknoll: Orbis Books, 1996) Latina feminist theological methodology applicable to biblical and contemporary interpretation.

Cave in the Snow: Tenzin Palmo's Quest for Enlightenment by Vicki Mackenzie (New York: Riverhead Books, 1998) Biography of contemporary Buddhist nun and advocate for women's ordination.

Cross-References:

- For biographical information on scholars mentioned, see Appendix A
- For manuscript sources discussed in these works, see Appendix B
- For definitions of technical terms, see Appendix C: Glossary

Appendix E: Discussion Guide for Book Clubs and Classrooms

How to Use This Guide

This discussion guide invites structured conversation, respectful disagreement, and comparative reflection across traditions. It's designed for flexible use—whether one chapter at a time, one Part at a time, or as a full-course companion. Each section includes:

- Shared Questions for All Chapters
- Comparative Exercises Across Traditions
- Tradition-Specific Prompts
- Capstone Prompts for Deeper Analysis
- Writing and Reflection Assignments
- Facilitator Tips for Sensitive Discussions

Educators and facilitators are encouraged to adapt the questions based on audience background (religious, secular, academic, interfaith, etc.) and learning context (in-person, online, asynchronous).

Shared Questions (For All Chapters)

1. What surprised you most in this chapter? Why do you think this figure or contribution was historically overlooked?

2. How did the sacred text or tradition both include and exclude women's voices? Were these exclusions deliberate, structural, or interpretive?
3. What kinds of evidence were used to reconstruct this woman's story? How do we assess credibility when sources are fragmentary or indirect?
4. If you were to teach or retell this woman's story in your own tradition or community, what would you emphasize?
5. How did this chapter shift your perception of who transmits or interprets sacred truth?
6. What intersections of gender with class, race, caste, or colonial power dynamics do you notice in this woman's story?

Comparative Exercises (Use Across Parts)

Mapping Erasure

- Compare how two different traditions marginalized female voices. What methods were used: omission, misattribution, reinterpretation, destruction, etc.?
- Chart these methods across time and tradition to identify shared patterns.
- Consider how colonialism, class structures, or racial hierarchies may have compounded gender-based exclusions.

Recovering Voices

- Examine the strategies women used to preserve or transmit sacred knowledge: mysticism, oral storytelling, scribal work, coded writing, patronage.
- Which strategies seem most effective? Which were most fragile?
- How did women navigate intersecting forms of marginalization?

The Role of Text vs. Performance

- In which traditions did sacred roles depend more on oral/ritual performance than on written texts? How did that affect whose voices were preserved?
- Compare Indigenous, African diaspora, and oral traditions with text-centered religions.

Cultural Crossings

- Choose one figure from a "major" tradition and one from the "other traditions" chapter. Compare how each interacted with power, authority, and sacred space.
- Consider how geography, colonial history, or cultural contact shaped their experiences.

Contemporary Connections

- Identify a historical figure from the book and research a contemporary woman working in similar roles today (scholar, spiritual leader, reformer, etc.).

- How do modern contexts both echo and differ from historical patterns?

Tradition-Specific Prompts

Christianity

- How do the stories of Mary Magdalene and medieval mystics challenge or confirm your understanding of early Christian leadership?
- What role did monastic communities play in preserving or constraining women's spiritual authority?

Islam

- How does Aisha bint Abi Bakr's story illuminate the relationship between personal authority and institutional power in early Islam?
- Compare the roles of female hadith transmitters with women scholars in other Islamic sciences.

Buddhism

- What does the Therīgāthā reveal about early Buddhist attitudes toward women's spiritual achievement?
- How did the establishment of the bhikkhuni order both empower and limit women's religious authority?

Judaism

- How do prophetesses like Miriam and Deborah compare with later rabbinic attitudes toward women's religious roles?
- What can we learn from Jewish women's liturgical and educational contributions in domestic settings?

Hinduism

- How do mythological figures like Sita and Draupadi function differently in devotional versus scholarly interpretations?
- Compare the agency of bhakti poets like Mirabai with women in more orthodox settings.

Indigenous and Oral Traditions

- What unique challenges and opportunities exist for recovering women's voices in traditions that prioritize oral transmission?
- How do colonial disruptions complicate our understanding of traditional gender roles?

Contemporary and Emerging Traditions

- How are modern women creating new forms of spiritual authority within traditional frameworks?
- What can we learn from LGBTQ+ and non-binary spiritual leaders about gender and sacred authority?

Capstone Chapter Prompts

Each Capstone (Chapters 7, 13, and Conclusion) includes a **Scholar Debate** and **"What Would Have Changed?"** sections. Use the following to engage deeper:

Scholar Debate Reflection

- Which scholar's view do you find most persuasive in this debate? Why?
- How does disagreement among scholars shape our understanding of women's historical roles?
- What methodological or ideological differences do you notice among the scholars?

What Would Have Changed?

- Choose one of the "What If" scenarios. In what ways would the tradition or community look different if that woman's voice had been preserved or centered?
- Reflect on how theological doctrines, practices, or hierarchies might shift.
- Consider both positive possibilities and potential new problems or conflicts.

Limits of Recovery

- What are the ethical implications of reconstructing women's voices from limited evidence?

- How do we balance honoring women's agency with acknowledging the gaps in our knowledge?
- When might recovery work risk imposing contemporary values on historical contexts?

Writing & Reflection Assignments

For College or Adult Learners:

Short Essay (750-1,000 words): Choose a woman from any chapter and write a profile including both what we know and what we must interpret from silence. Address the methodological challenges of your reconstruction.

Creative Assignment: Write a fictional but historically grounded letter, poem, or prayer from the perspective of a woman in the book who was not allowed to speak publicly. Include a brief reflection on your creative choices.

Research Project: Using Appendix D as a starting point, explore an additional woman not featured in the book and draft a short "chapter" in the same format. Focus on a tradition or time period that interests you.

Comparative Analysis: Choose two women from different traditions and compare their strategies for exercising spiritual authority. Consider both their successes and limitations.

For Book Clubs and General Discussion:

Personal Reflection: Which woman's story resonated most strongly with you? Why? How does her experience connect to contemporary issues?

Community Connections: Interview an older woman in your family or community about her experiences with religious authority, tradition, and change. How do her experiences relate to the historical patterns discussed in the book?

Creative Response: Create a piece of art, music, or poetry inspired by one of the women in the book. Share your creation and explain your artistic choices.

Facilitator Tips for Sensitive Discussions

Creating Safe Space

- **Set Ground Rules:** Establish expectations for respectful dialogue, including speaking from personal experience rather than making generalizations about entire traditions.
- **Acknowledge Discomfort:** Many of these stories challenge long-held assumptions. Normalize the discomfort that can accompany learning.
- **Honor Multiple Perspectives:** Make space for both traditional and critical viewpoints, especially when participants come from the traditions being discussed.

Managing Difficult Moments

- **When Someone Feels Attacked:** Redirect to the historical patterns rather than contemporary practices. Emphasize that critiquing past exclusions doesn't necessarily condemn current communities.
- **When Information Conflicts with Beliefs:** Acknowledge that scholarly and devotional approaches can coexist. Encourage curiosity rather than defensiveness.
- **When Power Dynamics Emerge:** Be aware of how gender, religious background, age, and other factors may affect participation. Actively include quieter voices.

Adapting for Different Contexts

Online/Asynchronous Learning

- **Discussion Boards:** Post weekly questions and require responses to both the original prompt and peer comments.
- **Virtual Breakout Rooms:** Use smaller groups for tradition-specific discussions before returning to the full group.
- **Multimedia Integration:** Encourage participants to share relevant images, music, or additional resources.

Interfaith Settings

- **Balance Perspectives:** Ensure representatives from discussed traditions have opportunities to share insider perspectives.
- **Focus on Learning:** Frame discussions around understanding rather than judgment or conversion.
- **Find Common Ground:** Highlight shared themes like the desire for authenticity and the challenges of preserving tradition.

Academic Settings

- **Connect to Current Scholarship:** Reference ongoing debates and recent discoveries in the field.
- **Encourage Primary Source Engagement:** Have students read excerpts from the Therīgāthā, Julian of Norwich, or other primary sources alongside the book.
- **Methodological Reflection:** Regularly discuss the challenges and ethics of feminist historical recovery work.

Additional Resources and Activities

Guest Speakers: Consider inviting:

- Local religious leaders (especially women)
- Women's studies or religious studies professors
- Museum curators with relevant collections
- Community elders with traditional knowledge

Field Experiences:

- Visit local religious communities to observe women's current roles
- Explore manuscript collections or religious art exhibits
- Attend worship services that highlight women's contributions

Extended Projects:

- Create a "lost women" exhibit for your local community
- Develop a documentary or podcast episode on one tradition
- Organize an interfaith panel on women's spiritual leadership

Reflection Questions for Facilitators

Before beginning, consider:

- What are my own assumptions about women's roles in religious traditions?
- How can I model intellectual humility while facilitating challenging conversations?
- What resources do I need to support participants from different backgrounds?
- How will I handle disagreement while maintaining respect for all perspectives?

Remember: The goal is not consensus but deeper understanding, respectful dialogue, and appreciation for the complexity of women's experiences across cultures and centuries.

About the Author

Kevin Meyer is a retired executive and lifelong student of subjects that challenge conventional thinking. Trained as a chemical engineer, he spent most of his career in executive roles in medical device manufacturing, where he developed a deep appreciation for the intersection of rigorous methodology and human-centered problem solving.

Meyer cofounded an e-learning company focused on continuous improvement methods, which he successfully grew and eventually sold. This experience reinforced his belief in the power of making complex ideas accessible to broader audiences—a principle that guides his current writing projects.

Born in the United States but raised for seven formative years in Peru, Meyer has traveled to over sixty-five countries, always with an eye toward understanding how different cultures approach fundamental questions about meaning, truth, and human flourishing. This global perspective shapes his approach to exploring diverse intellectual traditions with both curiosity and respect.

For nearly thirty years, Meyer has practiced *bhāvanā*—disciplined cultivation of understanding through deep, intentional study of subjects ranging from marathon running and scuba diving to philosophy, spirituality, and history. Each year, he embraces a new area of inquiry that pushes him beyond his comfort zone and challenges his assumptions.

Now retired and living in Morro Bay, California, Meyer finally has the time to fully explore the wildly divergent topics that have always fascinated him. He remains active in the local biotech startup community, bringing his experience in scaling complex operations to emerging companies.

This book represents Meyer's continued exploration of how human communities preserve and transmit their most treasured wisdom across centuries and cultures. While making no claim to scholarly expertise, he brings to this inquiry the same methodical curiosity and respect for evidence that guided his business career, combined with a deep appreciation for the spiritual significance these questions hold for millions of people worldwide.

Meyer can be reached through his website at KevinMeyer.com.

Other Books by Kevin Meyer

Sacred Editors Series

Sacred Editors: How Power, Politics, and Interpretation Shaped the Christian Scripture
The remarkable human story behind the formation of the Bible, tracing how scribes, bishops, emperors, and competing Christian communities shaped the New Testament canon through centuries of copying, translating, and theological debate.

Sacred Editors: How Exile, Law, and Dialogue Evolved Jewish Sacred Texts
An exploration of how the Hebrew Bible and Talmud came to be, examining the human decisions, political pressures, and scholarly debates that shaped Jewish sacred texts across centuries of transmission and interpretation.

Sacred Editors: How Preservation and Authority Defined Islamic Sacred Texts
The fascinating story behind the compilation of the Quran and the development of Islamic textual traditions, revealing the complex historical processes through which Muslim communities preserved and codified their foundational texts.

Sacred Editors: How Preservation, Transmission, and Insight Shaped the Buddhist Canon
The fascinating story of how the Buddha's teachings transformed from remembered words into the world's most

diverse collection of sacred canons, spanning cultures from Sri Lanka to Tibet to Japan.

Sacred Editors: How Tradition, Interpretation, and Devotion Shaped Hindu Sacred Texts

The extraordinary journey of Hindu sacred texts from ancient oral recitation to global digital archives, exploring how tradition-keepers, commentators, and communities across millennia have shaped the Vedas, Upanishads, epics, and Puranas.

Sacred Editors: The Women Who Shaped and Were Erased from Sacred Texts

A recovery of the forgotten women who transmitted, interpreted, and preserved the world's holy books across all major religious traditions. From Mary Magdalene's transformation from apostle to penitent, to the anonymous Buddhist nuns whose enlightened poetry survived in scripture, to the Islamic women scholars who safeguarded the Qur'an's oral transmission, this book honors the hidden guardians whose hands shaped sacred words that still guide billions today.

The Sacred Lost: The Violent and Vast Destruction of Sacred Texts and the Fight to Remember

A sweeping exploration of the vast destruction of sacred texts across world religions and the heroic efforts to preserve them. From the burning of Buddhist libraries at Nalanda to the digital preservation challenges of today, this book reveals how catastrophic loss, gradual abandonment, and technological change have shaped religious traditions—and how interfaith cooperation has often been the key to salvation.

Interfaith and Spiritual Exploration

The Beatitudes Path: An Interfaith Exploration of Sacred Blessings

A transformative journey through Jesus' most beloved teachings that reveals how the Beatitudes articulate universal truths about compassion, justice, and authentic living that transcend religious boundaries. Drawing on scholarship from Buddhism to Islam, Indigenous wisdom to ancient Greek philosophy, Meyer demonstrates how these ancient blessings offer profound guidance for seekers of every background wrestling with life's deepest questions.

Leadership and Personal Development

The Simple Leader: Personal and Professional Leadership at the Nexus of Lean and Zen

Filled with personal stories, practices, and insights from a thirty-year leadership journey, this book reveals the surprising connections between Lean manufacturing principles and Zen wisdom. Organized into eight practical parts—from reconnecting with your inner self to growing your organization—it shows leaders in any industry how to become more organized, effective, and balanced by integrating concepts like simplicity, flow, respect, and beginner's mind into their daily practice.

Biography

Harleigh Knott: Christmas Greetings From a Remarkable Life

A celebration of Harleigh Thayer Knott (1929-2019), a remarkable woman who lived her entire life in Morro Bay, California, while developing interests ranging from opera to history, polo to Indy car racing. Compiled from sixty years of her captivating and humorous annual Christmas letters, this book preserves the memory of an extraordinary life filled with Stanford education, world travel, and an insatiable curiosity about everything from frogs to the human condition.

www.ingramcontent.com/pod-product-compliance
Lightning Source LLC
Chambersburg PA
CBHW022057090426
42743CB00008B/637